Alexander Thom

Minutes of evidence at Trial of Drogheda Election Petition

Alexander Thom

Minutes of evidence at Trial of Drogheda Election Petition

ISBN/EAN: 9783742818812

Manufactured in Europe, USA, Canada, Australia, Japa

Cover: Foto ©Thomas Meinert / pixelio.de

Manufactured and distributed by brebook publishing software
(www.brebook.com)

Alexander Thom

Minutes of evidence at Trial of Drogheda Election Petition

DROGHEDA ELECTION.

COPY

OF

MINUTES OF THE EVIDENCE

TAKEN AT

THE TRIAL

OF THE

DROGHEDA ELECTION PETITION.

(1869.)

Ordered, by The House of Commons, *to be Printed*,
19 *February* 1869.

REPORT.

PARLIAMENTARY ELECTIONS ACT, 1868.

COURT for the Trial of an Election Petition for the Borough of Drogheda, between Sir F. Leopold McClintock, Petitioner, and Benjamin Whitworth, Respondent.

THE Petition (a copy of which is hereto annexed) between the aforesaid parties came on for trial before me at Drogheda on the 15th, 16th, 18th, and 19th days of January 1869, and thereupon I determined as follows:—

First. That Benjamin Whitworth, Esq., is not duly elected a Burgess to serve in the present Parliament for the borough and county of the town of Drogheda.

Second. That said election for said borough and county of the town of Drogheda is a void election.

Third. That Benjamin Whitworth, Esq., was, by himself and by his agents, guilty of undue influence at the said election for said borough and county of the town of Drogheda.

Fourth. That a system of intimidation was organised and carried out at the last election for the said borough and county of the town of Drogheda, subversive of the freedom of election, and outrages were committed which were calculated to deter, and did, in fact, deter a considerable number of voters from exercising their franchise at the last election.

Fifth. That Benjamin Whitworth, Esq., shall pay the costs of this Petition.

And I do accordingly hereby certify to the Right Honourable the Speaker of the House of Commons—

First. That the said Benjamin Whitworth, Esq., is not duly elected a Burgess to serve in the present Parliament for the borough and county of the town of Drogheda.

Second. That said election for said borough and county of the town of Drogheda is a void election.

Third. That Benjamin Whitworth, Esq., was, by himself and by his agents, guilty of undue influence at the said election for said borough and county of the town of Drogheda.

Fourth. That a system of intimidation was organised and carried out at the last election for the said borough and county of the town of Drogheda, subversive of the freedom of election, and outrages were committed which were calculated to deter, and did, in fact, deter a considerable number of voters from exercising their franchise at the last election for said borough of the county of the town of Drogheda.

Dated this Twenty-fifth day of January, One thousand Eight hundred and Sixty-nine.

WILLIAM KEOGH,
One of the Judges on the Rota for the trial of Election Petitions in Ireland.

This certificate is accompanied by a copy of the evidence given at the trial, as taken by the shorthand-writer of the House of Commons, sworn by me pursuant to the Statute.

WILLIAM KEOGH.

In the Common Pleas.

The Parliamentary Elections Act, 1868.

Election for the County of the Town of Drogheda, holden on the 19th November 1868, being the day of Nomination; the 20th November 1868 being the day of Polling; and 21st day of November 1868 being the day of the Declaration of the Poll.

The Petition of Sir *Francis Leopold McClintock*, of No. 21, Merrion-square North, in the County of the City of Dublin, Knight, Captain in Her Majesty's Royal Navy, whose name is subscribed.

1. Your Petitioner was a candidate at the above election.

2. Your Petitioner states that the election was holden on the 21st day of November, in the year of our Lord 1868, when Benjamin Whitworth, Francis Brodigan, and your Petitioner were candidates, and the Returning Officer has returned Benjamin Whitworth as being duly elected.

3. Your Petitioner states that upon several days immediately preceding the election addresses and speeches of an exciting and inflammatory nature were delivered in the public streets of Drogheda by the said Benjamin Whitworth and several other persons in his presence, and with his knowledge and consent, for the purpose of urging and inciting a number of persons to use force in order to intimidate and prevent the electors from voting for your Petitioner or the said Francis Brodigan, and to compel them to vote for the said Benjamin Whitworth.

4. A large number of men and women were hired by the said Benjamin Whitworth, or with his knowledge and consent, for the purpose of intimidating electors in order to induce them to vote for the said Benjamin Whitworth, or to refrain from voting for your Petitioner or the said Francis Brodigan.

5. Several members of the Roman Catholic priesthood improperly exercised their spiritual influence over many of the electors for the purpose of constraining them to vote for the said Benjamin Whitworth, and to prevent them from voting for your Petitioner or the said Francis Brodigan.

6. Upon the 19th day of November 1868, the day of the nomination of candidates, the Court-house, where the election was to be held, was taken possession of by a riotous mob, consisting of the friends and supporters of the said Benjamin Whitworth, who made an attack upon your Petitioner and his proposer and seconder, and several other of his supporters, and by actual force expelled them from the Court-house, inflicting severe bodily injuries upon them.

7. Upon the 20th day of November 1868, being the polling day, several thousand persons, friends and supporters of the said Benjamin Whitworth, armed, some with fire-arms and others with bludgeons and sticks, attacked voters who wished and had promised to vote for your Petitioner, and inflicted very severe wounds and other bodily injuries upon them, and forcibly prevented many of them from recording their votes, and also attacked a large escort of cavalry, infantry, and police, who were acting as an escort for the protection of voters, and caused such terror and alarm in the minds of the electors, that many who had promised to vote for the said Francis Brodigan, and some who had promised to vote for your Petitioner, were induced, by intimidation, to vote for the said Benjamin Whitworth; and many electors who had promised to vote for your Petitioner, and had come long distances to do so, and were most anxious to do so, if they could, without risk of their lives, were deterred from going to the poll and recording their votes.

8. Your Petitioner charges that the offence of undue influence at the said election was committed by the said Benjamin Whitworth and a great number of other persons, with his knowledge and consent; and that an organised system of intimidation and violence was established by the said Benjamin Whitworth and his friends and agents; and that the said Benjamin Whitworth could at any time have restrained the rioters from acts of violence if he had been willing to do so.

9. Your Petitioner alleges that if the electors had been allowed to vote according to their wishes, without any intimidation or coercion, your Petitioner would have been returned at the above election as a burgess to serve in Parliament for the said county of the town of Drogheda.

Wherefore your Petitioner prays that it may be determined that the said Benjamin Whitworth was not duly elected or returned, and that the above election was void.

F. L. McClintock.

LIST OF WITNESSES.

MINUTES OF EVIDENCE

Taken before the Right Honourable Mr. Justice *Keogh*, on the Trial of the Election Petition for the Borough of Drogheda, at the Court House, Drogheda.

Friday, 15th *January* 1869.

McClintock - - - - - - - - Petitioner.
Whitworth - - - - - - - - Respondent.

Mr. *McDonogh*, Q.C., the Hon. *David Plunket*, Q.C., and Mr. *Ryland*, appeared as Counsel for the Petitioner. Mr. *P. J. Magee* appeared as Agent.

Mr. *Denis C. Heron*, Q.C., Mr. *Christopher Palles*, Q.C., and Mr. *Hamill*, appeared as Counsel for the Respondent. Mr. *Henry Clinton* appeared as Agent.

Mr. *McDonogh* was heard to open the allegations of the Petition.

Thomas Plunkett Cairnes, Esq., sworn; Examined by Mr. *Plunkett*.

1. I believe that you are a Magistrate for the county of Meath?—I am.

2. And an elector of the town of Drogheda?—Yes.

3. The election for the town of Drogheda being held on Friday, the 20th of November, 1868, do you recollect on the Tuesday week preceding that Friday meeting Sir Leopold McClintock?—I think it was on the Wednesday.

4. The 11th?—Yes.

5. You came down from Dublin?—I went on the arrival of the half-past 11 train, to the station.

6. Then, just say what occurred shortly after your arrival in Drogheda?—I was introduced to Sir Leopold McClintock, and subsequently met him at a meeting of Conservatives, who came together for the purpose of hearing his views upon political matters.

7. And he was adopted, I believe?—He was at that meeting adopted by the Conservatives as their candidate, and resolutions were passed.

8. Mr. *Heron*.] What was the date of that?—On Wednesday, the 11th of November, one week before the day of the nomination.

9. Mr. *Plunkett*.] Then, I believe that Sir Leopold McClintock returned to Dublin?—He returned to Dublin on that evening, and returned here on the following Friday evening.

10. That was the 13th?—Yes.

11. Did you again meet him?—I met him again on the arrival of the train, and accompanied him with some other gentlemen on his canvass for a part of the town on the south side of the river.

12. How was he received?—He was very well received upon that occasion.

13. Was there any violence?—Not the slightest disposition to violence, and no incivility offered.

14. Did you pursue the canvass on the next day, or did he pursue it in your company?—I was with him for a very short time on the following day, but he pursued it, I understand, with others.

15. Whilst you were with him, how was he received?—He was very well received, civilly and respectfully.

16. Well, then, Sunday intervening, were you with him on Monday?—Yes, on Monday, accompanied by several gentlemen, we proceeded to canvass West-street.

17. Will you tell his Lordship how he was received on Monday?—There was a very different feeling exhibited then; much more disposition to interfere with our canvass. We were hooted as we went from house to house.

18. Will you tell his Lordship how Sir Leopold was received in West-street?—I say that there was distinctly much more disposition shown to interfere with our canvass, and they hooted us from house to house. A mob attended us during our canvass, who were evidently hostile.

19. Did you recognise any individuals among that

T. P. Cairnes, Esq.

15 January 1859.

that mob?—Not amongst those composing the mob. Upon coming out of Butler's shop, close to this in West-street, there was some disturbance. I was one of the last of my party who left the shop, and I found a great deal of excitement amongst the mob immediately about the door. Mr. Henry Moore, of West-street, was one of our party, and I saw him. I understand from those around me——

20. Mr. *Hoven.*] Just say what you saw yourself?—I saw Mr. Verdon and Mr. Clinton amongst the mob.

21. Mr. *Plunkett.*] Who is Mr. Clinton?—Mr. Clinton is Mr. Whitworth's conducting agent; Mr. Verdon is also a solicitor.

22. Did your observe their conduct there?—They were talking to Mr. Moore in a very angry and excited way. I could not hear the substance of what they said, but I heard Mr. Verdon call out, "We will have no Orangemen here." I then proceeded slowly along to the Town-hall, and I remonstrated with Mr. Verdon upon the impropriety of urging the townspeople.

23. Was Mr. Clinton also present?—He was present in the first instance, but whether he continued I do not remember.

24. What did he reply?—He replied that it was Mr. Moore's fault, that the disturbance had arisen from him. I then crossed over from here to Peter-street, through the mob, with great difficulty; an attempt was made to knock me down from behind. I stated to the mob who surrounded me upon that occasion that we wished merely to have fair play, and to have the contest carried on fairly and openly. I think Mr. Gardiner, the sub-inspector of police, was present on that occasion, if I do not mistake.

25. Was Sir Leopold McClintock's canvass continued the next day?—That was on Monday.

26. On the Tuesday?—I did not take a very active part on the next day. After that we consulted, and came to the conclusion that it was a hopeless proceeding to canvass in the town, from the state of the mob.

27. In what way was that Tuesday employed?—On the Monday evening after this occurred, we proceeded to canvass some of the out-voters in the country, and on the Tuesday we were occupied the greater part of the day in the tally-rooms, and I canvassed some voters here and there through the town. I did not afterwards attempt a house-to-house canvass.

28. You have already told us that you came to the resolution that it was useless to do so?—Yes.

29. Where were you on the Wednesday, the next day?—I went to Dublin on the Tuesday evening, for the purpose of voting for you and Sir Arthur Guinness.

30. I am much obliged to you for that; and on Wednesday?—I came down by the first train on Wednesday morning.

31. And you arrived in Drogheda, when?—I came here to the nomination.

32. Will you describe to his Lordship the state of affairs which you found?—I found the candidates and their friends assembled on the steps of the court-house; a cordon of police drawn up immediately in front, and a large and very excited mob in the street; I pushed through the police and took my place as well as I could on the steps, and I got next the Reverend Mr. Doyle, a Roman Catholic clergyman; he was in a very excited state, and shouted out as loud as he possibly could at intervals, "Down with the Orange faction;" I remonstrated with him, and said I was not an Orangeman, nor did I know of an Orangeman there; he said, "It is no matter, you have the old Orange blood in you," or words to that effect; there was an ugly feeling apparently at Sir Leopold McClintock, who occupied the highest step of the court-house door; after a delay of I should suppose about 15 minutes, one half the door was opened and a terrific rush ensued; I struggled to get in with the others, when Mr. Doyle to my surprise seized me by the coat, and assisted me in, saying, "You are an honest fellow at all events."

33. He said it to you individually?—He said it to me individually; I rushed in here, and occupied a position between the bench and the door, about where Mr. Gardiner is at present standing (*pointing out the same*). The sub-sheriff was within a yard or two of me; I found that I was separated from my party, but so great was the crowd that I found it impossible to get back to them; a scene of the greatest possible confusion then ensued; the whole body of the house was filled with a riotous violent mob of the lowest order of society, and a great number of them appeared tipsy; the mob appeared to be divided between Mr. Whitworth and Mr. Bodkin, but by far the greater number appeared to be in Mr. Whitworth's interest; I did not hear a single voice raised on behalf of Sir Leopold McClintock amongst the mob; we were crushed to the greatest possible extent, so much so as to become extremely alarming; the noise was so great, that though the sub-sheriff was within two yards of me, I was unable to say whether he read the writ; I heard him calling upon the people to hear the writ; I also called out with him for the purpose of endeavouring to make an impression upon the crowd; after a short time I saw Mr. James Matthews raised on a bench, and he appeared to be addressing the audience, but I was unable to hear one word he said; subsequently other gentlemen were raised into a similar position, and appeared also to attempt to address the audience, but not a single word of what they said was audible to me.

34. How close were you at that time to them?—I was at that time immediately behind that brass rod (*describing the same*), and a gentleman was speaking from where his Lordship is now.

35. Will you explain to his Lordship the circumstances under which you left the courthouse?—The mob surged and swayed over these benches, and on one or two occasions fell over the part of the bench where the respectable part of the community were, and at times they surged and swayed over, and fell over, the tops of those on the bench, and those underneath seemed to be in great danger; I heard some one say that Mr. Cottingham had fallen over, and was in danger of being suffocated; I then forced my way out as well as I could for the purpose of getting the assistance of the police to assist in rescuing, but I found that I had been anticipated, as somebody else had got there; a small number of the police came in; by this time a good number of the respectable part of the assembly had commenced leaving.

36. Did you see Sir Leopold McClintock at that time?—Not then; I was looking about anxiously for him and his other supporters, and I could not see him for some time; after some little time I found him on the step outside the side

side door, and I placed myself behind him: when I returned, after going for the police, I met the high sheriff somewhere adjoining the side door, and I asked him what had taken place; he stated that the candidates had been proposed and seconded, and he asked me who had (I am not quite sure whether it was) "seconded" or "proposed" Sir Leopold McClintock; he was in doubt as to the one or to the other; I told him; he also asked me as to a poll having been demanded, and I said "To prevent any mistake I demand it now;" when he said that would be sufficient; this occurred at that side door leading to the court and not in the court-house itself.

37. When you met Sir Leopold McClintock, what happened?—I found him standing immediately outside the side door. I placed myself immediately behind him so as to admit of the mob passing out. One man from amongst the mob came up to me and commenced screaming and yelling in a violent way, and threatening me and ordering me to leave that. He came within a few feet of me. I took no notice of him for some time, until I saw he was becoming so violent that he would probably assault me, and I then shook my fist in his face and threatened to knock him down if he touched me. The high sheriff came up shortly afterwards and used his influence to get these men out of the building.

38. How did you leave the court-house?—We then proceeded to the door of the court-house, and found such an angry mob in the street that we had to obtain an escort of police to force our way across it.

39. Was Sir Leopold McClintock with you at that time?—I am not certain whether he formed one of our party, but his immediate supporters were with us, and I think he was. We had to force our way literally through the crowd, so thick was it. As I got outside the edge of the crowd, on the opposite side of the street, a man ran across and deliberately struck me across the shins, endeavouring to knock me down. He was arrested, but subsequently discharged at my desire.

40. How were you principally employed on the Thursday?—There was no attempt at a house-to-house canvass on the Thursday either. I canvassed with Sir Leopold McClintock several voters on cars in the town and neighbourhood.

41. Was there excitement in the town of Drogheda on that day?—There was.

42. Was it greater or less than before?—I could not show my face without being hooted and insulted in every possible way, but up to this time I had seen no stones thrown.

43. Will you say what occurred on the day of polling after you left your own house?—I left my house about half-past seven, accompanied by Sir Leopold McClintock and several friends, and we proceeded into the town. With regard to the arrangement for bringing the voters into the town, I should have said that I made them with the stipendiary magistrate on the Thursday. I then waited on the stipendiary magistrate; they first called at Sir Leopold McClintock's tally-room to see what protection was required. I gave particulars of the numbers of voters and the roads they were expected to come by, and arranged as to the escort of police.

Mr. *Heron* objected to the opinion of the magistrate being given as evidence.

44. Mr. *Plunkett* (to the *Witness*).] What did they do?—I endeavoured to impress upon them the necessity of a large escort by the half-past 11 train, as we expected a great many voters by it. On the Friday we proceeded to the tally-room; on coming towards the town we were met by a crowd of girls.

45. At what o'clock was this?—Between seven and eight on the Friday morning; these girls were apparently factory hands, with green boughs. As soon as they recognised us on the cars they hooted and yelled, and threw dirt at us; there were no stones convenient. I proceeded to the tally-room and found that a voter who had freely promised to vote, and who had been in my employment for a great number of years, was absent, though he had promised to be there to meet me.

46. What was his name?—Patrick Boyle.

Mr. *Heron* objected that this name had not been mentioned until now, and applied that a list should be furnished to the Counsel for the Respondent.

Mr. Justice *Keogh* said that the Petitioner ought to be prepared with a proper list to guide the Respondent in his defence, and that if it was intended to go into any cases other than those mentioned by Mr. McDonogh in his opening speech, a list of the names had better be furnished at once to the Counsel for the Respondent, with the names of those persons by whom they were alleged to have been unduly influenced.

47. Mr. *Plunkett* (to the *Witness*).] Now will you tell us about those you expected at the tally-room?—I proceeded on an outside car, accompanied by Mr. Charles Smyth, from the tally-room to my brewery. When approaching the building I observed a crowd of factory girls, a great many of them with green boughs. I also saw the Rev. Mr. Matthews, of St. Mary's; when passing, he came quickly over to the side of the car in which I was and "booh'd" in my face very loudly; immediately the crowd of girls commenced hooting us, and followed us with vollies of stones all along James-street, striking the car several times.

48. What o'clock was this?—This was about eight o'clock; they followed us all along James-street. I then drove down to my brewery, and the girls assembled on the road commanding it, and commenced pelting vollies of stones whenever I appeared, and also breaking the windows; I saw the voter, and asked him why he had not come up as he had promised; he said he was alarmed——

Mr. *Heron* objected to a private conversation between the witness and the voter being given as evidence.

49. Mr. *Plunkett*.] Where was this conversation?—In my yard.

50. Was any one else present besides yourself and those voters?—Not immediately present.

51. Did you leave the yard afterwards?—I left the yard without the voter; I did not urge him to come. I attempted to leave the yard, but in every instance when I attempted to leave the yard I was saluted with vollies of stones, curses, &c., and after making several attempts I was obliged

T. F. Cairns, Esq.

15 January 1869.

obliged to send the escort with a note requesting that some police might be sent to remove the mob. After a delay of about 20 minutes, the mob left their position, and I returned to the tally-room.

52. Did you observe anything as you passed through James-street?—I saw the Reverend Mr. Matthews, with a large mob, following us up Paddock-lane as I passed round James-street.

53. How were they conducting themselves at that time?—They were cheering Mr. Whitworth.

54. Did they take any notice of you?—No; I escaped their notice; they were going in an opposite direction.

55. Then will you say what was the state of the town subsequently to that time after eight o'clock?—I then returned to the tally-room, and in the course of about an hour or so I voted here, accompanied by one or two others; on passing to and from the booth I was insulted, and hissed and hooted.

56. Did you go alone to the tally-room?—I was accompanied by two other voters. The violence of the mob from this time increased considerably; so great was it that at I think about 10 o'clock we considered it necessary to apply——

57. Mr. *Heron*.] Say what you did?—I was one of those who joined in applying for an escort of police, as arranged on the preceding day with the stipendiary magistrate; we got that escort, and subsequently to that every voter that was supposed to be obnoxious to the mob, or well known to them, was sent down in the centre of a police escort; I watched some of them going, from the window, and I saw the mob striking at them over the guns of the police; over the police.

58. Mr. *Plunket*.] Did you see any clergyman at that time?—I saw a Roman Catholic clergyman.

59. Do you know who he was?—I was informed——

Mr. *Heron* objected to this being received as evidence.

60. Mr. *Plunket* (to the Witness).] Have you since heard his name?—I have heard his name to be the Reverend Mr. McKee. I saw him taking off his hat; my attention was attracted by a noise in the street, and I saw a large mob, the majority of them armed with large sticks, coming in a very tumultuous way up Peter-street; this gentleman apparently leading them up. As they passed our tally-rooms they groaned and shouted, and brandished their sticks, shaking them at those in the windows.

61. Was there any stone throwing?—There were some stones thrown at the windows, but not many.

62. As to those voters whom you were expecting to arrive, what happened?—The voters expected by the 10 o'clock express, and the mail, and the half-past 11 o'clock train had not arrived up to this. There was a rumour that there was very serious rioting in the direction of the railway, and we were looking out anxiously for them.

63. Did you see anything of that yourself?—I was looking out anxiously for the expected body of voters from the train. I observed the escort coming round the corner of James-street. On looking through the window of the tally-room I had a complete, though distant, view of it.

64. Will you tell his Lordship exactly what you saw?—I saw the Hussars in front and at the sides, and an immense mob opposing their progress in Shop-street. I saw a great number of sticks in the air, whether brandished or thrown I could not say, close up to the Hussars. There was a halt on the bridge. I saw a Hussar's horse rear up, and they were thrown into disorder, and the Hussars retreated; and I saw the infantry formed across the bridge. I then heard a report of a shot. The mob fell back about 50 yards, and I saw a body lying in the intervening space. The Hussars then charged up the street, clearing it with extraordinary rapidity. Two of the horses fell at the turn, and the infantry subsequently charged. I saw one man held up from amongst the body of people who were with the military; it was literally torn to shreds with stones. Shortly after this a number of our voters rushed into the tally-room in a most excited state, bleeding from wounds inflicted on their way from the railway, and some of them in the tally-room were engaged for some time in dressing their wounds.

65. What was the conduct of the people outside at that time?—There seemed to be less disposition to violence after the shot was fired.

66. Immediately?—Immediately.

67. After the voters reached your tally-room, what happened?—We then discussed——

Mr. *Heron* objected to discussions of any kind being received as evidence.

68. Mr. *Plunket* (to the Witness).] What was the result of your discussion?—The result of the discussion was that Sir Leopold McClintock applied for an escort to bring the voters back to the railway station, as he considered it unsafe.

Mr. *Heron*.] You must only say what was done.

69. Mr. *Plunket*.] Did he obtain the escort?—The resident magistrate did not apply for some time; there was a delay of a considerable time owing to the resident magistrate being engaged, as we understood. He came after some delay, both Captain Talbot and Mr. Hamey; and Sir Leopold McClintock, I think, stated what he required, namely, an escort for the voters back to the station. Captain Talbot said——

70. Was that escort provided?—No; he declined giving it, and suggested that we should remain there till dusk.

Mr. *Heron* objected that the opinion of the resident magistrate was not evidence.

Mr. Justice *Keogh* ruled that the opinion of the resident magistrate could not be given.

71. Mr. *MacDonogh* (to the Witness).] But what did he do?—He left us without an escort.

72. Mr. *Plunket*.] Did those voters who arrived from Dublin all vote?——

Mr. *Heron* objected that this must be proved in a more regular way.

73. Mr. *Plunket* (to the Witness).] Do you know whether they all left the tally-room?—Not nearly the number who were expected arrived. There was a list of 30 made out.

Mr. *Heron* objected that legal proof must be

T. P. Cairnes, Esq.

18 January 1869.

be given that a particular voter had not voted.

Mr. McDonogh submitted that this was good evidence of general intimidation, if the witness knew of his own knowledge that the voter was not able to leave the tally-room.

Mr. Justice Keogh ruled that some names must be mentioned, as if the witness was not able to mention the names, he could not say whether or not the persons in question were voters.

74. Mr. Plunket (to the Witness).] Do you recollect the names of any of the voters who were in the tally-room at the time?—Mr. William Jameson, my cousin, and Major Smythe, and Mr. St. George Smythe, and the Rev. Mr. Rowe also.

75. Did those gentlemen leave the tally-room; did the Rev. Mr. Rowe leave the tally-room to go to the polling-booth?—Not that I am aware of; a number of others——

Mr. Heron objected to a number of persons being referred to unless the names were given.

Witness.] A number of other voters arrived subsequently, also injured, later in the day; amongst them one old gentleman who, I was informed, was Colonel Fairclough. He, amongst others, returned to the railway station in a covered car, accompanied by some of Mr. Whitworth's friends. I should have mentioned that Mr. Whitworth and several of his friends came up some time after the scene on the bridge to our tally-room and offered their services in protecting our voters to the booths.

76. Mr. Justice Keogh.] Who did so?—Mr. Whitworth and several of his leading supporters; the high sheriff, Mr. Frank Chadwick, and Mr. Richard Bradwell.

77. Mr. Plunkett.] At what time of the day was this?—I should say it was between two and three o'clock; but I would not swear very positively as to the exact hour.

78. Do you know, of your own knowledge, whether Sir Leopold's officers were withdrawn from the booths or not?—Yes.

79. Mr. Heron.] Were you at the booth?—I was not. I never left the tally-room after I voted, from the state of the streets.

80. Mr. Plunkett.] Did you see them in the tally-room?—I saw in the tally-room several of the people to whom I had seen books given in the morning, and whom I knew to be clerks employed there, and I heard them state that they had closed their booths.

81. Was that before or after Mr. Whitworth came with his friends to escort you?—Some, I think, before and some after.

82. Mr. Heron.] Are you sure?—I would not swear one way or the other. The greatest alarm prevailed in the tally-room for the next couple of hours. We were seriously apprehensive——

Mr. Heron objected to the witness's apprehensions being received as evidence.

Mr. Justice Keogh ruled that the witness might state the effect produced upon his own mind.

83. Mr. Plunket (to the Witness).] Were any stones thrown at your tally-room windows?—Some were thrown during the day at intervals. I was seriously apprehensive of danger in passing through the streets on my return home.

84. Did you see any violence from the windows of the tally-room?—Yes, there was a man assaulted.

85. Did you see it yourself?—I saw it, but not the details of it.

86. Do not say anything which you did not see yourself?—Of course not. I heard that a man was arrested and had been released again. I went down to Captain Gardner, and asked how it had happened that he had released him. I subsequently returned home, accompanied by Mr. Frank Chadwick, through the town, who volunteered to give me a safe convoy.

87. Mr. Justice Keogh.] Who is he?—He is a supporter of Mr. Whitworth's; Mr. Mayne being accompanied by the high sheriff.

88. Mr. Plunket.] Was he one of Mr. Whitworth's friends?—He was. When I returned to my office the following day I found the windows completely smashed, both some of the shutters and some of the sashes, and I found a quantity of stones inside, one a stone weighing nine pounds, and much larger ones lying in the area beneath.

Cross-examined by Mr. Heron.

89. I believe that Sir Leopold McClintock's address appeared first on the 14th of November. Will you look at the "Drogheda Argus" (handing a Paper to the Witness), and say did it appear before; look at the date to refresh your memory?—I am not sure. The 11th was the day on which he came down.

90. I know that?—I think there was a special edition of the paper (but I am not certain) during the election, and it appeared on the Wednesday.

91. Is that your recollection?—I will not say so.

92. Did his address to the independent electors of Drogheda appear before the 14th of November?—To the best of my recollection, it was placarded before that. Do you mean appeared in the papers or in placards?

93. I mean did it appear in print?—I believe it did.

94. What is the earliest date you will fix for that?—Either Wednesday evening or Thursday morning, the 11th and 12th.

95. Before Sir Leopold McClintock had addressed the electors, had you been trying to get a Conservative candidate?—Yes.

96. For a long time?—How long?

97. I mean for a fortnight or three weeks before that time?—Yes.

98. And had failed?—Yes.

99. Had the privilege of standing for the representation of Drogheda been offered to Mr. McClintock?—Yes.

100. To whom had it been offered; had he been here with Mr. Mayne to see the chance of a Conservative getting in?—Yes.

101. How long was that before Sir Leopold's address?—About a fortnight.

102. Had he declined the honour?—He had.

103. In addition, had you and the other supporters of the Conservatives here offered the privilege of the candidature to Captain Pepper?—Not to my knowledge.

104. Was there any candidate who came here, calculated

calculated the enclosure and departed?—Not to my knowledge.

Mr. McDonagh objected to this as being irrelevant.

105. Mr. *Heron* (to the *Witness*).] This is the last question I will ask you on the subject. How long before Sir Leopold McClintock stood had you and the other Conservative gentlemen been trying to find a candidate?—I cannot fix a time.

106. Were you a month trying?—What do you mean by "trying to find a candidate?"

107. Trying to induce a candidate to stand at the election; you understand that?—I do not quite understand what you mean by "trying to get a candidate." We were, of course, looking to the results of the last registry; we were anxious to get a person.

108. Anxious to get a candidate?—Yes.

109. On the morning of the polling did any other people come down from Dublin besides electors in your interest?—Not to my knowledge; but I believe there did.

110. Had you been with Mr. Mayne on the previous day to the railway station, to the telegraph office?—I had.

111. And were you and Mr. Mayne together when the telegram was sent to Dublin?—I was.

112. The telegram for persons to come down who were not electors?—Yes.

113. How many?—I heard 50. If you will allow me, I will state the transaction shortly to his Lordship; I am quite ready to do it, and I should have done it before but I omitted it.

114. That is the use of cross-examination; to bring out what is omitted unintentionally?—On my way into Drogheda, on Thursday morning, I was informed by Mr. Mayne that he expected a number of assistants the following day to assist his tally-men in the booths and in protecting the voters to and from the tally-rooms to the booths, and he discussed with me whether he could get accommodation for them in Drogheda that night. As we agreed that there would be very great difficulty in that, he asked me what was the earliest train he could get them down by the following morning. I told him the first train I was aware of was the mail at half-past eight; I said that was too late, and I proceeded to the railway station to ascertain the first train by which those men could be got down, who, I understood, were under 50. I was informed there was a goods train which arrived about eight o'clock and left at about six o'clock, but Mr. Symington could not say whether passengers would be taken by that train; he offered to telegraph to Dublin to ascertain whether passengers could be taken by it or not, and we waited till the telegraph should be replied to. While waiting, Mr. Mayne inquired what the expense of a special train would be, and he said it would be eight or ten pounds, and Mr. Mayne then sent a telegram to some person in Dublin (whom I don't know), ordering a special train for these assistants in order to have them down in time for the opening of the poll. I subsequently got a communication from Mr. Symington, stating that a third-class carriage would be given by the mail train.

115. What was the name of the person to whom the telegram was sent?—I am not aware.

116. Were you ever aware?—No; I did not see the telegram.

117. Do you mean to say that you did not know?—I did not see the telegram.

118. Do you mean to say that you did not know?—I did not see the telegram; I am not certain at this moment; I have my suspicions, of course.

119. I ask you now to give your suspicions?—Am I to give them? I may guess; it was sent.

120. I ask you to whom you now believe that the telegram was directed?—I believe it was directed to some one in Sir Leopold McClintock's interest at Dublin.

121. Do you not now in your heart believe you know the name of the person?—I am not certain at all.

122. Whom do you suspect?—Am I to answer that, my Lord?

123. Mr. Justice *Keogh*.] Oh, yes!—I rather think that it was to Mr. McClintock in Dublin; that is merely my guess.

124. Is that Mr. McClintock at the Custom House?—Yes.

125. What is his Christian name?—Alexander, I think.

126. Where were the 50 men to be procured?—In Dublin.

127. But from what place in Dublin?—I do not know.

128. Do you not believe that they were to be procured at the Conservative committee-room?—I do not believe anything of the sort.

129. Did you know what was to be paid to these men?—No.

130. Did you know that they were to get 1*l.* 2*s.* 6*d.* a piece?—No.

131. Did you see that some of them have since sued for their money and recovered it?—No.

132. Do you mean to say that you did not hear that?—No.

133. You have not seen it in the paper?—No, I did not notice it.

134. You were, of course, on Sir Leopold McClintock's committee here?—There was no committee; I was one of his prominent supporters.

135. Were you an active supporter, and did you canvass for him and do your best for him, backing your party like an honest Irishman?—I did, decidedly.

136. That is, you canvassed for him and with him, and did your best for him?—Yes.

137. On Mr. Mayne's statement, of course, you sanctioned the chosen 50 coming from Dublin?—Yes.

138. Were they to come with sticks?—I heard nothing of the sort.

139. Were they to come with sticks?—I believe not.

140. Did you see any of them when they came?—I saw some whom I believed to be them in the tally-room.

141. Had they sticks there?—No.

142. Were they taken from them?—They did not look like men who usually carry sticks. Some of them were old quiet looking men in the rank of clerks.

[The Witness withdrew.

The Reverend John Francis Moreton, sworn; Examined by Mr. *McDonogh*.

Rev. J. F. Moreton.

15 February 1869.

143. Are you a Clergyman of the Established Church?—I am.

144. Is yours a vicarage or a rectory?—A vicarage.

145. Where?—In the diocese of Limerick; the [illegible] of [illegible].

146. Are you a registered voter of the town of Drogheda?—I am.

147. Did you come to this town for the purpose of recording your vote?—I did.

148. Had you promised any of the candidates?—I had promised Sir Leopold McClintock.

149. When did you leave Dublin?—The day before the polling.

150. When did you leave your own house?—I left my own house before that day; I stopped with a friend on the way.

151. On the day of the polling did you come to this town?—I did.

152. At about what hour did you reach the Drogheda terminus?—I came by the half-past eight train; at about 10 o'clock, I suppose; at 10 or 11.

153. Did any other gentleman accompany you?—The Reverend Thomas Wallace.

154. Was he a voter also?—He was.

155. Was there anybody else?—Several were in the train, but not with me.

156. Upon reaching the terminus, what appearance presented itself to you?—Everything was quiet at that time; but there were symptoms of disturbance, on account of the large number of people that were about.

157. Did you see the resident magistrate?—Not at first, but soon afterwards.

158. That was Mr. Bond, I believe?—Yes.

159. Did you proceed to the town of Drogheda at that time?—No; we were advised to wait.

160. Did you wait accordingly?—Yes.

161. Until the next train?—Yes.

162. Did you happen to see what escort of military or what civil force there was there at the time when you were advised to wait?——

Mr. *Heron* objected that the advice was not evidence.

Mr. *McDonogh* supported his line of examination.

Mr. Justice *Keogh* reminded the learned counsel on both sides that as the facts of the case were to be dealt with by the Judge, and not by a jury, the drawing of inferences would be of no avail.

163. Mr. *McDonogh* (to the *Witness*).] Will you be good enough to state exactly what occurred. Having waited for the next train, did other voters come by that train?—They did.

164. At that time will you state whether, as a matter of fact, there was an escort, and of what kind and character?—There was a [illegible] escort in the town, but in the meantime there was considerable rioting at the station.

165. Did you see that?—I did.

166. Will you be good enough to describe that?—My attention was first attracted by an order given to the constabulary to form into order. They formed a curve about the entrance to the station-house, and immediately a mob rushed up to the station such as has been described already.

167. Will you describe it yourself?—They were armed with bludgeons and other weapons.

168. Were they numerous, or otherwise?—They were numerous, but not so numerous as the mobs which we met afterwards.

169. What occurred in your presence?—They commenced by yelling and shouting, threatening the voters who were waiting, and asking them to have the voters let out to them, and that kind of thing.

170. Did any one of them address you from the crowd?—Several. There was in particular one who attracted me on account of the deadly weapon which he had in his hand, an iron bolt.

171. What did he say?—He said, "If I had you out here I'd settle you," or words to the like effect. He seemed to be calling upon the police to let me out.

172. Did he say anything with regard to yourself about your station, or the profession to which you belong?—Nothing.

173. Did you see Mr. Hamilton there?—I did.

174. Had you known him before?—Yes.

175. Was that before the second train arrived?—It was.

176. Were there any voters in company with Mr. Hamilton?—There were several whom I understood to be voters.

177. Did you see anything occur to Mr. Hamilton or to those people who were with him?—Yes, and I saw some persons going about and saying to Mr. Hamilton, that it was a shame that people should not be allowed liberty of action, or words to the like effect. Then some persons came from the town and were urging some of those men who were with Mr. Hamilton to state for whom they were going to vote. I did not hear their reply, the noise was very great. One of them, as I understood, said he would not vote at all, and he was let go. I saw him go into the station. There was afterwards a scuffle amongst the men, and I think there were two of them carried away upon cars.

178. Mr. Justice *Keogh*.] Upon what day was this?—Upon the day of the polling.

179. Mr. *Heron*.] Did you see them?—I did.

180. Mr. *McDonogh*.] Did you see in what way the people laid hold of them or took them off?—They were (I was going to say) carried away by the mob; they were forced away by the mob.

181. Do you know Mr. Whitworth?—I saw a gentleman there whom I was told was Mr. Whitworth; I had not seen him before.

182. Mr. *Heron*.] Do you know him now?—Yes.

183. Mr. *McDonogh*.] Was it the person whom you have seen in court to-day?—I think I saw Mr. Whitworth here to-day, and he is the same person whom I saw at the station.

184. Mr. *Heron*.] He was beside me here?—Yes.

185. Mr. *McDonogh*.] When did you first see that gentleman?—At the station speaking to those voters.

186. Were those the persons that were with Mr. Hamilton?—Yes.

187. What did he say?—He asked them whom they would vote for.

188. Did

Rev. J. P. *Marston.*

18 January 1869.

188. Did you see him do anything towards Mr. Hamilton; tell us exactly what you saw consecutively, as well as you remember?—I saw that there was some altercation and some struggling; at length some of the mob came in and took away the men one at a time; there was some little interval between.

189. Was Mr. Whitworth present on that occasion?—Yes, he was.

190. Do you know Mr. Clinton, one of the conducting agents?—Yes; I am not sure that I know him personally, but I know his appearance.

191. Did you see him that morning?—I am not sure whether he was one of those who were addressing the mob; I would not know him at that time by name.

192. Did you see anything happen to Mr. Hamilton?—Yes, I saw him thrown down.

193. By whom?—By the crowd who were carrying away the man.

194. Did you see Mr. Whitworth take hold of any person?—

Mr. *Heron* objected to this as being a leading question.

Witness.] I saw Mr. Whitworth lay hold of the voter to whom he was speaking.

195. What did you see him do; tell us the whole as if now it was spoken for the first time?—As if he wished him to go with him.

196. Was it after that, that the mob took him?—It was; the mob in the first instance did not come until after Mr. Whitworth had been speaking for some time.

197. Did you happen to see how they took them away?—They took them upon separate cars.

198. What was the conduct of the mob at that place?—They were merely shouting, and yelling, and brandishing sticks threateningly.

199. Have you stated to us all that you remember about that occurrence of taking away the voters?—The man who said he would not vote went into the station, some of the mob afterwards rushed in and took him away with them.

200. Describe now the manner in which he was taken away, if you saw it?—A number of persons got about him and took him away. He was partially carried and partially dragged; he was put upon a car, and several men got upon the car with him. I do not know how many, but the car seemed crowded; the well-cushion and all seemed crowded.

201. Where was he put?—In the midst of them.

202. Was he sitting or lying, or in what position?—I really could not tell; there was great confusion, and the whole thing was a momentary occurrence.

203. After that, did you and the voters, when the second train arrived, proceed into the town?—Yes.

204. How was the escort arranged?—The cavalry in front, and the infantry on each side of the voters, with a single cavalry soldier outside of them; the Royal Irish constabulary brought up the rear.

205. Was it a large escort in point of number?—There were about 80 men in the constabulary. I heard the magistrates say there were 80 of the constabulary, and I suppose about half a company of infantry, and half a troop of cavalry.

206. Will you give us the names, as you remember them, of the voters who then proceeded with you down towards the town?—I knew but a few of them by name; there was Mr. Walker, Mr. Hamilton, Mr. William Dunbar, Mr. James Denison, Mr. Ball, and Mr. Eakens, and several others. I dare say I could remember the other names if I had time to think.

207. Were those whom you knew, gentlemen of respectability and position?—They were.

208. Did you observe, on starting from the railway terminus, what the state and condition of things was from that place down to the town, as to the crowd?—The crowd that had been round the station had in a great measure dispersed at that time, or rather retired, and when we started from the station there were not many persons in the way; those that were there commenced hooting as we went. As we approached the town, about midway between the railway station and the entrance to the town, the stone throwing commenced, and it grew more violent as we approached, until we got into James-street, and there it became very violent, particularly as we passed cross lanes; one leading down, I think, towards the iron works, on the right; the next was a very high steep one, on the left in the Bull Ring.

209. What about it?—There the stone throwing was very violent. As we reached the Bull Ring there was a temporary stop, and the escort were thrown a little into confusion. I do not know the precise cause, but there was great stone throwing at the time. I was not in the absolute front; I was immediately behind the cavalry. The officer in command seeing this, ordered the men to close in upon the voters, which was a great protection to us. In this position we went on till we reached the bridge.

210. Did you see whether or not any consequences followed from stone throwing?—Many of the soldiers and voters were bleeding at the time; I was bleeding myself at the time.

211. Where were you struck?—I might say all over; but the only severe wound I received was upon the head. It was from that that I was bleeding.

212. Will you resume your narrative?—Just here I heard the soldiers conversing with each other, and one said to another, "We shall catch it at the bridge."

Mr. *Heron* objected to this being received as evidence.

Mr. Justice *Keogh* ruled that it was admissible.

Witness.] I turned and asked the soldier to repeat what he said, and he repeated to me, "We shall catch it at the bridge." Then the men began to show symptoms of discontent. I heard them say, "We cannot stand this," speaking to one another. As soon as we turned the corner into the Bull Ring, I naturally looked towards the bridge, which I had just learnt was the great point of danger, and I saw great crowds at the end of the North Quay. There were also crowds at the Bull Ring, but they did not seem so dense as those on the other side of the river. We then got upon the bridge, and there we halted. The stone throwing there became very violent indeed. The stones seemed to come chiefly from the end of the North Quay, about the Telegraph Office, I think; but they came, in fact, from all directions, except from the west side; there was no means of throwing from that side.

213. Did

Rev. J. F. [illegible].

15 January 1869.

213. Did you happen to observe the size of those stones?—Some were very large; there were brickbats amongst them. I called the attention of my friend, who was with me, to the brickbats.

214. Did you see anything of Captain Dunn, the captain of the infantry?—I did not see anything of Captain Dunn.

215. Did you see him fall?—I did not see him fall; he was more in front of me.

216. What did you see?—I saw the cavalry thrown into great confusion, the horses plunging upon one another, and ultimately they seemed to wheel away from the stone throwing, and they fell back upon us; we were driven back then upon the constabulary at the [illegible] side of the bridge; then the cavalry re-formed and went forward again, and left the centre of the bridge for a short time quite clear. The stone-throwing continued at short intervals; the stone-throwing was very heavy, at times it was dreadful.

217. Were further wounds inflicted?—Further wounds were inflicted, and, about this juncture (the whole thing happened in so short a space of time that it is difficult to speak of things in perfect order; but so well as I remember) the men became very much discontented, and began to call upon the officer, saying that flesh and blood would not stand it, and "Will you allow us to stand here, sir, to be murdered," or "to be killed," or words to that effect. In the midst of this confusion I heard shots fired, and my friend Mr. Wallace next to me turned to me and said, "There is a man killed;" I did not see the man fall, nor did I see who fired the shot.

218. Did you see the body on the ground?—No; they ultimately charged up the street; they were [illegible] for a time in West-street, just opposite to this at the time the body of the dead man was carried past.

219. Where had you betaken yourself so as to enable you to see this?—On the footpath.

220. Were you with the military?—We were; we asked the officer what we were to do; he said he could not do anything more, that is to say, he could not escort us to the booth, for instance; but he said, "You had better stay with us," and we remained accordingly.

221. What did you see then?—While the body of the dead man was carried past, as I have stated, the mob [illegible] up Shop-street, and it appeared that the officers anticipated an attack; they ordered the men to load, which the men did instantly; they held their rifles in a position to be ready to fire if commanded.

222. Had the mob anything in their hands?—They were armed, we believe, with sticks and bludgeons.

223. Did you see what they did with them?—They were yelling at the military, and threatening them.

224. What did the officer do?—When the men had loaded, and held their rifles in a horizontal position, he immediately called out, "Do not fire," "do not fire," "do not fire." I do not know which of the officers it was; I think there were three officers or two officers.

225. Did the mob go off?—They remained a short time, and then they passed on up West-street.

226. What next occurred; where did you go?—I remained there for some time; a person was leaning against one of the shop doors, it gave way and went in, and it remained open, and Mr. Wallace and I got into this place.

227. What state were you in when you got in?—I was bleeding. The people in the house was very kind and gave me a glass of water, and offered other assistance, but I did not feel that I required it; besides, I was anxious to remain with my party, and we remained just at the door. I observed then that some of the men were very much wounded, and one young man near the door seemed faint, turned pale, and I took him by the arm and drew him in.

228. Was that a soldier?—Yes, the people of the house were very kind, and brought him into an inner room, where he sat upon a chair. I asked for a glass of water for him, which he took from my hand; then he fell forward and I caught him in my hand; he leaned his head upon my hand, and I supported him until he recovered again; and I asked some of the persons present to go out and tell some of his comrades to come in, for I feared, perhaps, that I had done wrong in bringing the man from the ranks without his officer's knowledge. Another soldier then came in, and I left them, and went out to the front again. The question then came, how we could get to the booths, and Mr. Wallace and I were anxious to keep together; but it was found that the booths were in different streets. He said that he would not go without an escort. Some gentlemen came and volunteered to escort him; I do not know who they were, but he declined; he said he must have authorised responsible persons to escort him, and the officer of the constabulary brought some police, and he went with them, I think, to Laurence-street. I went to Shop-street, having first taken the arm of Mr. McCann, I think it was. I knew him by appearance and addressed him; it was Mr. McCann, whose face I had known when he was a boy, and he very kindly gave me his arm, and I walked with him towards the booth, when one of the Messrs. Chadwick also came. I do not know Mr. Chadwick's Christian name. It was not that (pointing to a gentleman in the Court), it was your brother; he came on the other side and gave me his arm. I felt, of course, more or less exhausted, and I was glad to have his support, and I went to the booth and voted. I felt it my duty to vote, having come for the purpose. Mr. Wallace and I afterwards met in the Court here, and Mr. Chadwick, who is on the bench now, most kindly gave me his arm to conduct me to the railway station. The high sheriff, whom I also see here, gave his arm to Mr. Wallace, and I think there were two other voters with us, I do not remember whom, who also had, I think, some persons with them. Mr. Richard Kirk also rendered assistance to one of the voters, and walked up to the station with him. We remained at the station for, I think, two or three hours, until we got trains there and went on to Dublin.

229. Have you now stated all the facts as you remember them?—I think so.

230. As they occur to your memory?—As they occur to my memory. There are a great many more which one could not think of unless one sat down to think of them.

[The Witness withdrew.

The Reverend WILLIAM DISNEY ROE, sworn; Examined by Mr. *Plunket*.

The Rev. W. Disney Roe.

23 January 1869.

231. Are you a clergyman of the Established Church?—I am.

232. Where do you reside?—At **Newport**, county of Mayo.

233. Are you the clergyman of that place?—I am the rector and vicar of that place.

234. Do you remember coming to Drogheda, the day of the election here?—Yes; by the half-past eight o'clock train.

235. You are a voter of Drogheda?—Yes.

236. Just tell his lordship exactly what happened, without saying what was said; you may say anything that is said in a public way, but not a private conversation?—On arriving at the station at about 10 o'clock, we got out of the train; I intended to go down into the town, but when I went outside the station I saw a crowd of girls and boys, and some men; some of them had green boughs in their hands and sticks; there was a large force of constabulary also there, somewhere about 80 men, and while wishing to proceed, I heard that some others had also come by the same train for a similar purpose; there was a resident magistrate there, Mr. Reed; some person asked him would it be safe to go down without an escort, and he said that it would not be safe, and that he could not give us a sufficient force to protect us; but that if we would wait until the arrival of the next train, in the meanwhile he would send to the town for an additional force, and then escort all the voters to the Tholsel; we took his advice, and remained until the arrival of the half-past 11 o'clock train; whilst waiting during that time, there was a large crowd of persons came up at the arrival of the train from Belfast, I think it was about a quarter past 10 or 20 minutes past 10, and crowded into the station.

237. Whence did they come from?—From the town; they were principally men.

238. Had they anything in their hands?—They had sticks in their hands, short sticks.

239. What was their demeanour?—They seemed determined about sending the crowd into the station, and I and several others went into the waiting room and remained there; there seemed to be some confusion until the train moved off, and then those men retired. A man came up bleeding to the station from the town, and his face was covered with blood; he sat on a form at the station-house and his wound was dressed there; it was washed. Another man also came up from the town, he had lost his hat, and he had a pocket handkerchief wrapped round his head; I spoke to the man, and he told me ——

Mr. *Heron* objected to this being received as evidence.

Mr. Justice *Keogh* **overruled the objection.**

Witness.] He said that he was badly wounded; I asked him how ——

Mr. Justice *Keogh* ruled that this was not admissible.

Witness.] Mr. Hamilton came by the same train by which I came, and he had three men with him, those men seemed humble men; I saw Mr. Whitworth come up to the station during that interval, and he addressed one of the men, and asked him whom did he wish to vote for; there were a lot of people about who had sticks in their hands, and they were saying, "Vote Whitworth;" Mr. Hamilton was by, and Mr. Whitworth addressed Mr. Hamilton, and said it was a shame for him.

240. Mr. *Plunket*.] Did he do anything?—I saw him put his hand on the man's shoulder and ask him, "Would you not vote for me?" they seemed so angry that I retired from the window; I was told ——

Mr. Justice *Keogh*.] Never mind what you were told.

241. Mr. *Plunket*.] What did you see yourself?—Mr. Hamilton came back, and then the man was taken.

242. Did you see that man again?—I did not see that man again.

243. Then you came back again?—Yes.

244. What next did you observe; were the constabulary taking any active part?—The constabulary cleared the station, after the departure of the Belfast train, and meanwhile some hussars came up and a company of infantry, previously to the arrival of the half-past 11 o'clock train; Mr. Reed told the voters ——

Mr. *Heron* objected.

Mr. Justice *Keogh* ruled that the evidence was admissible.

Witness.] He told us that he would conduct us as far as the Tholsel, but that he would not conduct us anywhere else from the Tholsel; he also told us that a change would be made by the cavalry, if there was any necessity for such ——

Mr. *Heron* objected to the reception of this as evidence.

Mr. *McDonogh* argued that this evidence was admissible.

Witness.] He addressed those words to myself.

Mr. Justice *Keogh* directed the witness to confine himself to facts.

Witness.] At the time the train arrived we started from the station; the cavalry went first.

245. Mr. *Plunket*.] Whom do you mean by "we"?—A number of voters; the voters who had already come down by the half-past eight o'clock train, and the voters who arrived by the half-past eleven o'clock train. The cavalry went in front, and some cavalry at the sides; the infantry round the voters, and the constabulary guarding the rear. On leaving the gate outside the station-house some few stones were thrown, and when we came to the hill up to St. Mary's Church the stone-throwing was very great; one of the soldiers was struck, and I heard him saying, "Are we to be murdered in this way?" He was struck in the face. The stones rattled against the rifles of the infantry, and several of the voters were struck. I saw the Rev. Mr. Martin and Mr. Hamilton, who was alongside myself; he was struck on the back, and he complained very much of it; and about Jamestreet my own hat was knocked off, but fortunately I recovered it. I was struck in several parts of the body, but when we came to the Bull Ring the stone-throwing increased. One gentleman had an umbrella, and he lifted it up, and in a little time, said

The Rev. W. Disney Roe.

15 January 1869.

until that was broken, it gave some protection to him, and also to myself. Whatever was the cause, the cavalcade was halted, and there was a great scene of confusion, the mob shouting, and the stone-throwing having increased, until at length I saw the cavalry wheel round apparently in fright, and the infantry and cavalry rushed back upon the voters, and closed them up; and some gentlemen who were before me rushed against me, and the infantry also, and I turned, and I was pitched violently upon three or four gentlemen. There were some soldiers passing, and when I was pushed down I caught hold of one of them; he struggled to get away, but, however, I was the stronger man of the two, and I got up. When I got up the confusion still existed, the soldiers were running to either side of the bridge; at this time there was a shot fired; there was great cheering; when the shot was fired there was a peculiar sort of shout raised by the mob, as if of triumph. I did not see the man fire, but I heard the shot. Shortly afterwards another shot was fired. I fell back upon the constabulary, and as I just reached them the officer of the constabulary came down and told them to load. Some of the constabulary begged me to go into a house; I said, "No," and immediately a trumpet sounded, whether for charge or not I cannot say, but, however, the trumpet sounded, and there seemed to be a movement. The cavalry wheeled round their horses, and I saw the infantry rushing forward, and I rushed on with them, and there was a charge then up Shop-street, and I came with the cavalry and the infantry to the Tholsel. When I looked round I saw that only five other voters were with me—Mr. Minton, the Rev. Mr. Wallace (as far as I can remember), Mr. Jamieson, Captain St. George, and Mr. St. George Smythe—out of the whole number.

246. How much was that number when you started?—I cannot say; there was a number of them.

Mr. Heron objected to this evidence.

247. Mr. Plunkett (to the Witness).] Were there more than 20?—

Mr. Heron objected, unless the names of the electors were given.

248. Mr. Justice Keogh.] Do you know whether those parties had votes who were with you? —Not more than what they told me, that they intended to vote.

249. Can you say how many persons there were who were, to your own knowledge, voters within that number; you may not be able to enumerate all the names now?—I could not say that, except from hearsay.

250. Then you had better not say?—I could say how many started; I could say the names, but I would confine myself to the number.

251. Mr. Plunkett.] How many persons, whether voters or not, started with that escort?—Those that I enumerated, and there was another, Mr. Jamieson; there were two Mr. Jamiesons; there was a Colonel Fairclough, there was Dr. Brereton, there was a Mr. Filgate, and there were some others with whose names I am not acquainted.

252. Do you know how many persons started with the escort; you need not say exactly?—I was told ——

253. Never mind what you were told?—There seemed to be about 30.

254. You had just come to the place where you say you saw five of that party with them?—About five of that party when we came to the Tholsel here. I saw some of those gentlemen very badly wounded. When I arrived at the Tholsel I was told that a man was shot. I spoke to those gentlemen, and told them that it would be well for them not to remain out in the street, but to come into the Tholsel. They said they would remain under the protection of the military. I came in here, and I presented myself as a voter, here in this place, and I was told that my polling booth, commencing with the letter "R," was not where I presented myself, and I went up then to another place, where I was told that they were taking voters' names, and I was told that was not the booth for letter "R." I asked, then, where it was, and they told me in Lawrence-street. I was going down some stairs connected with this building, and I heard shouting outside, and I looked out at the window, and I saw the corpse of the man that had been shot laid on a shutter or a door, I cannot say which, and carried. The people seemed very angry. I saw, then, that if I should go out of the Tholsel, I should go at once to McClintock's tally-room, and decline going down Lawrence-street, as I saw a large crowd down there; and I thought at the time that that crowd had been driven on by the charge of the cavalry. However, I determined that I would not go down that street. I went to the tally-room, and I met Mr. Mayne, and I told him distinctly——

Mr. Heron objected to this evidence.

255. Mr. Plunkett (to the Witness).] Did you vote or did you not vote?—I did not vote.

256. What was the state of your mind at that time?

Mr. Heron objected to this question.

Mr. McDonogh supported this line of examination.

Witness.] I was horrified at the death of the man; and I did not think myself justified in running any further risk myself, or asking the police or the military to risk their lives.

257. Mr. Justice Keogh.] You did not vote, therefore, in consequence of apprehensions which you entertained?—Undoubtedly; as a question of it.

258. Mr. Plunkett.] You say that you did not vote; where did you go to?—To Sir Leopold McClintock's tally-room.

259. How long did you remain there?—Until shortly before the starting of a train which arrived in Dublin somewhere about four o'clock.

260. You went by that train to Dublin?—I went by that train to Dublin.

261. How did you get to the railway station from the tally-room?—Sir Leopold McClintock came out and told those voters——

Mr. Heron objected to this evidence.

262. Mr. Plunkett (to the Witness).] Never mind what he said; how did you get down?—I came down with the high sheriff, who kindly offered to conduct Mr. Filgate and Mr. Jamieson to the station.

263. Mr. Justice Keogh.] In fact, you were accompanied by the high sheriff?—By the high sheriff.

The Rev. W. Disney Roe.

15 January 1869.

Cross-examined by Mr. *Pallas*.

264. At what hour was it that you made up your mind that you ought not to vote?—I was coming down stairs after saying——

265. I know that; but I just want to fix the hour, if you can?—Well, it was about 12 o'clock. We came down as soon as we could after the arrival of the train, and I suppose it was about 12 o'clock.

266. Then from 12 until 4 you remained in the tally-rooms?—Yes.

267. Do you know now the position of the booth in Lawrence street?—No.

268. Then you are not able to say how far it was from the tally-rooms?—I was told that it was down Lawrence-street, and I saw a crowd there.

269. Will you swear that it was more than 30 yards to the tally-rooms from where you were?—No.

270. *Mr. Justice Keogh*.] Had you come from your residence in the county of Mayo for the purpose of voting?—Yes.

271. When had you left home?—I left home on the Wednesday.

272. What day of the month was that?—About the 18th.

273. Then you came to Dublin, and from Dublin to Drogheda?—I came to Dublin at about six o'clock on the Thursday, and then I came the following morning to Drogheda at about half-past eight.

274. And your business was to vote?—I had no other business.

[The Witness withdrew.

Mr. William Henry Filgate, sworn; Examined by Mr. *Ryland*.

Mr. W. H. Filgate.

275. Are you an Elector of Drogheda?—I am.

276. Did you come to vote at the last election here?—I did.

277. By what train did you come?—By the quarter to ten train.

278. At what time did you reach the station here in Drogheda?—At about 12.

279. Were there many other voters along with you at the station when you came?—There were several other gentlemen, whom I understood to be voters.

280. Were you amongst the party who were escorted by the military from the station into the town?—I was.

281. Did anything happen to you on the way?—Yes.

282. Will you describe what occurred?—I was struck on the back of the head by a man who had an iron bar in his hand; he came in through the file of soldiers, and went back again; shortly afterwards, I was struck by a stone on the side of my face, which cut me, and I got a third blow on my leg, with several other blows; those three blows all hurt me.

283. Whereabouts was it that you were when you got those blows?—The first blow was some time before I reached the bridge; the second blow was a stone also before I reached the bridge; and the third was on my leg, but I am not sure whether that was before I was on the bridge or after I had reached it.

284. What did you see at the bridge?—At the bridge I saw stones thrown at us, both from the front and rear; there were sticks, and I cannot tell what else.

285. Did you see the sticks thrown?—Thrown! the air was full of missiles of various kinds. When the troops had reached the end of the bridge, there was a call of "Back, back," and I found that the Dragoons in front were in disorder, and were coming back upon us, and I retreated a few steps; and the next thing that happened was that I heard the report of a shot; shortly afterwards, I heard, as I thought, two other reports, closely following one another.

286. Did you see any one injured by those shots?—No; I could not see in front. There was then a lull, and I next heard the word "Charge," and I then saw the Dragoons galloping up the street, followed by the troops, and the crowd in front. The police, who had very properly stopped at the entrance to the bridge on the Dublin side, then rushed past me. I then found myself standing on the bridge with two other gentlemen, one Mr. Francis Hamilton, who went towards the station, the other a tall, elderly gentleman, whom I did not know at the time, but who I since understand was Major Fairclough; his clothes were bloody, and he had a cut under the eye, and a very ugly-looking cut it was.

287. Where did you go then?—I walked towards the town, and the first house I came to, the door of which was open, I asked to be allowed to go in; I was very kindly permitted to do so, and I had my head and my face washed, and I remained there some time, until the blood had ceased to flow somewhat; I then went up to the tally-room.

288. In what state were you when you got to the tally-rooms; had you recovered from the effect of those bruises; I do not mean whether they were healed; were you stunned at all?—Well, I was not stunned, I was a little bothered.

289. Did you afterwards vote?—No.

290. What was the reason why you did not vote?—I understood at the tally-room that Sir Leopold McClintock's agents had been withdrawn from the booths, and that it was no use.

291. At what hour was it that you got to the tally-rooms?—Well, I cannot be positive, but I should think about a little after one o'clock; it might have been half after one or two.

292. How long did you stay in the tally-rooms?—I remained there until, I should think, nearly four o'clock.

293. Did you go back to the station?—I did go back to the station.

294. How did you go back to the station; did you walk or drive?—I walked, but I did not cross the bridge.

295. How did you get there?—I walked to the old station on the north side of the river; I got upon the railroad there, and I walked across the lattice bridge to the station.

296. Were you by yourself, or was there any one with you?—I was by myself.

297. Is there anything further that occurs to your mind that I may have omitted asking?—I am not aware that there is.

Cross-examined by Mr. *Hamill*.

298. Do you remember, at any time, hearing the word "halt" made use of, either in the

Bell

Ball Ring or on the bridge?—I did hear the word "link;" I don't know where the Ball Ring is; it was whilst I was on the bridge that I heard the word "link," and it was passed on.

299. From the rear to the front?—From the rear to the front; and it was passed on by the escort party, as far as I believe.

300. You say that you went into a house; do you remember that some gentleman or gentlemen came in and offered to bring anyone there who wanted to go up to the Tholsel to vote?—A man did come in, and I think he offered to escort me to the Tholsel; he did escort me to the tally-room.

301. And in going to the tally-room, you had to pass the Tholsel?—Yes.

302. Do you know whether that was the sheriff or some other gentleman; do you know who that person was?—No, I do not. I don't recollect his name, it was not the sheriff, for I saw the sheriff afterwards.

303. Do you know where your booth was at which you were to have polled?—Indeed I do not.

304. Mr. Justice *Keogh*.] Will you describe, as clearly as you can, how the cavalry went about; did they go right about, or did they merely back their horses?—They were in confusion; I saw their flanks; in fact, the horses were across the entrance to the street.

305. But was it a regular military movement?—Oh, no; they were beaten back in confusion.

306. How were the infantry affected; what movement did they make?—I could not see what the infantry were doing at that time in front.

307. But the cavalry were put in confusion, and thrown back?—They were, and they came back upon the escort party.

[The Witness withdrew.

Mr. *W. H. Palmer*.

15 January 1869.

Henry Alexander Hamilton, Esq., sworn; Examined by Mr. *McDonogh*.

H. A. Hamilton, Esq.

308. Where do you live?—At Balbriggan.

309. Are you a magistrate of the county of Dublin?—I am; and of the county of Meath.

310. Are you a voter for this town?—Yes.

311. Do you remember having come to the town upon the day of the polling?—Yes.

312. Were you accompanied by any other voters?—By four other voters.

313. Will you mention their names to his Lordship?—Patrick Donald, Andrew Semple, John Devine, and John Usher.

314. At about what time did they reach the Drogheda terminus?—Shortly before 10 o'clock; it was the half-past eight train leaving Dublin; I got in at Balbriggan.

315. Did they get in with you?—They got in with me.

316. Upon reaching the station, will you state to his Lordship exactly the state of things which you found there?—On arriving at the station there was considerable confusion, and I was anxious to get back to Dublin as soon as possible, and I addressed myself to Mr. Reed, who stated that he was the stipendiary magistrate, and was very anxious to go down to vote; and he pointed out the state of the place, and said he had but a small number of cavalry at his disposal, and it would be impossible to take us; and he suggested to us to wait till the arrival of the train which would leave Dublin at a quarter before ten; he would then have a large body of infantry and cavalry, and would escort not only ourselves, but the voters who came down by the second train; and I consulted then in trouble with some of the gentlemen who are here this morning. We remained at the station. I observed on the platform some streaks of blood when we were walking up and down. The mob had complete possession of the platform and of the rooms; they came in and out.

317. The rooms appertaining to the station?—The rooms appertaining to the station—the waiting rooms. They hustled me and drove me about, and those four men who were waiting with me; Semple said he should go off, and he went away.

318. Do you know where he went?—He went down to the town to vote, and the other three men remained for the present with me; they were walking round among the crowd, and going in and out the station-house with me. The mob were outside with their sticks, and I observed that a good number of them had in their hands those short iron bolts with a nut on them, which might have been found lying about a railway station; they had those in their hands brandishing them at us. That state of affairs went on for some time, and we waited. When I was standing outside, Pat McDonald stated to me——

Mr. *Heron* objected to this evidence.

319. Mr. *McDonogh* (to the Witness).] Was he one of the voters who came with you?—He was.

320. Was it said aloud in the crowd, or a private communication to you?—I considered it a private communication to me. The other two men, John Usher and John Devine, remained about the station-house; they were in different parts in and out, and I should say it was a little after 11 o'clock or so, or it might be after, when Mr. Henry Clinton, Mr. Whitworth's agent, as I understand, came up to me. We were at that time out among the mob; Mr. Henry Clinton came up to me in a very violent and very excited manner, and he said, "What are you doing with those men?" I said, "I am doing nothing with the men, the men are there." There were only two men there at this time, Usher and Devine, standing about in the crowd, and he spoke very violently, and that sort of thing, to me, in a very excited manner. Then a gentleman came up that I did not know; I have been since informed that he is Mr. Whitworth; I had never seen him before.

321. Do you now recognise him?—He had not spectacles on at that time. That is the gentleman that came up to me (*pointing to Mr. Whitworth*), and the mob was standing all round, with their sticks and those iron bars that I have before described, in a very excited manner. Mr. Clinton and Mr. Whitworth addressed first John Usher, and said, "For whom do you vote?" two or three times. Usher immediately said, "I will vote for Whitworth." Upon that, the mob seized him up, dragged him off in a car, and I saw no more of him.

322. Had that man previously promised to vote for Sir Leopold?—He sent me word that he

H. A. Hamilton, Esq.

15 January 1869.

he would do so; I had merely written him a note asking him to vote. He was with me at Balbriggan, and he gave me to understand that he would. In the train, coming down, there was a gentleman, an agent of Mr. Whitworth, whom I afterwards recognised in Drogheda.

323. Mr. *Heron.*] What was his name?—I cannot tell; he was the man afterwards in charge of a part of the mob, for I met him with green ribbons in his hat; he told me that he was one——

Mr. *Heron* objected to this evidence being received.

Mr. Justice *Keogh* directed the witness to state only what he knew of his own knowledge.

324. Mr. *McDonogh* (to the *Witness*).] Did you see him with the mob?—I did. There were three men dressed in the same way; he had two bands of green ribbons round his hat; he was one of the men talking in the train with me——

Mr. *Heron* objected to this evidence.

Mr. Justice *Keogh* allowed the objection.

Witness.] Usher was disposed of, and then there was only Devine standing some way off, when Mr. Whitworth rushed up to him, and Devine came to me, and he grasped me by his right hand, and he called out, "Will you save me?" Mr. Whitworth came up and caught him by the coat collar, in this way (*describing the same*), and he said, "Who will you vote for—who will you vote for?" I did not speak; I never opened my lips except to Mr. Clinton; I did address a few words, but when those other gentlemen came up I never opened my lips, or said one word. Mr. Whitworth put his fist up in my face, and backed me up against the wall, this old man holding my hand all the time, and he said, "You are a disgrace to the place; you are a disgrace to the place." He then called one of those men, whispering to John Devine, "For whom will you vote?" Mr. Whitworth then struck me in that manner (*describing the same*), which knocked me away from Devine, and I lost his hand, and I was thrown out into the mob. I was about six feet from Devine, and they still kept on at him, "Who will you vote for?" Devine called out, "I will not vote for anyone." I then saw Devine go into the railway station. A man came up to me of the name of Townsend; he was with me, and he asked might he take Devine back to Balbriggan; he wanted to go away; he was afraid. I said, "Yes, of course, take the man away;" and I saw them go into the railway station, and I saw nothing more for some five or six minutes. The mob rushed out of the station-house again with this man Devine. Devine caught hold of me in passing, and got me by the hand, and he grasped me very firmly. The mob then pushed us both on towards the goods station. Devine was knocked down with very great violence, indeed, and fell on the broad of his back, and received some blows. I fell on my knees, but not from the blows; I consider I was dragged down by Devine; I fell on one knee, I think, and my right hand came to the ground, and sprained my wrist entirely. I got up, and Devine got up; the mob dragged him off, and he was carried over to a car, close to the goods station. They were as full as they could be, close up to the car, and he was thrown on his back on the cushions, and he was held down by the arms and legs, and he was struggling to get off. I called to Captain Talbot, the stipendiary magistrate, who was riding past, and I said, "Will you give no protection to this man; this man is carried away against his will?" And he said, "I cannot do anything for you, sir." I saw him carried over towards the car, and immediately the car drove off amongst the crowd, and I saw no more of it.

325. Then those four men were disposed of?—Then those four men were disposed of.

326. Had Devine made any promise to you for Sir Leopold M'Clintock?—Yes.

327. Mr. *Heron.*] Had he promised to you?—Yes, that morning.

328. Mr. *M'Donogh.*] Will you proceed?—I had some conversation with the stipendiary magistrate, and he said that he would form the troops up at the door of the railway station. After all this occurred he sent in troops and police, and they cleared the place. He said, "I will keep the door shut, and if you will have the kindness to marshal the voters when they come down, I will have the soldiers in a sort of square that you will go into, and I will escort you to the polling." I waited for the arrival of that train, and saw a good number of my friends arrive by it. I thought there were 35; I told them there were 35.

Mr. *Heron* objected to this evidence.

329. Mr. *M'Donogh* (to the *Witness*).] Were there about 35 persons?—I thought so.

330. Did you know them to be voters?—I thought they were voters; I knew a great many of them; there were 15 I suppose, being acquaintances of my own, who arrived by that train.

331. Mr. Justice *Keogh.*] How did you know the 15 to be voters?—Except from knowing them, and seeing their names on the register.

332. Do you know that those 15, from your seeing their names on the register, were voters?—I went over the register with Sir Leopold M'Clintock one evening, and the men whose names I give you, I can state were on the register. There was Henry Sands, Marsh[illegible], my own cousin (Francis Hamilton, Mountjoy-square), two Mr. Smiths, Captain Smyth, Mr. Filgate, who was on the table, I saw him there; Mr. Morton, Mr. Rowe, Colonel Fairclough, Mr. Vanhomrigh, Mr. John and Mr. James Jamieson, a distiller of this town; and another, I think we call him Mr. Jamieson of Mornington; I do not know his christian name; Mr. Wallace; Mr. Brandon was there, I saw him; I do not at this moment recollect any others. Then the escort being ready the door was opened, and we all walked in while the troops were opening for us; the military were each side, there were some cavalry in front and a few of the cavalry each side; I was the second I think upon the left rank; we were about three abreast; we proceeded away from the railway station down towards the town; we got some way when the stone-throwing began very violently, and it increased as we got near the town; when we got to James's-street, I was struck with a large stone on the back, on the vertebrae at the back of the neck; it staggered me very much, and left me very faint from the blow, and as we were going along the stones, they began stone-throwing, and sticks and small pieces of

of broken and hoop iron I saw coming at us; persons all about me were more or less cut and injured. As we turned the corner from James's-street, a vast number of missiles came upon us, and pieces of broken glass; there was one of the troops, one of the 9th Regiment upon my left, who was cut on the side of the head with the bottom of a broken quart bottle; it struck him on the side of the head, and the man said, "What on earth am I to do?" I said, "You had better put your handkerchief to it;" the blood streamed from the side of his head; he took out his white handkerchief and bound his head up. We went on, and still the missiles came to us in all directions; the men were calling out, "Will you allow us to be murdered? Let us protect ourselves;" those were the troops. We pressed on, and had got about half way across the bridge, when we were stopped; we were told that the Riot Act was being read; while there, the stones were coming very thick indeed, and those other missiles also across us. The dragoons got into confusion; there were four or five in front of us; we were close behind them. The horses reared up; I saw the men striking at them with sticks and stones, and the horses became restive and plunged among the men. After the Riot Act was read, a very warm volley of stones came from the North Quay, which runs at right angles to Shop-street and also from Shop-street. The horses and the men were all driven back, the horses and the infantry in great confusion. I was thrown out from among the escort altogether; I was close to the bridge. I heard one man call to the others to make haste; I looked round, and a man was loading his Snider rifle, and two of his comrades were protecting him; just at that time I was struck with a heavy nob-stick; I threw up my arm and caught the blow on the right arm; he passed me and struck at the troops; immediately after that a man who was about 10 feet from me was shot dead; he was close to me. There were two shots fired as close as they could go; the ball passed me and shot this man, and he lay on the bridge, and his arm rose and fell; I was close to him; the dragoons had got each side of the bridge, up and down the pathway, and after the shot the mob fell back a slight way. I looked round there was no one on that part of the bridge but myself and the body of the deceased man. The dragoons formed behind me, across the bridge, and charged past me and the body. Being by myself, I immediately followed the dragoons close up after them. Missiles of all descriptions and filth, and earthen vessels, were thrown on us or on the dragoons as we passed up. Then I came up; I could not find a human being to speak to whom I recognised; the mob were bustling me; I got my back against the wall, the other side of the street; I could get no information as to where the polling places were, how we were to vote, or what we were to do. I afterwards saw Mr. Edward Verdon, a gentleman I have known many years; I asked where is the polling place, he said, "Oh, I will show you." He brought me across to the polling place, and I voted for Sir Leopold M'Clintock, and there was nobody I knew there; he got me some sherry; I was wholly exhausted from the blows I received, and from being knocked about and bustled. I got up to go and look out of the window, and I was immediately pulled back by a gentleman in the room, saying if I showed at the window I should be destroyed, and the place pulled down; I waited there a considerable time, and then went across to my friend Mr. Kearns; I was exceedingly anxious to get back to Dublin as I was much interested in the election for the next day. I said, "Oh, I must get off by the next train." I came out into the street again, and I tried to get down by the street here at the bridge; the place was in such confusion, and the mob so great, that I could not. I got Mr. Kearns to help me make my way up past the gaol; some of the mob followed, hooting and yelling, and calling out, "To hell with the Queen, down with your Church, and up with the stars and stripes." I then got across the Belfast Junction line to the north part of the town; I got to the north of the bridge over the Boyne; I was by myself; I crossed over the viaduct, and I got in that way to the railway station and remained at the railway station till the train came up; I went on to Dublin by the quarter before three train.

E. A. Hamilton, Esq.

15 January 1869.

333. Have you stated substantially what you remember?—Yes, all that I can remember.

Cross-examined by Mr. *Heron*.

334. What hour was it that you voted?—I will tell you as near as I can; I should think it was as near as possible to 12.

335. You mean a quarter after 12?—I came up immediately after the dragoons, immediately after the man was shot. I was about here for five or six minutes; it was before the body was carried through the streets. I had voted at that time.

336. You went and voted before you went to your tally-rooms?—Yes, by Mr. Verdon's kindness.

337. Where was it that you voted?—I think it is Peter-street; it is nearly opposite Sir *Leopold M'Clintock's* tally-room, the conjunction of Shop-street, on the right, up where the agent was; Peter-street I think it is called.

338. Did you know at that hour the state of the poll when you voted?—Not the least; I had not the slightest knowledge.

339. You did not go to the tally-rooms at all?—*No*; after I voted I asked to see Mr. Kearns, to direct me my way.

340. You were in a hurry to get back to the county election?—Yes.

341. The county election was the next morning; there was a little talk about the surprise in the country, like the surprise here?—Yes.

342. You have told us about those four voters?—Yes.

343. As to the man whom I have taken as Macdonald, accompanying you from Balbriggan?—Yes.

344. You do not mean to convey to his Lordship that McDonald, Devine, and Usher, live at Balbriggan?—No.

345. They live at Drogheda?—Two miles from Drogheda.

346. The northern side?—They are tenants to Mr. Cooper, for whom I am agent.

347. They live two miles on the northern side of Drogheda?—Yes.

348. In reference to McDonald, Devine, and Usher, are they not tenants-at-will, or tenants *from year to year*?—Yes, certainly.

349. You know it?—Yes.

350. Sample is not a tenant on the Cooper estate?—No.

351. Where

H. A. Hamilton, Esq.

15 January 1869.

351. Where does he live?—Three miles beyond Balbriggan, on the Dublin side.

352. How long had the four voters been on a visit to you before the election?—I know nothing whatever of them being there till the night before the election.

353. You know nothing at all about them?—I did not know that they were in the town.

354. You knew they were in Balbriggan, by some extraordinary coincidence, the night before the election?—No, two of them called for me.

> Mr. Justice *Keogh*.] The poll-books are here, and I suppose there is no objection for either party having the use of them.
>
> Mr. *McDonogh*.] Certainly not.

Witness.] Two of them called upon me. I came down to my own house on Thursday night, about half-past nine o'clock (I will tell you their names); Usher and Devine knocked at my door; I had no communication with them, except by letter; I wrote a line to each of them.

355. I only ask you when you knew they arrived at Balbriggan; you say the night before?—I had no knowledge of it, except what I have told you.

356. Do you remember the election of 1865?—No, I have no knowledge of it.

357. Do not you know that McDonald, Devine, and Usher voted in 1865, for Whitworth?—Neither directly or indirectly do I know of it.

358. You never heard it?—No.

359. You do not know how they voted in 1865?—No.

360. There was no Conservative candidate in 1865?—I took no interest in the election at all. I do not know who the opposition to Whitworth was at the time.

361. Do you know McDonald, Devine, and Usher to be Roman Catholics?—Yes.

362. And Semple a Protestant?—Yes; the Church of Scotland.

363. Semple is on Colonel Taylor's estate?—He is now; he has got the farm within this last year.

364. Did he vote out of his farm on Colonel Taylor's estate?—No.

365. He was the tenant on Colonel Taylor's estate at the time he voted?—He came down to vote, but Colonel Taylor's estate is not in the borough.

366. Where did McDonald, Devine, Usher, and Semple lodge on the night before the polling?—I have not the least knowledge.

367. Have you a rent warden on the Cooper's estate?—Yes.

368. What is his name?—Hodson.

369. Was he in Balbriggan the night before the polling?—He lives there; I did not see him that night.

370. Do you believe he was there?—Yes.

371. Had you any communication with him?—Not at that time.

372. But immediately before?—No.

373. Did you give him any word about having the Cooper tenants all right?—No; and so guarded was I that I would not allow him to come with me that morning in the train; he asked to come.

374. So guarded were you of what?—Of having anything said against me bringing these men against their will, which was said. I would not allow the bailiff to come with me; I turned him back.

375. Was he coming with you?—Yes; he said, "I will come with you to Drogheda." I said, "No, you will not do it." I did not see these men, except by note, as I wrote.

376. What rent does that McDonald pay?—About 25 *l.* a half-year.

377. What rent does Devine pay?—[illegible] a year.

> The learned Judge intimated that it was not necessary to enter into the question of the rent paid.
>
> *Witness*. They are very respectable men.

378. Mr. *Heron*.] Do you mean to convey to his Lordship that Mr. Whitworth struck you?—I do.

379. Was it a hard blow?—It was sufficient to separate me from the hand of Devine, and drive me out into the mob.

380. Were you holding on to Devine as hard as you could?—No; Devine was holding on to me; his hand was in mine; he held me as hard as he could hold.

381. You said you let Semple go by himself?—I did not let him; the man said he would go, so did McDonald.

382. Semple went off and voted by himself?—I do not know whether he voted; he went off.

383. I may tell you he voted for McClintock; McDonald went away then?—I do not know.

384. Did not you inquire whether McDonald, Devine, Usher, voted or not?—My impression is that they never voted at all.

385. That is what you heard?—From hearsay. I believe none of the three voted at all.

386. Mr. Justice *Keogh*.] Who do you mean by the "three"?—McDonald, Usher, and Devine. I believe now that Semple did vote.

387. Mr. *Heron*.] He did vote for McClintock?—Yes.

388. What hour did Semple go away to vote by himself?—He stayed with me about the station for some time; he went about half an hour after we arrived.

389. What hour was it?—About half-past 10.

390. Semple went off by himself?—Yes; the other three remained.

391. They remained with you?—They were about the station.

392. They remained with you?—They remained with me, because we could not get protection to the poll.

393. Did not Semple go and vote?—He went by himself.

394. To vote for McClintock?—Yes, he told me so.

395. You believe he did vote?—Yes.

396. Could McDonald have walked down with Semple?—He did not.

397. Could he?—I do not think he possibly could, for I could not.

398. In what position of life is Semple?—A farmer; a most respectable man.

399. He is a most respectable man, and is perfectly well known?—I believe he voted for Whitworth at the last election.

400. No, you are wrong?—He told me he did.

401. Who paid the railway fare for the four men?—I do not know; I did not.

402. What other voters got in at Balbriggan?—None, to my knowledge; there was no five. I made a mistake about a man named Green, who did not vote; he is one of Colonel Cooper's tenants; he did not vote.

403. Is

403. As this day you did not pay the railway fare for the men, did you pay your own railway fare?—I did.

404. Have you no suspicion who paid the railway fare for the men?—No.

405. Was it Hudson?—Hudson did not to my knowledge.

406. You gave no money for the payment?—No.

407. You do not know where the men lodged the night before the polling?—No.

408. Have you a suspicion?—No.

409. Were they in Hudson's house?—They told me they went backwards and forwards to Dublin; they had been threatened, and they came there to hide themselves.

410. To your house?—No, not in my house; I was not in Ballinggan at all the many days before the election.

411. You entertain a great interest in this Conservative cause all over Ireland?—Undoubtedly.

412. Now, as to this expression you heard from the mob; I must repeat the terms, "To hell with the Queen, down with the church, and up with the stars and stripes"?—Yes.

413. We all know stars and stripes is the American flag?—Yes.

414. Now, I would ask you, as magistrate, having some experience, this question; you heard Mr. McDonagh's speech?—Yes.

415. And you heard there was what was called a Fenian element?—He used that expression.

416. Do not you think the expression of "stars and stripes," was likely to come from that element?—There are Fenians in America, as we all know by hearsay.

417. Do not you think that expression was likely to come from a mob of that sentiment?—That is my opinion.

Re-examined by Mr. *McDonagh*.

418. You told Mr. Heron that the two men, I did not catch which man, had told you that they had been threatened; what two was that?—Usher was the man who told me he was threatened to be thrown into the Boyne, and McDonald as well, and Cleary; they said they dare not cross the bridge, they would be thrown into the Boyne.

419. When was it they told you that?—The night before, at my house.

420. Mr. Justice *Keogh*.] You said you got back yourself by the Boyne viaduct?—Yes.

421. Is that by the railway bridge?—Yes; I crossed by the north of the bridge, the railway station is to the south of the viaduct.

422. It was the railway bridge you crossed?—Yes, the large viaduct; I was by myself.

423. After this occurrence, you mentioned an altercation between you and Mr. Whitworth; what time intervened before you entered that square formed by the military, to go down to the voting?—Fifty minutes.

424. Before you entered the square?—Yes; I know by the arrival of the train.

425. Did you see Mr. Whitworth or his agent there after this occurrence which you have mentioned?—What occurrence?

426. The conflict between you and him, such as it was?—I did not see Mr. Whitworth again after the man had said, "I will not vote for any one;" he appeared to me to go into the mob by the railway station; I did not see him after.

427. When you speak of the mob which met you as the military were going, were they a distinct mob at the railway station?—The mob at the railway station, there were some women among; I saw no women in the mob at the bridge; they all seemed to be men armed with sticks, but from the railway station to the bridge, we were continually pelted; I ought to say this; when we got off the railway premises, there is a road running parallel from the railway station to the country road, while we were going along that, still on the railway premises, we were not interfered with; but opposite the poor-house, coming on the main road, I first saw the stones coming, and it increased in violence until we got to the large square on the bridge.

[The Witness withdrew.

Mr. Richard Macabe, sworn; Examined by Mr. *McDonagh*.

428. Are you by profession, a short-hand writer, or reporter?—Yes; I am.

429. For many years, have you been engaged in the practice of the court?—Beyond 20 years.

430. Were you in this town on the night before the day of the polling, and under the balcony of Siloam's hotel?—I was in the drawing-room of the hotel.

431. Were you listening to the speeches delivered on that occasion?—Yes.

432. Will you look at that report (*handing the same to the Witness*), is that in your hand writing?—It is.

433. Does that report, which is in your handwriting, give——

Mr. *Heron* objected to the course of examination, on the ground that the original notes ought to be produced and read.

434. Mr. *McDonagh* (to the *Witness*).] Did you take it in shorthand?—Partly in shorthand, and partly in longhand.

435. What has become of those partly shorthand and partly longhand notes?—I do not know; I threw them into my waste basket at my desk.

436. When you were done with them?—Yes; it may be that, had I known that I would have been examined on this to-day, I would have preserved them.

437. Have you searched for them since?—Yes.

438. Have you been able to find them?—I have been unable to find them.

439–40. You threw them into the waste basket?—Yes, the waste basket was removed in the usual way, down to the kitchen.

441. Is that a faithful and honest report of what occurred, which you hold in your hand?—Yes.

Mr. *Heron* objected to the paper being read, unless the shorthand and longhand notes which were taken at the time, were produced.

Mr. Justice *Keogh* overruled the objection.

442. Mr. *McDonagh* (to the *Witness*).] Is that a true and faithful report of what occurred?—Yes, a true and faithful report of my notes.

443. Do you know the name of the clergyman who

H. A. Hamilton, Esq.

13 January 1869.

Mr. R. Macabe.

Mr. R. [illegible]

15 January 1869.

who spoke first?—The Rev. Mr. Murphy, a Catholic curate.

444. He was the first speaker?—Yes, I think so.

445. Who was the next speaker?—There is a portion of this not my report.

446. Not in your handwriting?—No, not in my handwriting.

447. We will not allude to that at all, give nothing but you own handwriting?—It is merely an addition.

448. Mr. *Pollen.*] State which of it is not in your handwriting?—This last page.

449. Mr. *McDonogh.*] Whatever is not in your handwriting, we will take off. Do not read anything that is there but what is in your own handwriting. Who is the next speaker to Mr. Murphy?—The Rev. Mr. Murphy, a Catholic curate, the Rev. Mr M'Kee.

450 What is the next person who spoke?—The Rev. Mr. Glyn. He is the next, but he is a gentleman I did not know. I took the names of gentlemen as I heard them.

451. You took the names of the other gentlemen?—Yes; the Rev. Dr. Murphy came next, and then follows the Rev. Mr. Govan, a Catholic curate.

452. Mr. *Heron.*] When did you write that out?—I think I transcribed it on the same night that I took the report, on the 19th, the day before the poll.

453. For publication?—Yes, I speculated as a correspondent upon them.

454. Did you send that document away anywhere?—Upon my word I think I delivered it at the office.

455. What office?—The Drogheda Conservative Office. I think I delivered it myself; I might have sent it by my son.

456. When did you get it back?—I have not seen it till it was handed to me now.

457. Mr. *McDonogh.*] Do you know whether Mr. Whitworth was there upon that occasion?—He was not present during the speeches, but he came into the room afterwards, and addressed the crowd, telling them to go home.

458. Where was he during the delivery of the speeches?—I could not see him in the room, and had he been there, I think I should have seen him.

459. Do you know whether the room where the balcony is, was employed for Mr. Whitworth's purposes?—

Mr. *Heron* objected to the question.

460. Mr. *McDonogh.*] Was there any other gentleman there, besides the reverend gentlemen whose names you have given, during any portion of the time?—Yes, there were many parties in and out.

461. Who were they?—There were more than a dozen in the room altogether; I perhaps could enumerate them.

462. You were minding your business, I presume?—Yes.

463. Now read the Rev. Mr. Murphy's speech?—"The Rev. Mr. Murphy was the first speaker; he commenced by observing that they had arrived at a great crisis—a contest between Protestant ascendancy and equality. The great question of the day was, whether the Protestant Church was to be disendowed and disestablished in Ireland. Any person who wished that that should be so would vote for McClintock; anyone who wished to sustain Protestant ascendancy in Ireland would be opposed to Mr. Whitworth. He, therefore, hoped no Catholic in Drogheda would vote against Mr. Whitworth. Anyone who voted against him would prove himself an enemy to his country, and a supporter of the Protestant Church. He might tell them, for they had already abundant proof of it, that Mr. Whitworth was as much opposed to Protestant ascendancy as Cardinal Cullen is himself, and he longed for equality. He hoped they would not be led astray, for he would again tell them that anyone who voted against Mr. Whitworth was an enemy to his religion, and to the priests of his church, who would sacrifice their lives for the people. If they were wise, they would vote on the side the priests want, because they know the priests had never deceived them. Did not Father Kelly and Father M'Geokin lose their lives by attending patients in fever, and were the priests not every day risking their lives attending upon their flocks on their sick-beds? They should vote, then, for Whitworth, which would be voting for liberty and the destruction of Protestant ascendancy. He had that day heard it reported that a mob of 500 Orangemen were to come down from Dublin next day—the polling day (Friday)—to disturb the peace of the town. He thought they might not have heard it, and he wished, therefore, to put them on their guard. Will you, men of Drogheda, tolerate this in your Catholic town? He would advise them, then, seriously, to be fully prepared, for the Orange party in Drogheda was anxious and panting to crush them. Every man who is opposed to Whitworth is on the side of the Orange candidate. Let them remember that. Although he never wished any man to do wrong, he must again call on them to be prepared, for the Drogheda Orangemen had secured the assistance of 500 of their brethren in Dublin. The Catholics opposed to us are Orange Catholics. They must despise them, no matter who they are. There were some of them he esteemed and loved, but he must stand by his church. Those Catholics who were on the side of the Orangemen must be put down. They must be crushed at any risk; they should, therefore, be prepared for them, for it was a terrible crisis. He was sure many parties had been deceived by Brodigan and his committee; but there was time to relent, and if they now came round to the side of Mr. Whitworth they would be received with open arms. By promising support to Brodigan they had brought a thorough enemy into the camp, and everyone who was an enemy to Whitworth was an enemy to his church, his country, and his principles. Let everyone bring up all the voters he can in his neighbourhood to-morrow, and by so doing he will be materially assisting in disendowing and disestablishing the Protestant Church. The Conservative party were promising bribes which they never intended to pay. They will deceive the Catholics who trust to them; but if the Catholics go with their priests they will never do wrong." That finished the Rev. Mr Murphy.

464. Now for the Rev. Mr. M'Kee?—The Rev. Mr. M'Kee said, "This would be a momentous contest. It was a contest against their deadly enemy. He was a North of Ireland man, a native of Ulster; he was born within a few miles of the Yellow Ford, where Hugh O'Neil gained a victory over the English; he had read of the persecutions which had occurred in Dro-

Mr. E. [illegible], 15 January 1869.

hods. in bygone times. They had all heard of the butcher Cromwell, who gave glory to God for the murder that he butchered in Drogheda, in one day. That church which stands at the head of Peter-street had a wooden steeple; when Cromwell came to Drogheda, more than 200 years ago, Cromwell went first to St. Mary's Church, where they had, the other day, to fight a battle over again. Cromwell was opposed there by the good priests, who mounted the walls to resist him, but they were beaten back and fled for refuge to St. Peter's Church, which then belonged to the Catholics. Their priests and men fled to Peter's Church for refuge; but Cromwell came with his invading army, and what did the butcher do? He found he could not force them to surrender, and he set fire to the steeple, and when they fled from the church he butchered them without the slightest mercy. When the Cromwellians gained the victory they robbed their forefathers of their property. Who are the party that are now coming forward to act a similar part? The descendants of Cromwell's soldiers, whose ancestors being their forefathers at the Tholsel of Drogheda." The Rev. Mr. M'Kee next stated that "the present bishop of Glasgow's father was flogged at Millmount, and that the father of Mr. Brodigan, the present Member, went up to see the infamous act performed. He (Mr. M'Kee) knew what an Orangeman was; he was sorry to say that Orangeism had its origin in the county Armagh. Orangemen say they will be true to the Government as long as they give them places and emoluments; as long as they give them the loaves and fishes they will be loyal. The Orangemen are loyal as long as they get everything in the country; as long as they feed on the vitals of the Catholics. A few months ago one of the ministers, in the North of Ireland, said that sooner than they would submit to a change from Protestant ascendancy, he would see the Crown of the Queen thrown into the Boyne. Now, he asked them were they to become slaves; the Orangemen of Dublin were, on next day, to come down to Drogheda. If these men should come down let them hurl them into the Boyne. Let the people meet them in the morning, at the train, and give them a warm reception." I would state that I have not taken a full verbatim note.

465. Is that substantially what took place?—Yes.

466. Have you a distinct remembrance of their saying something about throwing them into the Boyne?—Yes, I am as distinct as that I am looking at the judge.

467. The Rev. Mr. Glynn said what?—" The Rev. Mr Glynn next addressed the crowd: he confessed he was ashamed to stand there as a Catholic priest; he was ashamed of the people of Drogheda to allow the battle of the Boyne to be fought over again, which was fought 200 years ago on the banks of that river, and a terrible battle it was. On that occasion there were two contending armies; one party fought under the flag of 'No Popery,' 'Church Ascendancy,' and 'To h—ll with the Priests.' The flag of the others was, 'Religious Equality,' and 'Peace and Harmony among all Classes of their Fellow-citizens.' Who is the successor to-day of that Catholic army? Who is the general to-day? Mr. Whitworth. They were that night on the eve of another great battle of the Boyne. Their general was an Englishman, anxious for religious equality, and the battle was for Ireland. When they had the Protestant Church dis-established, and dis-endowed, they would then get anything they wanted, and the priests of Ireland would be found in their ranks. Now, was there any Catholic amongst them who would be so base as to go into the ranks of the enemy? If there was, his name would be recorded in history as the vilest wretch in creation. He advised all who heard him to bring their friends to the poll; to marshall their forces early in the morning, and when they were about to charge, say, 'Friends of freedom, charge them home; foes of freedom, faugh-a-ballagh.'" That concludes it.

468. The Rev. Dr. Murphy again?—" The Rev. Dr. Murphy next addressed the assemblage; they had arrived at a very important crisis in the history of their native land. The would-be Catholic Member, Mr. Brodigan, and Orange emissaries from h—ll, had come amongst them. At this critical juncture he advised the people to be faithful in following the advice of their clergy, secular and regular, and the Catholic traitors, and Orange demons, would soon be routed from Drogheda. Up to this moment the greatest peace has existed amongst the people; he trusted the same quietude would mark the proceedings, up to the hour of closing the poll next day, and a glorious victory would be theirs." That concludes that.

469. The Rev. Mr. Gavin is next, is he not?—Yes. "The Rev. Mr. Gavin now came forward, amid loud cheers. He said he knew by their voices that they proclaimed him a friend, not an enemy. He knew by their voices that they believed he was prepared, as their forefathers were to go to the block, lay down his head and sacrifice his life for their interests. When he last spoke to them he told them that there was a crisis arrived at in reference to the three kingdoms, England, Scotland, and Ireland, but particularly to Ireland. He told them, last evening, that there was a question not only before the three kingdoms, but before all Europe; a question was brought before the people to decide, and that question was the disendowment and disestablishment of the Protestant Church, which was generated and nurtured in lust and crime, while it was fatted on the spoliation and robbery of the Catholic property and the Catholic Church of Ireland. The people of England were not acquainted with our grievances until their eyes were opened by a continuous rebellion. The question of disestablishment and disendowment of that church which was placed upon your shoulders is now understood in England to be a grievance in this country, and the question for you is, will you give your voices against it. Up to a very recent period he had not intended to identify himself with the politics of the town; but when he saw a man, by the way, a most respectable and an educated man, of the name of Mr. M'Clintock, coming into Drogheda to be returned by the voices of the Liberals and Catholics of Drogheda, his blood rose to his face, and he blushed for shame that such a man would get a chance of becoming representative for the town. All that he wanted to tell his hearers in conclusion was, that on yesterday, in the city of Dublin, some of the friends of ascendancy in this town hired 800 [illegible] to come and butcher the Catholics of Drogheda. He asked them, would they meet them. He assured them, on the word of a priest, that what he said was a fact, that some party in the favour of the Orange candidate have went to Dublin and purchased the rag, tag, and bobtail of

Mr. R. Macnie.

25 January 1869.

of Orangemen to come down and butcher them to-morrow. He did not want the people of Drogheda to treat these hirelings as they deserved, but he merely wanted to show to what extremes the Orange party are capable of going, seeking for victory, in order that M'Clintock may be another, who will, by his vote, assist to perpetuate that badge of conquest and blot on the English constitution, the Protestant Church. Did any of them know the Irish language? Did they know what a cauthon was? He would explain it to them. It was a calf with a dirty tail. No matter, although Mr. M'Clintock may be a gentleman and a man of education, he called him a cauthon; for, from many of those of his supporters it was clear he had a dirty tail. No matter how learned a man and great mind Mr. M'Clintock may be, he may sound well with his plummet, remarkably well; but when he comes to use it here, seeking for sand and dry, he will find amongst no adamantine rock to the bottom."

470. Is that your own handwriting you have been reading at the houses?—Yes, that is my handwriting.

471. Have you now finished your report?—Yes.

Mr. Heron applied for a copy of the speeches read by the witness.

Mr. Justice Keogh ordered a copy to be supplied.

[The Witness withdrew.

Mr. Samuel Devlin, sworn; Examined by Mr. Plunket.

S. Devlin.

472. Are you a Councillor in Dublin?—Yes.

473. Did you come down to Drogheda on the morning of the polling day?—I did.

474. Who accompanied you, do you know?—Mr. Bell, of Bell's Grove, living in Dublin; Mr. Harris, and Dr. Brennan, and two or three more; I do not recollect their names.

475. Did you hear Mr. Hamilton mention a number of gentlemen's names?—I was not here when Mr. Hamilton was examined.

476. Will you tell us what occurred when you arrived at the railway station in Drogheda?—When we got within 100 yards of the railway station, the train stopped, and we wondered it did not come up to the platform; the station master came down running along the steps outside the train, and he asked whether there were any voters.

Mr. Heron objected to what the station master said being received as evidence.

Witness.] He said there was a great deal of excitement at the station, and that we should take care of ourselves, and advised as many of us as we could to get together in one compartment if possible. A number of people got into a first-class carriage, and all the seats were occupied, and when he made some arrangement with the other carriages, we proceeded to the platform, where we got out. A number of gentlemen met us, and said we were to be escorted down by the cavalry. "Take time and get yourselves into line." There were about 30, and we proceeded in that way from the station, and the stone throwing commenced immediately after; hooting first, and then stone throwing, till we got into James-street; then we got it quite hot and heavy. I used the caution of putting my umbrella up; I saved my head; I got well pelted about the back; two gentlemen who passed me were bleeding from the head; the blood was running down their coats when we got there; there was a sort of halt.

477. Where?—At the bridge, and I distinctly saw a great crowd in Shop-street; in fact, the street was full. I looked and saw bludgeons and sticks, and saw the cavalry. There was a rush, and I was knocked down and picked up; when I got up I saw a man bleeding from the head; about that time I heard the shots. I saw the man, I might say, firing; I saw him on the ground. After that the crowd got thin, and soon after the charge was made up the street. I looked about for the voters; some went into a house; I followed and got into Kelly's. There I found some gentlemen had got in; Colonel Fairclough along with the rest; he was bleeding very much. We went upstairs, in the back room. The person of the house said, "For God's sake, do not make any noise." There was a great noise outside, and every moment they expected the fellows in. We got some water when we were upstairs, and tried to stop the blood. He bled for an hour and a-half. A person in the house allowed us to go in the front room, but we were told not to go near the window, the crowd were watching us. We waited till half-past two, two hours, then the landlord came up.

Mr. Heron objected to the evidence.

Witness.] We remained there till the high sheriff came, and we were told that the high sheriff and some gentlemen were downstairs and wished to see us. During the time we were there, there was a great deal of excitement, but we were determined they would get the worst of it if they came upstairs. I have a book with me in which I got the gentlemen to write their names. I said, "We may forget one another, will you write your names in this book, and we shall know one another." I kept the book.

478. Mr. Plunket.] Is this the book?—

Mr. Heron objected to the book being produced.

Witness.] We remained there till the high sheriff came and told us the town was tranquil, and we might go up and vote; some would not vote; I said I would not vote; I would not risk my life any farther; at last we got there; I found I had lost my hat when we got up there. Mr. Chadwick was with us, and I heard the clerks were withdrawn from the polling booths, and that we could not poll.

479. Mr. Plunket.] What o'clock was that?—Three, or a quarter to three; we were very anxious to get to the train. Mr. Chadwick conducted me to my brother-in-law's in West-street; we got a car and went the back way out of the town.

480. You went back by train?—Yes, by the mail train.

Cross-examined by Mr. Palles.

481. I suppose it was about twelve o'clock when you got into this house; that was the hour when the occurrence took place, was it not?—Yes.

482. What

482. What hour did you first leave the house?—I think about half-past two; twenty-five minutes to three.

483. Where did you go to then?—Up to Peter-street.

484. From Peter-street where?—To West-street.

485. Where was the tally room?—In Peter-street.

486. When you say you went to Peter-street, you mean you went to the tally room?—Yes.

487. How long did you remain in the tally room?—Half-an-hour.

488. Where did you go to then?—My brother-in-law's.

489. Where was that?—West-street.

490. How long did you remain there?—I remained there less than half-an-hour.

491. From West-street you went to the station?—Yes, straight.

492. There were six gentlemen in the house originally with you?—Yes.

493. Was Mr. George Bell one of them?—No.

494. Look at that and tell me the names?—There were Mr Vanbrakey Macready, Charles Henley, Francis Hamilton of Bird's Eye-square, Colonel Fairclough of 8, Upper Leinster-street, Robert Smith, and myself.

495. Are you aware whether any of those persons voted?—Yes, Macready voted, he told me after.

496. You know that Mr. Macready voted?—He told me so; I did not know it till I saw him in Dublin.

497. Do you mean to swear that you would not have been able to vote if you wished?—I could not swear that. I did not know what I might meet between the bridge and the polling-place.

498. The poll did not close till five o'clock, did it?—I do not know that.

499. When did you know that McClintock had no chance?—I did not know it.

500. When did you suspect it?—I did not suspect it.

501. When you were going away by train, you did not suspect that McClintock would be beaten?—He was beaten, and we were all beaten.

502. Did you suspect McClintock was beaten?—I had no suspicion at all. I came down to vote, and I was prevented.

503. Did you pass the polling booth when you were going to West-street?—I do not know where the polling booth was.

504. Did you ask?—No.

505. You remember when those gentlemen came in about half-past two and offered to escort you to vote?—Yes.

Mr. S. Barklie.

15 January 1869.

506. Did you believe you would be safe in going under their escort?—I had my doubts.

507. That is the reason you did not go?—I did go.

508. You did not go to vote?—I could not.

509. The reason you did not go to vote was, that you believed you would not be safe under the escort?—Yes.

510. You thought the escort which would take you to West-street would not be sufficient to take you to the polling booth?—I do not think I did.

511. Was Mr. Bradbrooke one of the persons who offered to bring you to the polling booth?—No one offered to bring me.

512. No one offered to form an escort?—No one.

513. Had you Mr. Bradbrooke, Mr. Chadwick, and Mr. Carroll?—Yes.

514. Did they ask every one of the party if they wished to vote?—Not that I know of.

515. What did they say?—What the sheriff said was, they were very sorry they were obliged to run up there for shelter; they said it was very poor shelter he gave us.

516. Did they, or not, say this or anything like it, "If you wish to vote we will conduct you to the poll and give you any protection you require"?—Yes.

517. They said that?—It was said in the room.

518. You understood it as addressed to you all?—Yes.

519. Did some of them answer that they would go?—Not in my hearing, not one.

520. Did some of them say they would not?—I said I would not go.

521. Did some of them say they thought there was no use in their voting?—I did not hear it.

522. Will you swear they did not?—I did not hear it.

523. At this time there was some discussion about the price of some refreshments, was there not?—No.

524. About who should pay for the refreshments?—No; you were never more mistaken.

525. The party were having a discussion as to whether Sir Leopold McClintock ought not to pay for the refreshment?—No; your brief is wrong there.

[The Witness withdrew.

Mr. Edward Townley Hardman, sworn; Examined by Mr. Ryland.

Mr. E. T. Hardman.

526. Were you an elector?—Yes.

527. Did you come down to record your vote on the day of the poll?—Yes.

528. By what train?—The train that was supposed to leave Dublin at half-past nine; the train that was supposed to leave; it did not leave at the proper time.

529. Did anything take place before you arrived at Drogheda?—Yes; when we came within a short distance of the terminus the train was stopped; the station-master came to the carriage in which I was, and asked in a very excited manner if there were any voters there. No person in the carriage answered. Then he said, if there were any they had better tell him. Then we saw the voters being brought out. I should mention there were two other voters, friends of mine, in the carriage; Smith and Bisset. When we got out we were put into the next carriage, with a number of others, and the train then proceeded to the terminus. We were then brought out and placed under an escort of military. The infantry formed two deep, with the cavalry outside, and we were brought down this way into the town. We were not molested until we got some distance from the railway. When we got outside the railway gates stone throwing commenced, and the whole way from there into the town we were pelted, more or less; in Palace-street especially. We were hurt very much. I was struck two or three times. I saw several

Mr. E. T. Hardman.

15 January 1869.

several gentlemen under the escort struck, and also soldiers as well. When we arrived at the bridge a halt took place. I did not know at the time what the reason was. In a short time we were again marched on, when another halt took place, and the soldiers and everyone were driven back by the violence of the stone-throwing; the horses reared and almost fell back on us, so that the voters attempted to get back out of the way, and in their doing so most of them were knocked down, I among the rest. When I picked myself up I found the rest of the voters were vanished; I could see none of them. Then the cavalry came behind where I was standing, and prepared to charge. On seeing that, I withdrew off the bridge into Mr. Harbert's.

530. On which side of the bridge?—The west side. I waited there some time till the crowd had become less. However, I saw the crowd was very thick on the bridge. Previously as we were leaving the bridge I saw the soldiers drawn in a body in front, and I heard two shots. I then left the bridge and went into the saltworks, and seeing the crowd was still very thick on the bridge, I attempted to leave the other way, by John-street. I intended to go round by another bridge further up the river, and through West-street to the tally-room. However, as I went through the yard I was met by three men. One asked me whether I was going to vote for Whitworth; they were armed with sticks and looked very ferocious; and I said of course I was. Then one of them said they would escort me through the town, and he came with me. Just outside we were met by three others; he told them I was going to vote for Whitworth, and they came round me and marched up Sheep-street with me. As I passed several crowds, these men said I was going to vote for Whitworth. When we came to the polling-booth in Sheep-street I went in expecting I should vote for Sir Leopold M'Clintock; but the men came in along with me and surrounded me, and I felt that if I voted for Sir Leopold M'Clintock at that time, my life was in danger. One of these men then said that I was going to vote for Mr. Whitworth. Some person in the booth said I could not do so unless I had a ticket obtained from his tally-room. Then the men said they intended to escort me to his tally-room. I went out with them, thinking I could easily escape from them outside and go to Sir Leopold M'Clintock's tally-room. However, they insisted upon my going to a room which happened to be one of the polling-booths, which they mistook for Mr. Whitworth's tally-room. There I was met by a gentleman, who asked me whether I was going to vote for Mr. Whitworth.

531. Who was that?—I have heard since that it was a Mr. Matthews; he was the same gentleman I met there.

532. Would you know him now?—I think so; he was a young man; I do not see him here.

533. Go on with your description?—I said there was plenty of time to vote; I was not in a hurry. At the same time I was thinking how to get away from my escort.

534. At what o'clock was that?—I should say very nearly one o'clock.

535. Now about the three men?—Three of the four men were in the body of the polling-booth speaking to some of the people in it; the other man was standing with me at the door; he said to me, "Mr. Hardman, you had better go home or vote for Mr. Whitworth; you will certainly be killed if you do not; if you vote for Sir Leopold M'Clintock you will certainly be killed."

536. Mr. *Heron*.] Who said that?—One of the men who escorted me up the town. I asked him would he take a drink; he said he would. He came there, and I took him into a public-house and gave him a drink. Still he kept with me, and we were walking up the street together, when I slipped into a house and he passed on; I waited until I thought he had gone, then I came out of the place and walked up the street to the tally-room, where I remained the greater portion of the day.

537. Mr. *Ryland*.] Did you vote?—Certainly not.

538. What prevented you afterwards voting when you got to the tally-room?—There was an immense crowd at the polling-booth, and I thought my life in danger.

539. Was that the reason you did not vote at the polling-booth?—Yes.

540. Were you struck yourself, or did you see other persons struck?—Yes; when we were walking down, I turned round and saw a gentleman walking just behind me, one of the voters who had evidently been struck.

541. Mr. *Heron*.] What was his name?—I do not know his name.

> Mr. *Heron* objected to the witness stating that the gentleman who was struck was a voter.

542. Mr. *Ryland*.] Was he a gentleman who was escorted?—I saw the blood streaming down his coat, and I found some of it on the back of my coat and trousers afterwards; I saw a gentleman who was walking before me struck there on the back of the head; I saw several of the soldiers struck, and I saw two of the soldiers turn round who were struck.

[The Witness withdrew.

Captain William Daunt, sworn; Examined by Mr. *McDonogh*.

Captain W. Daunt.

543. During this election were you a Captain in Her Majesty's service?—Yes.

544. Were you in charge of that portion of the military?—On the 20th of November?

545. Yes?—I was in charge of 84 of the 8th Regiment, and also I had a party of the 14th Hussars under my command.

546. Were you assisted by any officers of your own regiment?—I had four other officers of my own regiment under me.

547. Had you any officers of the Hussars?—Captain Knox, of the Hussars.

548. The whole detachment was under your charge?—Yes.

549. Do you remember when you were called upon?—I was ordered somewhere about 11 o'clock to go down with 40 men and reinforce a party already down there, which consisted of 20 of the 8th Regiment, and some of the Hussars.

550. Did you receive the order from your colonel?—I received the order from Colonel Knox to manage the whole troop there.

551. You proceeded there accordingly?—Yes.

552. When

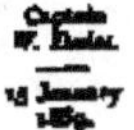

552. When you reached the station, did anything attract your attention?—When I reached the station I saw some of the Hussars there, and I also saw this part of my regiment there. One of the stipendiary magistrates, Mr. Hood, came up to me and told me that there was a party of voters immediately expected by train, and that I was to escort them up to the polling-booth; and he requested me to get my men ready to escort them up, and get them between my men.

553. And you proceeded to make your dispositions accordingly?—Yes; I then proceeded to make my dispositions so that the voters should get immediately between my files. In a short time the party arrived. I was told by Mr. Hood that I was to escort the voters. He then came up to me, and said "Here they are."

554. How many persons were there altogether who came by the train?—About 40; they crossed to me by the way they came into my files.

555. Then I presume each took up his position just as you directed; the infantry, and cavalry, and police?—Yes; I had the voters between my files; some cavalry on each side outside my men; and the rear was protected by a body of the constabulary.

556. You moved towards the town in that order?—Yes.

557. What occurred next?—When we got about 20 yards from the station there was a few people outside; when we got outside they increased in number, and when we got 30 yards from the station, stone-throwing commenced. After a little time, being in front, my men in the rear, the cavalry; I turned round and saw several of my men bleeding profusely from cuts about the face. As we proceeded further into the town the crowds were much thicker. There was a very large crowd as we came into James-street; they were shouting and yelling at us, and cursing us, and brandishing their sticks at us. All this time stone-throwing was continuing, and also other missiles. I saw pieces of brick-bats pass close to me. There seemed to me to be all sorts of missiles, some of these thrown from the houses; I should say so from the direction in which they came. By-and-bye the crowd became denser and denser, till we came to Bull Ring, but we continued to get on till the cavalry got just over the bridge, to this side of the bridge; then there was a halt; a stoppage took place, and I saw the horses of the cavalry were plunging and rearing about. In the meantime stones were flying in showers at us; I saw several gentlemen whom I was escorting, and who I presume to be voters, bleeding; and I also saw several of my men bleeding. I had tried to get at the front as soon as the halt took place. I saw that active measures must be adopted, and I wanted to get a magistrate in front, but I could not get there owing to the plunging and rearing of horses; I then fell back; there were two horses rearing there immediately, and I had to retire to prevent myself being kicked or knocked over by the horses. As I did so, I saw three or four of the Hussars wheeling to the right to get away past my right flank, past my men. I must tell you that when the halt took place the horses of the cavalry pressed back and broke the formation of my men entirely; they fell back and broke the formation in which we marched. After this I saw three or four of the cavalry wheeling to the right to get to the rear, I presume, of the party; just then I was hit by a large stone in the chest,

which caused me to stagger back, and I fell against some of my men behind, and just as I was regaining my feet (I did not fall, I staggered back only) I was struck by a stone on the side of the head; I fell, and I know nothing more about it.

558. You became unconscious?—Yes; the next I knew of it, when I was being helped up off the ground by some of my men; I heard a shot fired just as I was in the act of being helped up off the ground, and I saw several of my men loading; I stopped their loading; there was then a great lull in the uproar, but the uproar previous to this had been tremendous; I called out to the magistrate, but my voice was drowned in the tremendous uproar; when I heard this shot fired, I noticed there was a lull, and after seeing my men loading, and stopping it, I turned round and saw a man lying 15 or 20 yards from me at the commencement of Shop-street. The crowd had spread out considerably then; I could almost see up the street; I could not see the front as far, because the horses were in front of me; I saw a great crowd on the quay to the right, who kept up a tremendous fire of stones at us; I saw a man lying in the road; the crowd opened; I formed my men up then about the bridge, and turned round to Mr. Hood; I saw the crowd were then closing in again; I requested leave of Mr. Hood to charge; it was impossible to stand that sort of thing any longer; he told me that the Riot Act had been read, and that I was to charge; while I was speaking to him, the cavalry came up from the rear and charged up Shop-street, past my right flank; I then charged up about 30 yards after them; there were still stones thrown from the windows on the left-hand side of Shop-street; we charged about 30 yards on the double up; I formed the men a minute or two, and charged up the side of the street facing the court-house.

559. Had you any of the persons placed under your escort with you then?—I saw a few of them standing behind my men after they were drawn up in front of us; they were standing behind.

560. Did the mob come up again and pass you?—The mob came up again bearing the body of this man on a shutter or door on their shoulders, and using most menacing language and shaking their sticks at us; they seemed so excessively violent and infuriated, that the men were all ordered to load.

561. And they did, I presume?—Yes, we loaded.

562. Do you remember whether you said anything about their firing, or prohibiting them?—I told them not to fire until orders were given.

563. Did the mob pass on then?—The party who were bearing the dead body passed on, but still there was a great mob left in front of us.

564. Did anything else occur?—Some stones were thrown at us, even after we were drawn up, and I saw one make a deep mark on a cart; it passed where I was standing; I saw an immense number of sticks and stones; they were large thick sticks.

565. Did anything else occur that day?—We afterwards marched up to the prison, and two men were delivered up to the civil power.

566. Did you examine the state of the rifles which your men had?—I examined them when I returned from election duty to Dublin.

567. What day was that; how soon after?—The

Captain W. Dunn.

15 January 1869.

The beginning of December, but they were examined by officers the same day.

568. How many did you find injured?—

Mr. *Heron* objected to the evidence on the ground that the examination of the rifles was at a remote day from that on which the alleged damage took place.

Mr. Justice *Keogh* allowed the objection.

569. Mr. *M'Donogh*.] Are the other officers here?—One of them is here who inspected some of the rifles.

570. Were many of the men injured on that day, or hurt?—Yes, four officers and 14 men.

571. Were any of them seriously hurt?—Oh! yes; there is one very ill and in the hospital still.

572. What is his name?—Serjeant Campbell.

573. Were you at Stoncke's Hotel?—I was billeted at Stoncke's Hotel for a week.

574. Were you there at night when speeches were delivered by clergymen?—I heard part of the speeches delivered on the 19th, Monday, the day before the polling.

575. Do you remember any expression in relation to any of the people coming from Dublin?—I heard attention called to this: "Men of Drogheda recollect the battle of the Boyne that was fought here nearly 600 years ago, and be prepared to fight this battle again to-morrow." I also heard that we must adopt every measure to return a man who votes for the disestablishment and disendowment of the Irish Church, which has been built up by the spoliation and robbery of the Catholic religion.

576. Do you remember anything said about the men coming from Dublin?—There was an immense amount of cheering after this, and as I was not particularly interested in it, I withdrew from the window, and afterwards I heard the words, "Orangemen, down with them, down with them;" but nothing more than that.

Cross-examined by Mr. *Hamill*.

577. At the time you were upon the bridge, did you hear the word "halt" cried out?—No.

578. Did you hear any command given to the cavalry to wheel round?—No.

579. Nothing of that kind?—No.

580. They were under the command of Colonel Knox?—Yes.

581. Did you hear him examined on a former occasion?—Yes.

582. Did you hear him say that he had given the command to the Hussars to go to the rear?—I cannot remember now.

583. Did you hear him admit that it was the word "halt" that made him——

Mr. *M'Donogh* objected to the question.

584. Mr. *Hamill*.] Were the cavalry in advance of you?—Yes, four yards in front of me.

585. There was an officer; is he here; is that officer here?—He is here.

586. Did you see the cavalry wheel before this happened to you?—I saw about three or four pass me, and just at that moment I was knocked down.

[The Witness withdrew.

Captain John Hunter Knox, sworn; Examined by Mr. *Plunket*.

Captain J. H. Knox.

587. You are Captain of the 14th Hussars?—Yes.

588. Were you quartered at Drogheda at the time of the late election?—Yes.

589. How long were you here before the polling day?—I was here a few days; I came here on the Saturday, I think, before.

590. Were you here on the nomination day?—Yes.

591. Were you kept in readiness to act on that day?—Yes, I was left in readiness.

592. Now, tell us what happened on the day of the polling?—On the night before the polling I got an order from Colonel Knox, who was in command of all the troops in Drogheda, to take half my troop out the following morning, and to parade down at the court-house at a quarter past eight, I think it was, or a quarter before eight, and accordingly the following morning I paraded. There had been orders that I was to take half the troop under my command. I had one officer who was to be left in with the other half; accordingly I paraded 16 of my men in front of the court-house, and reported myself to Colonel Knox. He introduced me to some of the magistrates, and told me to render them any assistance they might require. I remained there for some time, and had not anything to do. There was a great crowd, and so on, but there was nothing for the soldiers to do for some time. Afterwards I was told to take half my troop to assist some men in taking prisoners up. We did so, and came down to our own position to the court-house. Soon after, about half-past nine, I think, I went with Captain Talbot down to the railway station. I was told that I was to bring in some voters that were coming in by train. I brought my men down through the town; the streets were full of people, but they did not interfere with us beyond hooting, yelling, and crying, but they did not molest us. We arrived at the railway station; there was a very large crowd there. I was told that there were some voters inside. They would wait till the next train with more voters arrived; they came in together, and the magistrates who were there (Mr. Reed was one and Captain Talbot the other) consulted me, and asked me if I thought we had sufficient force to bring the voters into the town. There were 16 men of my own and a portion of the infantry, 9th Regiment, and some police; I do not know the strength altogether at the time; I said no, I thought the force was not sufficient if they did not allow the men to use their arms; if they chose to let them use their arms, if necessary, I thought the force sufficient; but if they wanted to do the thing peaceably they ought to get a larger force. There was a note sent off, and they got up another company of infantry under the command of Captain Talbot. We formed an escort, and attempted to bring the voters into the town.

593. You were in charge of the infantry and others?—Yes. When I went first to the railway station there was a large mob in and about the station and down the line. We waited at the railway station a considerable time; I should think over an hour; and after some time the mob dispersed and went back to the town. When we started at first the road was quite clear for some way. When we got into the town the stone-throwing commenced; not many at first, but it got worse and worse until we got to the bridge, and there it was very bad.

594. Were

Captain J. H. Kane.

15 January 1869.

594. Were any of your men injured?—Yes, they were all hit, but none of them injured severely, but they were all hit; I was hit myself by several blows on the back of my head.

595. Mr. Justice Keogh.] Did you say you were thrown?—A stick was thrown and hit me on the back of the head; I was also struck on the right arm with a stone. My horse was struck in several places about the head and fore legs and hind quarters; in fact, he was struck all over.

596. What occurred next?—I had Captain Talbot with me mounted, and the high sheriff was also with me. He seemed to have a great effect on the people; they cleared away. He kept a great many people away from us, and just as we got on the bridge the words "halt and front" were passed along; but we should have been obliged to halt if the word "halt" had not been passed. We could not go on at a walk; the horses would not face the mob and the sticks and stones; they were plunging and rearing about. My men were divided. I had a few with me when I started; the others were each side of the escort.

597. The formation had been broken, had it not?—Yes, the formation had been broken very much; my men were scattered about when I first started. Just as we got over the bridge I turned round and saw what was going on, and saw that I was no use whatever, and my own men were no use where they were; and to the few men behind me I said, "Get in rear of the infantry; get back." They wheeled their horses round, and they went in rear of the infantry. Just as as I passed the front of the infantry there was a shot fired, and a man fell in front of the mob. Well, there was a lull, and the mob ran back. There was a vacant space left, but a few seconds afterwards they seemed to be coming on again. I turned round to Captain Talbot and said, "What am I to do?" he said, "Charge and clear the streets." The men drew their swords and galloped up the street, and the mob ran in every direction, and I trooped up the other half of my troop in front of the court-house.

598. When you formed up, did you see then the persons you were escorting?—No, I did not see them; I do not know what became of them.

599. What next occurred?—Afterwards the body of the man who was killed was carried past on a shutter, and the mob threw sticks and stones, and I saw the infantry in the loading position; we went up to the gaol afterwards.

600. What was the demeanour of the mob when carrying the dead man past?—Very threatening; it seemed that if we had not got arms, and the infantry were not ready, they would have attacked them; that was their demeanour.

Cross-examined by Mr. Heron.

601. Had you the slightest difficulty in clearing the street by your charge?—No, not the slightest; the shot that had been fired cleared the street in the first instance; the two shots that were fired.

602. Had you passed the bridge yourself on horseback before the word to halt was given?—I had just got over the bridge at the time.

603. Who gave the order?—I do not know; it was passed from the rear; the whole escort were attacked all round; I looked round in the saddle.

604. Was the word passed from the rear?—I heard the word from the rear, "halt and front." I will not be certain that I did not hear, "We cannot keep up, we are attacked," or some words to that effect.

605. Was the word given by some one in authority?—I do not know who gave it at all.

606. Did you give the word to halt to your men?—No.

607. But they did halt?—Yes, they were halted by the mob and the sticks as much as anything else.

608. Did you direct your men to wheel round?—No, there was no regular formation; there was no regular word of command; it was not necessary to give a regular distinct word; I turned round and said, "Get in rear of the infantry."

609. And up to that time you had been facing towards Drogheda?—No, not always; at times the horses were rearing up in the air, sometimes sideways, and sometimes turning round.

610. You told your men to get in rear of the infantry?—Yes, the two or three men near me.

611. They then did so?—Yes.

612. Your men did not retire to the rear of the infantry until you gave them the word?—No; I told the few men near me to do so; the others were at the side of the infantry.

613. Was it after you got into the rear then the infantry opened out to let you charge?—After we got to the rear I formed my men up; they were scattered when we first started; I formed my men up and went round one side of the infantry, and galloped up the street.

614. Mr. Justice Keogh.] Were there any of your men thrown off their horses?—Yes, there was one man, when we were galloping up the street, or two men and horses came down; one horse came down, the other horse struck him and came down.

615. It was not the result of blows or stones?—The second horse, I believe; I did not see it. His fall, I believe, occurred by a chamber-pot; it came down out of a window; it fell in the front of the horse; he swerved round and fell.

[The Witness withdrew.

Captain R. M. Jephson, sworn; Examined by Mr. Ryland.

Captain R. M. Jephson.

616. Of what regiment are you?—The 9th Regiment.

617. Were you at Drogheda during the election?—I was.

618. Where were you?—With Captain Dennis' Company, who went to the railway station to escort the voters.

619. Will you describe what you saw at the railway station?—We had been escorting the voters, and after leaving the station 200 or 300 yards, stones began to be thrown; the mob used threatening language, and I heard, "Bring them out, pull them out," alluding to the gentlemen, I believe, we were escorting. Some stones were thrown, and the shower of stones increased as we got to James-street. There the mob was very violent, and then the shower of stones increased. Then when we got on to the bridge, on this side of the bridge, the mob seemed to have concentrated their forces, and we were obliged to be

Captain E. M. Ingham.

15 January 1869.

be brought to a halt; the cavalry were thrown into confusion and fell back, and threw us into disorder also.

620. Did you see the man shot?—I saw him on the bridge just after the cavalry, or most of of them, wheeled and went past our right flank, and just after that I saw the gentleman lying down on the ground in front, and the mob were stoning him; I went up; I thought he was in danger. I went up to do my best to assist him; I tried to lift him; as he was rather heavy, my first attempt was ineffectual. All this time the mob seemed bent on stoning the gentleman almost to death.

621. Was he one of the party you had been escorting?—I had not seen him before in the party.

622. Was he in the party at the time of the stoning?—He had got in front somehow or the other, and I went and tried to lift him up, and one of the crowd came up and threw his arm round the gentleman's head to shelter him from the shower of stones, and another came up and took him to his horse. I returned to my company a few steps behind, and I heard a shot fired. I saw Captain Daunt immediately after, and I inquired who had fired the shot, and then after the shot was fired, the mob opened out and the cavalry charged, and we followed them up to the court-house here.

623. Did you receive any injuries yourself?—I got a slight blow on the cheek from a stone.

624. Were many of your men hurt?—Yes; I saw a number of our men bleeding, and the several of the gentlemen we were escorting.

625. Have you examined the arms of any of the men?—I examined all the arms of the company that I belong to.

626. On what day did you examine the arms?—On the same day.

627. How many rifles did you examine?—I examined either 26 or 29; I am not quite sure of the number.

628. In what state were the rifles?—Out of the number, there were 23 or 24 injured. I had them marked down as injured.

629. What was the nature of the injury to the rifles?—Blows from stones, the barrels scratched or dented, and also the stocks injured.

[The Witness withdrew.

Mr. FREDERICK ST. CLAIR RUTHVEN, sworn; Examined by Mr. *Plunket*.

Mr. F. St. C. Ruthven.

630. I BELIEVE that you are an officer in the constabulary?—I am.

631. Were you in charge of any of the constabulary on the day of the polling in Drogheda?—Yes, I was in charge of a party of 14 men; that number was afterwards increased to 29.

632. When you had the 14 men, what part of the town were you in?—I was at the railway station.

633. Will you describe what happened?—When I arrived in the morning, sometime between 5 and 6, at first everything was quiet for sometime till after the arrival of the first train, by which some 40 or 50 people came down from Dublin and went into Drogheda. Sometime after they went to Drogheda two of them returned to the station bleeding and bruised from the beating they had received at some place in the town, or in its vicinity, and they stated——

Mr. *Heron* objected to this evidence.

634. Mr. *Plunket* (to the *Witness*).] What did you see them after they came in?—I went down towards the town with my party, and I met Mr. Reed, the resident magistrate, coming up with a party of constabulary, and he remained with me for the rest of the day with 15 more constabulary.

635. What happened afterwards?—The mob greatly increased at the station till they amounted to several thousands, and they were very furious, and armed with sticks and bludgeons of various kinds.

636. Mr. Justice *Keogh*.] Will you tell us what occurred?—I kept my party at the station for a long time to keep the mob from entering the station, but some of them got round by the ends of the station, and got into the station. It was reported to me that they had beaten some people——

637. Do not say what was reported to you?—I then cleared the station.

638. Mr. *Plunket*.] After you had cleared the station, what happened?—I saw some people in the railway carriages were bleeding very much from the wounds which they had received, and I kept the station clear till the arrival of the next train. We then started for the town with a number of people who were voters.

639. As you went down with this escort, what happened?—Immediately before the escort moved the mob seemed to have been mainly withdrawn from the station, and shortly after we got out of the railway premises the stone throwing commenced. It was principally meant for the persons whom we were escorting in the first instance. The stone throwing increased very much as we got into the town, and became very bad in the Bull Ring, and from that on to the bridge.

640. When you came to the bridge, what happened?—The mob was very violent, and sticks and stones were thrown in great numbers, and I saw the military disorganised, and they partly retired on the constabulary, who also retired, and were in some confusion. I saw several of the people we were escorting struck with stones, and at the bridge two of them were knocked down, and then Mr. Reed, who was with me till that time, went to the front; and shortly afterwards Colonel Talbot directed me to go to my party and fix swords to keep back the mob, who were coming up in the rear of us, which I did. I heard two shots fired, and I saw the military charge up the street, and I charged up after them. I placed some of the persons whom we were escorting in the centre of the escort, but some of them I think, did not remain there; they got into some house afterwards.

641. In fact, had you any difficulty in protecting the voters by your men?—Not except from the stones and sticks that were thrown at us. We marched in the rear. We marched behind the persons whom we were escorting.

642. Were you hurt yourself?—I got a slight blow of a stone.

643. Were

643. Were any of your men injured?—There were four of my men injured.

[The Witness withdrew.

Mr. Justice *Keogh* put it to the Counsel for the Petitioner whether it was wise to accumulate evidence on points on which no question was raised.

Mr. EDWARD TOWNLEY HARDMAN, sworn; Examined by Mr. *M'Donogh*.

644. WERE you present on the occasion of the polling-day in this town?—I was, as check clerk at one of the booths.

645. Were you present when the Rev. Mr. Matthews and a voter of the name of Kelly were together?—I don't think it was the Rev. Mr. Matthews. There were four clergymen. I do not think Mr. Matthews was among them. There were four gentlemen in clerical attire.

646. Do you know the names of any of them?—No, I do not. I know their appearance.

647. They were Roman Catholic clergymen?—Yes.

648. Where was Kelly?—Kelly came up to the booth in charge, as it appeared, of two or three persons who were insisting upon his voting, and he refused to vote, and declared that he would not vote at all, and he went down-stairs; immediately afterwards I was obliged to go down myself to a call of nature, and on going down-stairs I saw this man in the hall with several of these clergymen; they were pressing him to vote.

Mr. *Heron* objected that unless some of these persons were identified this evidence was inadmissible.

Mr. Justice *Keogh* thought the objection was premature.

649. Mr. *M'Donogh* (to the *Witness*).] For whom were they pressing him to vote?—For Mr. Whitworth.

Mr. *Heron* submitted that if this was sought to be made a case of undue influence, it must be made out to be a case of undue influence by the respondent or his agents.

650. Mr. *M'Donogh* (to the *Witness*).] Tell us what occurred?—One of these gentlemen said to him that he should vote for Mr. Whitworth. "If you do not you will disobey your church, and you know what the consequence of that will be;" then said Kelly, "This election has nothing to do with my church;" and he emphasised the word "my" very strongly, so much as to say whatever it had to do with any other church, it had nothing to do with the Catholic Church; he succeeded in getting away from them, and as he was going out he turned down towards the court-house, and a policeman standing in the doorway put out his hand and took him by the coat and directed him to turn the other way; to turn up the street.

651. And did he accordingly?—He did.

652. At the time the clergyman said this, do you remember any other expressions used?—He said afterwards, subsequent to this, that he would be damned, or some word of that nature; that he would be lost.

653. Was that the substance of what he stated?—That was the substance of what he stated; he said, "You are disobeying your church, and you know what the consequence will be."

654. Did the man vote, or refrain from voting?—The man went away and did not vote at all; he was brought up by parties who called upon him to vote for Whitworth, and he refused to do so; he said, "I will satisfy you so far, that I will not vote at all."

655. Did you see Mr. Whitworth on that occasion?—Mr. Whitworth was present.

656. Was he present at the time that the clergyman was endeavouring to induce him to vote for Mr. Whitworth?—They were all together.

Mr. *Heron* said that he should not have raised the objection if this had been stated before.

657. Mr. *M'Donogh* (to the *Witness*).] Had you yourself suffered any injury from the mob during any portion of the time?—I had been several times struck and abused, and one day I was very badly beaten.

658. When was that?—The first occasion was, I think, the Monday week before the election; I got a blow; a single instant blow; there had been a good deal of excitement several days before, but on the day before the nomination I was knocked down and trampled upon and very badly beaten, and very much hurt; I still feel the effects of it.

659. Where did that attack on you take place?—Just at the post office here, in the street up there, I was posting a letter, and there was a meeting being held here at the "Tholsel" at the time, and the crowd coming out from it, and I wished to avoid coming down through the crowd, and I crossed the street and went down a lane that leads to the other street; as I was going down I heard feet coming very suddenly after me, and I was suddenly caught by the back of the neck, and struck across the shins and thrown on my face; I got my hands over my face on the ground for fear anything should happen to my face, and I suppose the whole thing lasted three or four minutes.

Cross-examined by Mr. *Heron*.

660. You say that you were first beaten on the Monday week before the nomination?—I think it was Monday week, but I am not certain; I did not say I was beaten.

661. You were assaulted, to use the legal phrase?—I was.

662. Ten days or a fortnight before the polling?—I think it was the Monday week before the polling.

663. Whom were you acting for then?—No human being; I took no part in the election from the beginning to the end.

664. You were not acting for Mr. Brodigan at all?—Certainly not; I never asked a man for his vote for any candidate.

665. Were you, in no shape or form, Mr. Brodigan's agent?—In no shape or form.

666. Paid or unpaid?—Paid or unpaid.

667. And never got a shilling?—I acted as a clerk in the booth at Mr. Mayne's personal request, because he was short of hands, his men not having come down that morning.

668. What booth were you in?—In No. 3, I think, in Peter-street.

Mr. E. T. Hardman.

15 January 1869.

669. Were you promised to Mr. Brodigan?—No.

670. Did you give him a promise?—No.

671. Did you give him a promise that you would vote for him ever?—Mr. Brodigan knew very well that I would vote for him unless a Conservative came forward.

672. The result was that you did not vote at all?—The result was that I did not vote at all; and between you and me, I think I showed my discretion.

673. How many hours were you in the booth?—From the time it was opened till the time I was ordered to retire; till 10 minutes past one.

674. From eight o'clock in the morning?—Yes.

675. What booth were you in?—In Peter-street; it was No. 3, I think; I may mention that I think I exercised a sound discretion in not voting; I will tell you why.

676. I don't ask you for any explanation; were you in the employment of Mr. Simcox at any time?—Yes; I was his assistant.

677. Were you dismissed by him?—No.

678. Were you accused by him of perjury?—No.

679. Never?—No.

680. On your oath?—On my oath.

681. Were you summoned?—I heard something of it, but it never went on; I believe there was an error.

682. Of yours?—No, none whatever.

683. Was it a summons against you?—Yes; I heard such a thing was in contemplation, but it never went forward; I never saw a summons.

684. Why did it not go on?—I suppose they found that they were wrong.

685. Was that the reason?—I give you the best answer I can.

686. Did you pay any costs about it?—No.

687. What was the charge against you?—I heard indirectly. There never was any charge made against me personally at all. I heard, through a third party, that I was accused of claiming a qualification that I did not possess.

688. On your oath, were you served with a summons?—It is so long ago.

689. On your oath, were you served with a summons for perjury?—I believe, on my oath, that no summons was ever served.

690. Do you know Dr. Pentland?—I do, very well.

691. Did you ask him to interfere for you, and prevent the exposure?—Not that I am aware of, and I have no recollection of anything of the kind.

692. Do you mean to tell his Lordship, when I ask you whether you were summoned for perjury, and whether you asked Dr. Pentland to interfere to save you, that you have no recollection?—That is exactly my answer; and I may go further, that I do not believe I ever did.

Re-examined by Mr. *M'Donogh.*

693. With his Lordship's permission, will you give an explanation about this?—It is rather a hard case. The fact and truth of the matter was this: I was with Mr. Simcox nearly 10 years ago, but on one occasion there was a dispute between us, and a professional agent of Mr. Simcox's asked me a question with reference to my qualification as to infirmary surgeon. He asked me was I a member of the London College. I said I was not. He said, "Are you a member of the Edinburgh College?" I said, "I am not; but I have been in Edinburgh, and have studied there." They took down this as claiming the qualification; and there is the whole explanation.

694. Was Mr. Simcox in the same trade as yourself?—Yes.

The Witness withdrew.

Mr. Michael Kelly, sworn; Examined by Mr. *M'Donogh.*

Mr. M. Kelly.

695. Are you a voter of the town of Drogheda?—Yes.

696. Do you remember the last election?—I do.

697. Do you remember having been applied to to vote for Mr. Whitworth?—Yes; he sent me a card.

698. Do you remember any clergyman applying to you?—I do.

699. Will you tell me who they were?—Father Mathews.

700. Was he the first?—Yes.

701. At what hour of the day did you see him?—It was about eight o'clock.

702. Eight o'clock in the morning?—Yes.

703. At that time did any number of persons come to your house?—Not at that time.

704. Was he there before the time that they came?—He was.

705. How soon after he left you did the mob come?—There came no mob at all to me whilst I was there.

706. You remember that whilst you were there they did not come?—Yes.

707. What did Mr. Mathews say to you when he came to you to solicit the vote?—I was in bed when he came there first, and he spoke to the mistress, and I heard his voice below, and I came down. He asked me was I coming; and I said, "Where?" So he said, "To vote for Mr. Whitworth." But, I said, "I will vote for no one." He and I spoke to that purpose for a good while; and I said I would not vote at all. With that, he came there at 10 o'clock and asked me to vote; and I would not. So, with that, about 10 o'clock, I went up the street and took a few bye-lanes, intending to vote for Sir Leopold M'Clintock; and I was not long in West-street when a party of people got round me and catched me, and dragged me and bustled me about. With that, Father Mathews came over to me, and he in the crowd. "Will you vote yet?" said he. "I did, sir," said I. "For whom?" said he. "For Whitworth," said I. "I will see that," said he. So that the crowd held me there while he went away. So he came back and said, "How dare you tell me a lie?"

708. He left you there with the crowd?—Yes.

709. How long was he away?—About three minutes.

710. What did he say when he came back?—He said, "You scoundrel, how dare you tell me a lie?" I said, "I did so to save my life." "Take him along," he says; and they brought me to the court-house, and I was not long here before I was ordered to Peter-street, and carried partly up there to the booth room. So I asked for the judge of the room when I went in, and I asked him was I to be covered; and he made answer not

not. "Why did not you vote?" said he. "I cannot please everybody," said I. So I told him I would not vote that day; and they provoked me as long as they could. So I asked the judge to give me my liberty; and I turned down the stairs back, where I met Mr. Whitworth, Father Powderly, Father Doyle, and one of the Christian Brothers. So the crowd followed me down, and told Mr. Whitworth that this man did not vote, and would not vote. So Mr. Whitworth——

711. What did he say to you?—He told me to be the same as all the people of Drogheda, and to vote the same as all the people of Drogheda, and showed me the state of the poll; and I told him I would not vote, and I would please myself. So with that, one of the Christian Brothers said to me, "Let him go; he is going to Hell. If anything happens between this and home, what will be the result? you will be damned for ever." So, at all events, in respect of my vote, I was giving my vote to Sir Leopold M'Clintock, on account of Mr. Cooper, and I would give 20 more if I had them. That was all I had over that election.

712. Did you promise the vote to Sir Leopold M'Clintock?—I did, on account of Mr. Cooper being a neighbour of mine; we are next-door neighbours.

Cross-examined Mr. *Fallon.*

713. When did you promise to vote for Sir Leopold M'Clintock?—I suppose it was about a week before the election.

714. Who was it asked you?—Mr. M'Clintock and Mr. Cooper; and these parties all came into the house.

715. Had you ever any conversation with any one as to money, in reference to your vote?—The Christian Brother spoke of money to me, and I told him if he wanted 100*l.* I could lend it.

716. With the exception of that, had you any conversation with any one about money for your vote?—Not then. I am a voter in Drogheda for 18 years back now, and I never got anything from any of the Members.

717. You had no conversation with Father Mathews; as to money for your vote?—Yes; he said he would call at 10 o'clock for me; I said, "If you do, bring 100*l.* with you."

718. With the exception of that, had you any conversation about money with Father Mathews?—Never.

719. Did you ask him would he give you 20*l.* for your vote?—That is what I am saying; 100*l.* if he was coming to me again.

720. Which was it, 20*l.* or 100*l.*?—It was 100*l.*

721. Then it is not the fact that you asked Father Mathews would he give you 20*l.* for your vote?—I told him 100*l.* if he came to me again.

722. You did not say 20*l.*?—Not a word.

723. You are quite clear as that?—I am quite certain.

724. Why did you say that you had voted for Mr. Whitworth, when you had not?—I did not promise Mr. Whitworth.

725. But did you not say that you had voted for Mr. Whitworth when Father Mathews asked you?—To save my life with the mob.

726. Do you mean to tell his Lordship that you thought your life would not have been safe unless you told that lie?—I considered my life was in danger if I voted at all.

727. And you think that you were in a great deal better position because you said you had voted for Mr. Whitworth?—To save my life.

728. Then, though they found out that you had not voted for Mr. Whitworth, you are still here to tell it?—Sure, I could vote for Sir Leopold M'Clintock, or Mr. Whitworth, if I liked.

729. Who is your landlord?—Mr. Hamilton, of Dublin.

730. And who is Mr. Cooper, to whom you say if you had 20 votes you would give them to him?—We are the next-door neighbours in respect of land.

731. What lease have you of your farm?—Sixty-one years.

732. How many of them are out?—Ne'er a one; about eight years have expired.

733. You say that when Mr. Whitworth spoke to you, he said he had been already partly returned?—Yes.

734. Do you remember what numbers he told you?—I did not take the numbers in my hand; it was Father Doyle that had them.

735. He had at least three times as many as any other candidate at that time, had he not?—He had three clergymen, and the Christian Brother, and himself.

736. I mean the votes that he said he had. Did you know what I meant by my last question?—Put it again to me, and then I will know; I did not know.

737. Tell me the state of the poll, as told you by Mr. Whitworth?—I cannot tell that.

738. Do you remember that the figures, whatever they were, showed that Mr. Whitworth had about three times as many as any other candidate?—This was about half-past 10, but I do not know what figures they were.

739. Was he in a large majority?—He was.

740. What is the name of this Christian Brother who you say used those expressions to you?—I cannot tell you.

741. Did you ever see him before?—I did.

742. How many Christian Brothers are there in Drogheda?—I am not able to say that.

743. Have you formed no opinion as to his name?—No. If I saw him I should know him.

744. Who else was present at the time that those expressions were used by that Christian Brother?—The police were there.

745. Anyone else?—Mr Whitworth and the two priests.

746. The two priests whose names you have mentioned?—Yes.

747. What took place when you were canvassed by Mr. Mayne to vote for Sir Leopold M'Clintock?—I was in my own house when they came in, and I said, "I give my vote to Mr. M'Clintock, on Mr. Cooper's account, and if I had 20 more I would do the same."

748. Of what religion are you?—A Roman Catholic.

[The Witness withdrew.

[Adjourned to To-morrow, at Half-past Nine o'clock.

Mr. *M. Kelly.*

15 January 1869.

Saturday, 16th *January* 1869.

SAMUEL HANNAN, Esq., sworn; Examined by Mr. *Fyland*.

S. Hannan, Esq. — 16 January 1869.

749. Were you one of the resident magistrates sent to Drogheda, at the last election?—I was.

750. On what day did you arrive in Drogheda?—I arrived here on the evening of the 19th of November.

751. That was the evening before the poll?—Yes.

752. Will you describe what you saw, if you saw anything remarkable in the town on that evening?—I felt that mischief was coming.

753. Tell us what you felt?—When I got half way between this court-house and the bridge, there was a small crowd of persons. The porter carrying my luggage was in advance. The luggage having been heavy, I took part of it to relieve him. I was carrying a writing-case, and when I got to this crowd they commenced kicking at this bit of a writing-case, and I didn't take much notice. I passed on, and then they commenced kicking myself; I turned and told them that I was not a candidate, or a voter, or an agent at the election. They came on to the court-house so far, and it got worse. I got past the court-house, and then they got very violent, and kicked me, and tried to throw me down. At last, things were so bad that I had to leave the street and get against a door, and put my back to it. It opened inside and I went in backwards, and in the act of getting in they seized my writing-case, and another matter I had in my hand, which they took from me. I got the writing-case and got in safe, and I was hardly safe inside, when the owner of the house told me I must leave it, as they would break his house if I stopped there; so I was turned out. Then I got into the crowd again and they were not so violent, and I got on; and, in fact, a gentlemanly sort of man came forward and appeased the crowd, and told them they should let me alone, and let me go to the hotel; so I got to the hotel, and when I asked for my luggage it was gone, and they did not know where. They suggested the other hotel, and I went there, and then I conversed with my brother magistrates, two other stipendiaries. They had made the arrangements which of course I did not interfere with. The next morning we were all here at an early hour, and the matters that you have already heard recited occurred, which of course I saw at a distance. I allude to that affair at the bridge; I saw it.

754. Were you in sight of it at the time?—I was standing exactly at this corner. I was watching for the escort. The high sheriff had spoken to me, and expressed his uneasiness at the escort having remained out so very long, and expressed a wish to go and assist; I believe I dissented at the first, wishing to have him an efficient officer close to myself; but, however, I consented in the end. Of course he was fully competent to go without me, but we were acting together; but he went, and shortly after he went I saw the escort approaching. I saw a number of persons from about the middle of Shop-street, I think they call it, going down, and with sticks attacking the cavalry. The colonel commanding was standing beside me, and he being an elderly person, I called out to him what I saw, as it occurred, which impresses it more upon my memory now. I told him I saw them attacking the cavalry with sticks; that I saw the cavalry disorganised; and then I exclaimed in great excitement that the cavalry were beaten back and were retreating, or, as the officer described it, going round. I watched very anxiously for another few moments, and I could not distinguish whether the infantry were beaten back. I saw them struggling with some members of the crowd, and I couldn't distinguish. Of course I know that they were not driven back, but I could not at that moment distinguish. Then the two shots were fired, and in an instant the crowd vanished as if annihilated; the street was perfectly cleared. The cavalry then charged up and the infantry after them, all in the height of excitement, and the stipendiary magistrate who was riding with the cavalry fell so close to me that his hat struck me, in fact, in the fall. Then word came up that a man was shot, and then the excitement exceeded anything from all ranks and classes, and the stipendiary magistrate came forward, and there was a great clamour, people calling out, "Why did you order the men to fire? why did you read the 'Riot Act?' There was no occasion for the men to fire;" the magistrate asserting that he did not order the fire. However, the evil went on, and I am most reluctant to mention names, but I think Mr. Whitworth was there, and he and some others invited me into the magistrates room, that we might consult what was best to be done; of course, I assented, and Mr. Whitworth and some of his friends, and the colonel commanding, and myself, met, and then I asked for the other two stipendiaries, but they were obliged to stay with the troops, because the troops would not stay in the streets unless a magistrate was with them. Mr. Whitworth and his friends gave every assistance, and the result we came to I believe you know already, also; that is, that the clergymen were requested to have the body removed, which was at the court-house at the time, and the colonel gave up the names of the two men who had fired. I issued a warrant for them. The colonel then at my request delivered them at the jail and not in the street, but he delivered them to the jailer.

755. Have you been at many contested elections in Ireland?—I have.

756. And at some where there have been disorder and disturbance?—Very great disorder. I have seen many at Tipperary, Waterford, Dungarvan, and those places.

757. Have you ever seen one so riotous and disorderly as the last one here?

Mr. *Heron* objected to the question.

Mr. Justice *Keogh* said that the proper question to ask the witness was, what was the

the state of the town and of the people during the election.

Witness.] Exceedingly violent; in fact, it made me as anxious as ever I was upon any occasion in my life, having the charge of the troops and having the charge of the people. I never felt more anxious upon any occasion. The troops were there with loaded arms, and there was that excitement that I thought it necessary twice to go forward to the colonel, and remind him that he should not allow his men to fire without express orders from me. I asked him where he wished me to remain; he told me, "In front of the troops." I told him, "No; remember, colonel, I am senior magistrate here; do not on any account fire without distinct and positive orders from me."

Cross-examined by Mr. *Heron*.

758. When were the troops withdrawn from the street?—The troops were withdrawn from the street just after the warrant was written out and signed by me.

759. At what hour?—I really don't know.

760. Was it immediately after the meeting of the magistrates that the troops were withdrawn?—Immediately.

761. Did you remain about the streets until five o'clock?—I should say so. S. [illegible], Esq.

762. Do you not remember?—I really don't know the hour. 16 January 1869.

763. Until five o'clock, until the polling closed?—Certainly.

764. And you knew the polling was going on?—Well, I fancy I did not, because I avoided going into a polling booth.

765. Do you know that the election was going on until five o'clock?—I cannot say that I know when the polling booth was closed, or when they ceased.

766. Or the legal hour?—I believe it is something about five o'clock; but you asked me whether I knew of their being polled or not. I will give any information with pleasure, if you will tell me what you want to know, if it is in my power.

767. Mr. Justice *Keogh*.] You say that you saw Mr. Whitworth?—Yes.

768. Did you see Mr. Whitworth at any place when the attack was being made upon the military?—I did not.

769. You do not know where he was?—I do not.

[The Witness withdrew.

Mr. THOMAS IDDON, sworn; Examined by Mr. *Plunket*.

770. Were you in Drogheda on the day of the polling?—Yes. Mr. T. Iddon.

771. Were you in Drogheda on the evening before the polling?—Yes.

772. Were you in a street opposite to "Simpson's Hotel," when speeches were delivered from the balcony?—Yes.

773. Did you hear any of the expressions used on that occasion which you can call to mind?—I did.

774. Would you mention to his lordship what you heard?—I heard one of the clergymen calling upon the crowd to meet the Orangemen that were coming from Dublin and to hurl them into the Boyne.

775. Was there anything else?—I also heard one of them say that there were 300 Orange ruffians hired in Dublin to come and butcher the Catholics of Drogheda to-morrow.

776. Was there anything else you heard at that time?—Except such expressions as "Down with the Orangemen," I do not remember any.

777. Did you see any persons on that balcony except clergymen who were there?—I saw one gentleman.

778. Do you know who he was?—I believe his name is Mr. James Duff Matthews.

779. Do you know Mr. Whitworth?—I do.

780. Did you see him there?—I don't remember seeing Mr. Whitworth there.

781. Do you know a man of the name of Michael Kelly, of James'-street?—I do.

782. Did you happen to see him in any of the polling booths on the day of the polling?—I saw him in one polling-booth in Peter-street; I saw him come into the polling booth along with three other persons, and the three other persons that were along with him wished him to vote for Mr. Whitworth, and he refused to do so, and said he would not vote for any person; and after remaining there for some time he went down.

783. Do you remember anything else in connection with that transaction?—Shortly afterwards I was getting out of the polling booth when Kelly was there, and being spoken to by a clergyman.

784. Did you hear what passed between them?—I cannot exactly swear to the very words; I can give the substance of the words; one of the clergymen was coercing Kelly, at least in language, to vote for Mr. Whitworth.

785. What was the substance of the language which he used, so far as you heard?—So far as I heard, I believe these were the words: why can't he vote for Mr. Whitworth, and that of course he knew now it would be voting against his church if he did not.

786. Was there anything else?—I don't remember any words except that I heard the word "hell" used by one of the clergymen to Kelly, and something about his bread being taken away. That is the substance of the words used by the clergymen.

787. Do you know whether Kelly is a baker in the town of Drogheda?—He is.

788. And you heard the word "hell" used by one of those clergymen?—I did.

789. Do you know the names of any of those clergymen?—I think there was a Christian Brother there.

790. Was he one of the clergymen who was present?—He was; I should recognise him again if I saw him.

791. Mr. Justice *Keogh*.] What was his name?—I don't know his name, I know him very well by sight.

792. Mr. *Plunket*.] Was there any person present on that occasion, that you saw, except the clergyman?—Mr. Whitworth was there.

793. Was he taking part in the conversation?—I heard Mr. Whitworth say, "Why cannot you do as you are told" or "asked" (I do not know which); "see the large majority I have got."

Cross-

Mr. *T. Liddon.*

26 January 1859.

Cross-examined by Mr. *Pallas.*

794. I believe Mr. Whitworth was present only part of this time?—I cannot say; I was there when he used those words.

795. Just say all the words that you heard Mr. Whitworth use?—Those were the only words that I heard Mr. Whitworth use.

796. Did you hear him say, when Kelly said, "I have made up my mind not to vote at all," "I have made up my mind not to ask any man to break his word"?—I did not.

797. You do not remember those words?—I do not remember those words. He might have said them, but I did not hear them.

[The Witness withdrew.

Mr. Frederick Charles Biggar, sworn; Examined by Mr. *McDonagh.*

Mr. *F. C. Biggar.*

798. Were you in Drogheda on the night before the polling?—I was.

799. Were you outside "Simcox's Hotel"?—I was at the other side of the street, under Mr. Moore's.

800. Did you see any persons on the balcony?—I did; the balcony was full of people.

801. Are you acquainted with the person of Mr. Whitworth?—I am.

802. Did you see Mr. Whitworth that night?—I did.

803. Where?—Standing beside one of the clergyman that was speaking.

804. Did you see whether anything occurred to Mr. Moore's house during that night?—Yes, I saw a great many panes of glass broken; they fell down round me while I was under the house.

805. What broke the glass?—Stones, I suppose.

806. At what time was that?—It was about seven o'clock.

807. About what time in relation to the speeches; were the speeches before the breaking or after?—They were speaking about the time the glass was broken.

808. Who were speaking?—Some reverend gentleman, I do not know his name.

809. Were you able to catch any of the expressions?—Yes; they said that there were 500 Orangemen coming from Dublin, and that they would meet them at the bridge, and fight the battle of the Boyne over again, and hurl them into the Boyne.

810. Do you happen to remember whether Mr. Whitworth was on the balcony at that time?—He was.

811. Where was he when the glass was being broken?—I could not exactly say where he was on the balcony, but he was on the balcony; I do not recollect the exact place.

812. Were you well acquainted with his personal appearance?—Yes; I knew him personally.

Cross-examined by Mr. *Harvey.*

813. Have you sworn that Mr. Whitworth was on the balcony when these words were used; was that your intention?—Yes.

814. Have you been in court during the rest of the trial?—I have.

815. And have heard the other evidence about the words used on the balcony?—Yes.

816. But you swear that Mr. Whitworth was there standing beside them?—He was standing beside some reverend gentleman.

817. You have no doubt at all about that?—I have no doubt at all about that.

818. Do you know a man named Owen Cameron?—I do.

819. Who is he?—He is a flour porter at Smith and Smyth's.

820. You are in the same office?—Yes.

821. Were you with Owen Cameron at the hiring of any people?—No.

822. Do you know Owen Cameron?—I do.

823. Did you see him pay any mob?—No.

824. Do you know anything about it?—No.

825. Do you know what I allude to?—Yes.

826. What?—You allude to men being hired.

827. For whom?—To protect Messrs. Smith and Smyth's premises.

828. Were men hired to protect Smith?—The men belonging to the mill were.

829. How many of them?—I do not know.

830. How many men belonging to the mill?—Fourteen, I think.

831. Were those men hired that day?—The mill was closed.

832. And the men hired?—No, they were sent out.

833. Sent where?—Up the town, to protect the gentlemen belonging to the firm polling.

834. They were sent up to town to protect the firm when polling?—Yes.

835. How much were they paid, do you believe?—I do not know what they were paid.

836. Were they paid?—I do not know.

837. Did these men get the tickets of the Rowing Club; are you secretary of the Rowing Club?—I was last year.

838. Did these men get tickets?—No.

839. Are you sure of that?—Yes.

840. Had you any tickets?—No.

841. Did you see any tickets of the Rowing Club?—No, they were all destroyed after the races; all the tickets belonging to the club.

842. And you never heard how much these men were paid, upon your oath?—No, upon my oath.

[The Witness withdrew.

Mr. Montague Maxwell Carpenter, sworn; Examined by Mr. *McDonagh.*

Mr. *M. M. Carpenter.*

843. Where do you reside?—I am at present residing with my mother, in the town of Drogheda.

844. I thought you had come this morning by the train; were you at the railway station on the morning of the day of the polling?—Yes.

845. Did you see Mr. Hamilton there?—Yes, I did.

846. Will you tell us what occurred in your presence with respect to Mr. Hamilton?—I went up to the station in the morning; I escorted a lady up to the train, and when I arrived there I

saw

saw Mr. Hamilton and several other gentlemen there waiting to be able to come down to town; waiting for an escort to bring them to the town; and I saw Mr. Hamilton with some man talking to a number of men, telling them that they must keep together, that it was the best way, and that when the escort came up they would all get down to the town. When I was there I saw a car drew up, on which was Mr. Whitworth and another gentleman; I heard since that his name was Mr. Clinton; I saw them come and take two people away whom I understood came there with Mr. Hamilton to vote for Sir Leopold McClintock.

847. What did they do when taking them away?—One man in particular was very obstinate, and said he would not go, and objected to going; and they took him away by force.

848. You saw that?—I saw that; I was standing beside the car.

849. Did you see him approach Mr. Hamilton, that man that you say was very obstinate and wished not to go?—I saw Mr. Hamilton objecting to their taking this man away. I did not actually see him shoved away, but I saw that they pooh-pooh'd, in fact, what he said, and took the man away.

850. Was Mr. Clinton there at that time?—Yes, he was the gentleman who assisted Mr. Whitworth in taking him away. I did not know Mr. Clinton at that time.

Cross-examined by Mr. *Palles*.

851. Were there two men taken away at the same time?—They were taken away during my stay at the station.

852. But were they taken away at the same time?—I cannot say exactly that. They were taken away one after the other.

Mr. M. M. Carpenter.

16 January 1869.

853. Did you hear Mr. Whitworth say anything upon that occasion; were you near enough to hear anything?—I did not hear him say anything particular. I heard him ask this man for whom he would vote, and then I did not hear what occurred; but I saw them take the man away.

854. Was that the first or the second man?—That was the first man.

855. How long afterwards was the second man taken away?—I cannot exactly say how long afterwards; it was during my stay at the train.

856. Mr. Justice *Keogh*.] Did you see Mr. Whitworth there at the time that the man was taken away?—Yes.

857. Was he near the man?—He assisted Mr. Clinton, or the gentleman I have since heard to be Mr. Clinton, in taking the man away.

858. Do you know him to be Mr. Clinton now?—I had heard that it was Mr. Clinton at the time, but I did not know Mr. Clinton by appearance.

859. Now, knowing Mr. Clinton's appearance, supposing he was in court, would you know him?—I might.

860. Look round and see if you can see him in court?—No, I would not recognise him in court. The man had a hat on when I saw him.

861. Do you know Mr. Whitworth?—Oh, yes, I know Mr. Whitworth very well.

862. Do you see him in court?—Yes, I see him in court; Mr. Benjamin Whitworth.

[The Witness withdrew.

Serjeant James Vincent, sworn; Examined by Mr. *Ryland*.

Serjeant J. Vincent.

863. What regiment are you in?—The 2nd battalion, 8th Regiment.

864. Were you in Drogheda at the time of the last election?—I was.

865. When did you come to Drogheda; did you come any time before the election?—We came down on the 14th, I believe.

866. Were you one of an escort which came down with people from the train on the day of the polling?—Yes, I was one of the escort.

867. Did you see any stones thrown, or anything of that sort?—Yes, there were stones thrown at the voters just after we were leaving the railway station till we got to the bridge; but the stones were not thrown at the soldiers till we got to the bridge, or close by the bridge; and then they were thrown at the soldiers as well as the voters.

868. Did you see any person struck with the stones?—There were eight of my men struck and bleeding; there were seven of them treated by the doctor that day.

869. In what part of the escort were you; were you in front or at the side?—I was next the cavalry, in front, in the vacant space between the two sub-divisions of the infantry.

870. In what state were the crowd at the time; the people that were round the troops on the outside when you were at the bridge?—They were in a very excited state.

871. Did you see the rifles of the men afterwards?—I did; I saw them inspected in the barracks after that.

872. Was there anything the matter with them?—About 50 of them were cut with stones and injured.

873. Captain Dent was the officer in command, I believe?—Yes.

874. Did you see anything happen to him?—He was knocked down, but I did not see him knocked down.

875. Were you hurt yourself?—I was struck three times, but I was not injured.

[The Witness withdrew.

John Nacey, sworn; Examined by Mr. *Plunket*.

J. Nacey.

876. You were one of the escort that came down with the people from the train on the polling day?—Yes.

877. Had the crowd on that day anything in their hands?—They were all armed with heavy cudgels and sticks.

878. Did you see anything in their hands besides the cudgels?—Not before I came to the bridge at the end of the Bull Ring.

879. What did you see then?—I saw a revolver in a respectable young man's hand.

880. What was he doing with it?—He had it pointed

J. Neary.

16 January 1869.

pointed in his right hand, and at the same time Captain William Dunnt, commanding the escort, was on the ground.

881. In what direction was the pistol pointed?—It was over Captain Dunnt, but I could not probably say whether it was for him, or meant for one of the voters whom we were escorting.

882. Did you do anything when you saw that?—Yes.

883. What?—I made a plunge with my bayonet at the man. There was a grey-headed old gentleman, one of the voters, that we were escorting from the station house, who was knocked down by a stone of about two pounds weight.

884. Do you know who that voter was?—I do not.

885. When you made a plunge with the bayonet, did you strike the man?—Yes, I struck him on the arm above the elbow, slightly.

886. What did he do next?—He dropped the revolver. At the time he dropped the revolver I was knocked down senseless on the bridge myself by a cut, which I have the mark to show.

887. Before you were knocked down, did you see what became of the revolver?—The youngster, as I recovered again, was running away with it. I think he was between 13 and 15 years of age, but he had a heavy cudgel and a stick in his hand at the time.

888. Mr. Justice *Keogh*.] You say you saw a young fellow running away with the revolver; was that the same respectable young man who had the revolver before?—No, it was another person.

[The Witness withdrew.

ANDREW O'CONNOR, sworn; Examined by Mr. *McDonogh*.

A. O'Connor.

889. Do you remember the night before the polling?—I do.

890. Were you orderly on that occasion with Captain Dunnt?—I was Captain Dunnt's orderly.

891. Were you at the hotel?—I was.

892. Did you see any clergymen there that night?—I did.

893. Where were they?—On the verandah.

894. Did you hear them speaking?—I did.

895. Did any of the expressions used strike you so as to make you remember the substance or the words?—Yes.

896. What were they?—On the night of the 19th, I heard a clergyman saying to the mob that he hoped they would all meet to-morrow, to meet five or six hundred Orangemen that were coming from Dublin, and that he hoped they would fight the battle of the Boyne over again.

897. Anything else?—And a young gentleman alongside of him, on his left, said, "To hell with the Orangemen."

898. Was he also on the verandah?—He was; he was leaning over the verandah.

899. Would you know that young gentleman?—I would not.

900. Did any other expressions attract your attention?—Yes; the mob addressed him, "Yes, father, we'll meet them to-morrow with sticks and stones."

901. You heard that from the mob?—I did; presently some of the mob began to pick stones at the opposite side of the street at a shop.

902. In what state did the people appear to be?—They appeared to be an outrageous mob to me.

903. How many Roman Catholic clergymen were there there?—I could not tell you.

904. Are you yourself a Roman Catholic?—I am.

905. Do you know Mr. Whitworth?—No, I could not swear to the man.

Cross-examined by Mr. *Hamill*.

906. Where were you standing?—I was in my bedroom, looking out of the window opposite, overhead of the verandah.

907. And you were looking out and listening to the speeches?—Yes.

908. Enjoying all you saw?—Yes.

[The Witness withdrew.

SAMUEL SMITH, sworn; Examined by Mr. *McDonogh*.

S. Smith.

909. Were you the orderly of Colonel Knox?—Yes.

910. Were you at the hotel the night before the polling?—Yes, on the 19th.

911. Do you know Mr. Whitworth?—No.

912. Where were you while the speaking was going on?—I was in my bedroom in the hotel.

913. Is that above the verandah?—Above the verandah.

914. Were you in the same room with the former witness?—Yes.

915. Were you looking out of the window?—Yes.

916. Did you hear the expressions which were used by any of the clergymen?—Yes.

917. What did you hear, the substance of it, as you remember?—The first clergy that spoke said, "People of Drogheda, do you remember what took place two or three miles out here?" and with a long pause he shouts, "The battle of the Boyne;" and he says, "On to-morrow there is 500 or 600 Orangemen coming down from Dublin to put Sir Leopold McClintock in. Be prepared to meet them, and we will fight the battle of the Boyne over again." And he referred back to the history of 200 years ago, when Cromwell had possession of the lower part of Drogheda; "The Catholics fled up to St. Peter's church for protection, and Cromwell followed them. At that time the church steeple was a wooden one; he set fire to the steeple, and as they were leaving he butchered them. At that time it was a Catholic church, and now it is a Protestant one."

918. What else do you remember?—He said no more.

919. Did any other clergyman address them, as you remember?—There was some others.

920. What did he say?—I could not say exactly what he said.

921. Did your hear anything called out by the crowd?

G. Smith. 16 January 1869.

crowd?—I heard the crowd say that they would meet them with sticks and stones to-morrow.

922. Did you hear or see anything occurring then to any of the houses?—I saw that a great many of the crowd were very violent at the time, throwing stones at Mr. Moore's windows, across about 40 yards from the verandah.

923. After the crowd had said they would meet them to-morrow with sticks and stones, did you hear another clergyman address the mob?—There was another addressed them.

924. Do you remember anything of what he said?—No.

[The Witness withdrew.

Mr. WILLIAM THOMAS BRISCOE, sworn; Examined by Mr. *McDonogh*.

Mr. W.T. Briscoe.

925. You reside in Dublin?—I do.

926. Are you a voter of Drogheda?—I am.

927. Did you come down to vote?—I did.

928. By what train did you come?—By the quarter to ten train I left Dublin.

929. For whom did you come to vote?—For Sir Leopold McClintock.

930. Did you vote?—I did not.

931. Were you one of the party escorted into the town?—I was.

932. Were you yourself struck?—I was very severely struck.

933. Where were you struck?—In the forehead and the back of the head, and my limbs were all blackened.

934. Where did you take shelter?—I ran to a house in the Bull Ring; I was thrown out of the escort by a blow I got, and then I lay on the bridge for a moment or two; and then as soon as I recovered myself I crossed over to a shop, and they shut the door in my face; and then a man struck me in the face, and I haven't recovered since; I have been very nervous since.

935. The first blow you mentioned put you out of the escort?—Completely.

936. While you were lying on the bridge did the escort pass off?—The escort passed off.

937. And was it after that that man assaulted you?—It was.

938. At which side of the bridge was it that they closed their doors against you?—At both sides; they slammed the door in my face and told me I shouldn't come there; had it not been for a man who seemed to have some control over them I should have been murdered, I verily believe.

939. Do you know who he was?—I do not, indeed.

940. With whom did you take refuge, then?—He brought me out of the town.

941. You never were at the tally-rooms?—Never; I was not able to cross the bridge; I was afraid to go by the train because I saw a number of people there, and I walked, bleeding as I was, to Laytown; I think it was four or five miles off; I had a severe cut on the back of my head; I knew nothing until I was a mile or two out of the town, and I was told by a woman on the road that I was all bleeding.

942. When did you get to town?—I got by the three o'clock train that left Laytown.

943. Mr. Justice *Keogh*.] When you say you walked to town, that is to say you walked some miles in the direction of Dublin?—Exactly; I walked to Laytown, the next station.

944. Mr. *Heron*.] That is five miles, I believe?—It is three miles, I believe.

[The Witness withdrew.

The Reverend THOMAS WALLACE, sworn; Examined by Mr. *McDonogh*.

Rev. T. Wallace.

945. WHERE do you reside?—At Belfield, Kingstown.

946. Are you the son of Mr. Wallace, the Queen's counsel?—I am.

947. Did you come down here to vote?—I did.

948. Are you a voter of this town?—I am.

949. Did you come by the first or second train?—I came by the first train.

950. Did you see Mr. Hamilton after the first train?—Yes; I came with him, in fact.

951. Did you see the men he had with him, the voters?—I did.

952. Did you see anything happen to them?—I saw Mr. Whitworth; I saw, before Mr. Whitworth came up, two men, who professed to be Mr. Whitworth's agents, who were trying to induce the man to go with them; the man said nothing, but appealed to Mr. Hamilton for protection. Some time afterwards Mr. Whitworth came up with a crowd, and I saw Mr. Whitworth take hold of one of those men, and with the crowd hustle him off with one of his agents and put him on a car, having assaulted Mr. Hamilton, who was holding the hand of the voter who was thus taken away, who was appealing to Mr. Hamilton to protect him.

953. Who was it assaulted Mr. Hamilton?—There was a great crowd; I cannot say who it was; I saw him knocked about.

954. Was Mr. Whitworth there at the time?—He was.

955. What became of the man?—He was taken away by Mr. Whitworth and his agent and put on a car; I don't know what became of him.

956. Were you one of the escorted party?—I was.

957. Were you injured upon that occasion?—Yes, I was.

958. Did you make your way notwithstanding to the polling place?—I did.

Cross-examined by Mr. *Heron*.

959. You voted?—I voted under an escort of police.

960. Mr. *McDonogh*.] Did you see that old gentleman, Colonel Fairclough?—I saw two gentlemen lying on the bridge knocked down; I did not know who they were.

961. Were you yourself badly beaten?—Well, I was struck four times, and my head was cut very much, and my hat cut through.

962. Where did you get the escort of police?—Opposite the Tholsel; I was standing behind the military at the time, and I spoke to Captain Talbot first, and Captain Talbot said he could do nothing for me; and I think it was that gentleman

Rev. T. Walsh. 15 January 1869.

man standing there (*pointing to a person in court*) who then got me an escort of police, and I was brought to the tally-room and to the booth, and I voted.

963. Mr. *Heron*.] Then you voted before you went to the tally-room?—I was not there at all. I made a mistake. I ought to have said the booth.

964. You went to the booth, and you did not go to the tally-room?—I didn't.

965. Did you write within a quarter of an hour after the occurrence on the bridge?—No; not for an hour. I cannot exactly say. It was a long time that I was writing under the escort. I should think it was about an hour. It was a long time.

[The Witness withdrew.

Mr. Charles M'Carthy, sworn; Examined by Mr. *Plunket*.

Mr. C. M'Carthy.

966. I believe you are a student of Trinity College?—Yes.

967. Were you engaged to come down to a tally-check on the day of the election at Drogheda?—I was engaged as a tally-clerk to come down for Sir Leopold M'Clintock.

968. Did you come down?—I came down by the train, arriving as nearly as I remember, at half-past eight at the Drogheda terminus.

969. When you arrived, just tell his Lordship what happened?—I saw a crowd, numbering about 200 or 300, principally composed of young girls who looked like factory girls, and men and boys armed with sticks and stones, and we walked down very quietly, and just outside the railway was a priest. I was told afterwards his name was Father Green, one of the agents of Mr. Whitworth——

970. How do you know that he was an agent of Mr. Whitworth's?—Because I saw him afterwards talking with Mr. Whitworth and with Mr. Verdon.

Mr. *Heron* objected to the reception of this evidence.

Mr. *Plunket* said that it would be seen presently that this was not an unfair question.

Witness.] Just as we came out of the railway this priest hissed the mob on our party, who numbered about six, making use of the words, "McClintock's bloody Orangemen, boys; don't hurt them!" There was a Mr. Malley along with me, and we went along the little side-path on the left-hand side of the road, and walked by ourselves there; and when we got a little way from the railway the crowd began throwing sticks and stones, and the priest was walking beside them and hissing, and urging them on with his hands and laughing, and pointing out some whom the crowd had not thrown stones at. We could see them distinctly, being behind him. The crowd, thinking we did not belong to the others, did not throw stones at us, as our party commenced running down towards the booth, and we walked. We walked down, then, past a building on the left—I think it is the poorhouse—and while we were passing there we saw a man take the back rail out of his cart and strike one of our party on the bridge of the nose, nearly knocking him down. We went round there, and turned by a road up to the left, intending to go round that way by the town, as we were afraid of our lives to go down to the town by the common straight way. There was a large and tremendously excited crowd, and half way up the hill we were met by a crowd of women and men. We, to save our lives, declared we were for Whitworth, and so we were allowed to pass; and when we were at the top of the hill we met an agent of Mr. Whitworth's——

971. What makes you say "an agent of Mr. Whitworth's"?—Because he had a card in his hat. I have a card in my pocket of the same kind.

[The same was delivered in, and is as follows:—]

"Drogheda Election—Whitworth.

"Mr. Voter.

"Polling Place, Booth No.

"at

"The polling will commence at eight o'clock a.m. on Friday morning next, 20th November, and will close at five o'clock on same day.

"Your early attendance at the poll is requested.

"☞ Please bring this card with you."

Witness.] We declared to him that we were Mr. Whitworth's friends. "Well," says he, "it is not safe for you to go down through the town, but I will bring you down; if you say you are Whitworth's friends." So he brought us down, and just when we got into the street the crowd closed round us threatening our lives, and saying we belonged to the "bloody Orangemen." He said, "No, boys, they are Whitworth's friends," and beckoned with his hands, and said, "All right, boys;" and he had to keep saying it the whole time down to the tally-room. So we went down there, and I procured three of those cards in the tally-room, and he introduced me there to Mr. Whitworth and another priest. I think it was the same Father Green whom we had seen at the railway. So we walked then down to the town, trying to look for our booths, but we were afraid to ask anybody, because if the crowd had known we belonged to any side except Mr. Whitworth's, they would have taken our lives. About one o'clock I saw a frightful crowd rushing down towards the railway down Shop-street, and we heard them using frightful work; they were wrecking some voters coming from the rail. I was going down Shop-street, and I saw a crowd of horse soldiers and foot soldiers on the bridge, and I said to Mr. Malley, who was with me all the time, "We had better get out of this crowd." So we went up into a window——

972. Never mind what you said to Mr. Malley?—We went up into a window, and while there we saw the scene on the bridge.

973. Tell us what you saw there?—I saw the horse soldiers in front moving, and behind them were some foot soldiers surrounding some voters, and the crowd beat back the horse soldiers, and they retired. They went back as if they were beaten by stones.

974. Did you hear a shot fired?—I heard first of all a shot fired, which seemed to come from a window as I looked down, and immediately after two

that two shots were fired; and immediately after the crowd scattered like rabbits into a burrow, or like feathers blown off your hand. Immediately after that I saw a body lying across the street, and then the horse soldiers came again and charged up the street, followed by the infantry.

975. After that where did you go?—I went up to the court-house; trying to look for Mr. Mayne, or for our tally rooms; I did not know where they were. While at the court-house I saw two Roman Catholic clergymen standing at the door of the court-house, and an old gentleman with grey hair and a grey beard came in to vote, escorted by some police; he went into vote, followed by the clergyman, and he voted for Sir Leopold McClintock; and the priest made some remonstrance, or said something to him; I didn't quite catch what; and followed him out, and pointed him out to the crowd as having voted for Sir Leopold McClintock, and stones were thrown at him and sticks; and I saw the same clergyman do the same thing to two or three different voters at the court-house door.

976. Mr. Justice *Keogh*.] Do you know his name?—An old woman in the crowd told me his name was Father M'Kee or M'Creagh, I am not sure which.

977. Mr. *Plunket*.] Was there anything after that?—I saw nothing after that.

978. Did you succeed in getting to the tally-rooms?—I did not succeed in getting to the tally-room, because I was afraid of my life, and I went up with Mr. Whitworth's card in my hat.

979. You say that you were introduced to Mr. Whitworth?—The agent introduced me to Mr. Whitworth as a friend of his in his own tally-room.

980. Did anything else occur to you that you recollect?—Nothing, except that Mr. Whitworth was talking to the clergyman.

981. To which clergyman?—I think it was to Father Gavan; I am not quite sure.

Cross-examined by Mr. *Fallon*.

982. Where were you engaged to come down to Drogheda?—In Dame-street.

983. In the Conservative committee-rooms?—Yes.

984. Who was it engaged you?—Mr. Purcell engaged me for a Mr. Kennedy.

985. Mr. Kennedy was acting for Sir Leopold McClintock?—He was, as I understood.

986. Were you at those Conservative committee-rooms the evening before you came down?—No, I was not; at least not at the time that the other men were engaged, but I was afterwards.

987. What is the number in Dame-street of those committee-rooms?—I think it was 17, but I am not quite sure.

988. You say you were not there when the other men were engaged?—No.

989. But you were there afterwards?—Yes.

990. Do you remember being there when some of the men who had been engaged were there?—Yes.

991. And when Kennedy was there?—No; Kennedy was not there.

992. You did not see Kennedy there at all?—No.

993. Did you see at the Conservative committee-rooms any of the men who afterwards came down in the train with you?—I did; some of them.

994. How many?—One or two.

995. Only one or two?—Only one or two that I recognised.

996. Can you say that you did not meet 20 at the Conservative committee-rooms, who afterwards came down with you by that early train?—I couldn't swear to 20 faces where I could swear to one or two.

997. May there have been 20, although you did not recognise them? Certainly.

998. How many came down with you in the train?—In the carriage where I was there were about 12 or 15.

999. In the carriage in which you were not, can you say how many there were?—I should think not.

1000. Were they full. How many carriages were there on the train. Now how long were you waiting before you got into the carriage from the time you arrived at the station?—I should think half an hour.

1001. I suppose in that half hour you were very well able to see the number of people that there were in the station?—Yes.

1002. How many were there?—I should think there were between 40 and 50.

1003. Was Kennedy there?—He was.

1004. Did Kennedy buy the tickets for all the party?—I did not see him buying them.

1005. Who gave you your ticket?—Kennedy.

1006. Had you a bludgeon with you on that occasion?—No.

1007. Any stick?—I had a light stick.

1008. Had you that stick with you the evening before at the Conservative committee-rooms?—No.

1009. Are you certain of that?—I am certain of it.

1010. Had you any other stick if you had not that one?—I always carry a cane.

1011. On the evening before, at the Conservative committee-rooms, were you flourishing something, and saying what you would do in the way of protecting voters the next day in Drogheda?—Not that I remember.

1012. Will you swear that you didn't?—I say I don't remember.

1013. That is the farthest you can go?—Yes.

1014. Will you swear that in the Conservative committee-rooms, the previous evening, you had not a thick stick, and that you were not flourishing it and saying what you would do in Drogheda the next day?—I don't remember.

1015. How many of the men that came down with you were armed with bludgeons?—I did not see any with bludgeons.

1016. How many with sticks?—As far as I remember, two men in the carriage with me had sticks.

1017. How many not in the carriage with you had sticks?—I cannot answer that.

1018. How many of them had a revolver?—I didn't see one, or even a heavy stick.

1019. You said you came down as a poll clerk?—I did not tell you so.

1020. You told my learned friend, Mr. M'Donogh so; did you act as a poll clerk?—No, because I could not get to the rooms.

1021. At what hour were you in Drogheda?—I think it was about half-past eight; I hadn't a watch with me.

1022. But at all events the election had commenced before you arrived in the town?—I cannot say.

1023. Do you know what "roughs" are; do you

Mr. C. M'Carthy.

18 January 1859.

Mr. C. M'Carthy.

18 January 1869.

you know the ordinary meaning of the expression "roughs"?—I do.

1024. How many of the men that came down in the train with you, were roughs?—I don't think any of them were roughs. I think most of them were engaged in the office in Dame-street, or in the one on the opposite side.

1025. And they were all coming down as poll clerks?—Yes.

1026. Mr. Justice *Keogh*.] You say that you saw two old gentlemen come into the court-house to vote, and that they did vote?—One old gentleman with a long grey beard.

1027. I thought you said there were two; another with him?—No; I saw other voters treated in a similar way by the same priest.

1028. But you said that the clergyman came in after them?—He followed them into the booth-room where they gave their votes.

1029. What did you see him do afterwards?—He remonstrated with them for voting against Mr. Whitworth, and then he followed them out to the door of the court-house where the excited part of the mob outside formed a phalanx round the door; he pointed out particularly to one old woman who seemed to be leading the mob, that those gentlemen had voted against Mr. Whitworth; he pointed at them, and said "McClintock."

1030. What took place?—Then the mob set on one old gentleman, and beat him the whole way down the street, and the constabulary had actually to turn round and beat the fellows off with the butt end of their muskets to prevent the old gentleman being killed.

1031. Can you say who that priest was?—I asked a woman who he was, and she said it was Father M'Creagh.

1032. Would you know the gentleman if you saw him again?—I don't think I would.

1033. What time was that; was that after the attack on the military?—As well as I remember, it was.

1034. Mr. *Fleming* (through the *Court*).] Do you know who the old gentleman was?—I do not know his name, but he was a very remarkable looking old gentleman with a long grey beard; he was rather below the medium size. He was a very peculiar looking old gentleman, and he seemed to be very well known in the town, because they all called him by a name which I forget.

1035. Would you know it if you heard it again?—I think I would. I would know the old gentleman again, certainly, if I saw him.

1036. Mr. Justice *Keogh*.] Do you recollect the name that they called him, or anything like it?—It was something ending in "son," I think, or something like it.

1037. Mr. *Pallas* (through the *Court*).] I forgot to ask you how much you were to be paid for your day's work?—I did not bargain at all.

1038. Was there no contract made?—There was no contract made.

1039. Look about among these gentlemen, and see if you see the clergyman that you refer to?—I think that was one of the clergymen standing at the door of the court-house (*pointing to a person in the court*); but Roman Catholic clergymen are so like each other that I cannot swear to any one in particular.

1040. Mr. *McDonogh*.] Do you mean to say that that was the clergyman who went in and remonstrated with the old gentleman?—I wouldn't swear that, because there were so many things happening that day.

Mr. Justice *Keogh* inquired the name of the person who had been pointed out, and it was stated to be the Reverend James Powderley.

Witness.] I wouldn't swear that was him, but it was very much like him.

1041. Mr. *Pallas*.] Have you any memory upon that subject at all?—Not as to his appearance. I remember the fact of his going in quite well. The only thing I remember about it was, asking this old woman.

[The Witness withdrew.

St. George William Smith, Esq., sworn; Examined by Mr. *McDonogh*.

St. G. W. Smith, Esq.

1042. Where do you reside?—At Newtown, near Kells, county Meath.

1043. Are you a voter of Drogheda?—I am.

1044. Did you, on the day of the polling, come to this town?—I did.

1045. Was it by train?—By train from Kells; it came into Drogheda about 10 o'clock.

1046. Did you remain at the station, or did you come into the town?—I remained at the station till the 12 o'clock train came in with the voters.

1047. You were one of the escorted party, I suppose?—I was.

1048. Have you resided in the neighbourhood of Drogheda for any time, so as to be known by the people?—Oh, yes, for an age; the family always resided near it for an age.

1049. You are one of the Annesbrook family, I believe?—Yes.

1050. Were you known in the town?—By every one nearly.

Mr. *Heron* stated that he would admit this.

1051. Mr. *McDonogh* (to the *Witness*).] Were you beaten on that occasion?—I was.

1052. How many blows did you get?—Three before I ever entered Peter-street at all; one on the right side, breaking the brim of my hat, another on the left cheek, and another very severe one on the crown of my head, which cut in my hat and almost stunned me, and made me unconscious for a time. The blood flowed very freely, and I found great difficulty in keeping up with the escort through James'-street; it was so narrow, and they were getting so pressed there, that there was danger in going through that part of it, and we were getting scattered.

1053. Did you vote?—I did not.

1054. Where did you take shelter?—When the affair took place on the bridge, after the charge of the cavalry, I went up with the infantry, and charged with the infantry up the street, and I found great difficulty in keeping pace with them, because I had met with an accident, and I had a large heavy coat. The men were rushing out of the houses and lanes with clubs at us, and one fellow with a bludgeon aimed a blow at me, and I do not know how I escaped. I got up then to the Tholsel, where, out of the number of 30 or 40 that left the railway, I think there were not more than seven or eight of us.

1055. Were you in terror and apprehension at that time?—Every moment; you did not know whether your life was safe a bit. After we got to the bridge we all slouched our hats and turned our collars up to prevent our faces being smashed to pieces.

1056. For whom had you intended to vote?—For Sir Leopold McClintock.

Cross-examined by Mr. *Morell*.

1057. You say you got up after what was called the cavalry charge?—I got up with the infantry.

1058. Did you pass this house?—I stopped at the Tholsel.

1059. There was nothing to prevent your going in there?—I went up to the tally-rooms, and when I went there I was told they had withdrawn their clerks from the poll, and that the election was over.

1060. Did not they tell you not to vote?—They told me there was no necessity for my voting.

1061. Did they not tell you not to vote?—I said, "Are you going to the poll"? They said, "It is no use, we have withdrawn our clerks."

1062. Were you at Kelly's, a person in the Bull Ring?—No.

1063. Were you in any house at all?—No.

1064. You were not in any house?—Not in any house.

1065. Do you remember the sheriff coming to you?—The sheriff never came to me.

1066. At the tally-room?—No; I went into the room, and I heard some noise in the room.

1067. Did you see the sheriff there?—I saw some gentlemen; the sheriff, I think, was amongst them.

1068. Did he come and say to you, and to others, that if any gentlemen wanted to go down to vote he was ready to go with them?—I heard him say he was ready to escort them.

1069. But you declined it?—I did not decline it, but it was no use; the election was over; they had withdrawn the clerks, and our own were scattered.

[The Witness withdrew.

Mr. G. W. Smith, Esq.

16 January 1869.

EDWARD BOYD, Esq., sworn; Examined by Mr. *Plunket*.

E. Boyd, Esq.

1070. Are you a Doctor of Medicine?—I am.

1071. Where do you live?—In Kingstown.

1072. Are you a voter for the borough of Drogheda?—I am.

1073. Did you leave Dublin on the morning of the polling day in Drogheda?—I did, by the half-past eight train.

1074. When you arrived in Drogheda, tell his Lordship, shortly, what occurred?—I arrived here at about a quarter to 10, coming down by the mail, and my brother and I were alone together; we walked out of the carriage, and came down here in the direction of the town. After we had got about 200 yards, we noticed, for the first time, a number of men lounging upon the parapet of the railway along there. I had a newspaper in my hand, and I put it in my pocket, which attracted their attention, and I carried it there with my hand in my pocket for a little distance. The crowd immediately closed on me; they thought it was a signal, I suppose, and said, "For whom do you vote; vote for Whitworth." So they gathered round us, and one man in particular was a little drunk, I think; he tried to upset my brother three or four times, and caught him by the collar and put his foot out, but he did not succeed. But they closed round us, and put their sticks over our heads, and said, "Vote for Whitworth." So my brother having one of Mr. Whitworth's cards (he was the only one who canvassed us), showed it them, and they said, "All right."

1075. Had you promised to support Mr. Whitworth?—Certainly not. Then they made way for us. We came up along, I think, the north quay, the other side of the bridge, and came up by the upper road, and then down through the crowd. Then we came in and voted for Sir Leopold McClintock.

1076. After you had voted, what happened?—Then we came up the other way, and by mistake took the wrong road, and came round by the chapel to the railway station.

1077. Did anything occur to you as you went along?—We did not suffer any personal violence; we asked the road to the railway station, and said we were strangers. The woman whom we asked inquired for whom we voted, and we said, "For Whitworth, to be sure," or something to that effect. She said, "Oh, you Orange ones, you would not be coming this way if you were Whitworth's men." That was all. When we got to the railway station, I found a tremendous crowd of people there, but I got in unmolested, and passed through the police.

1078. Did you see Mr. Whitworth there?—I saw a gentleman on horseback, who I afterwards heard was Mr. Whitworth, but I do not know; I could not identify him.

1079. Would you know him?—I know him since I came into court.

1080. Where did you see him?—At the railway station.

1081. Do you see him in court now at all?—Yes; he is here (*pointing to a person in the court*).

1082. When you arrived at the station, did you get off quietly there?—My brother and I were both safe, because we were inside, but the crowd collected round a number of men, who, as it appears, were Sir Leopold McClintock's clerks, and attacked them. The people said, "What a shame of Mr. Whitworth not to come in and put an end to the row, he being outside at the time."

1083. Mr. Justice *Keogh*.] Who said that?—Some of the people in the crowd.

1084. Mr. *Plunket*.] Do you mean the crowd outside or the crowd inside?—The people in the railway station.

Cross-examined by Mr. *Heron*.

1085. Do you remember having seen Mr. Whitworth on horseback?—I did see a gentleman on horseback.

1086. And you now recognise him to be Mr. Whitworth?—No.

1087. Do

E. Hoyt, Esq.

10 January 1859.

1087. Do you now recognise Mr. Whitworth as the gentleman on horseback?—Certainly not.

1088. Was he the gentleman?—I could not tell you; I was told he was on horseback outside by the crowd; that was all.

1089. Did you see Mr. Whitworth on horseback?—I saw a gentleman on horseback.

[The Witness withdrew.

HALL DRENNON, Esq., sworn; Examined by Mr. McDonogh.

H. Drennon, Esq.

1090. Are you a medical gentleman?—Yes.

1091. A doctor or surgeon?—Both.

1092. Where do you live?—In Great Brunswick-street, in Dublin.

1093. Are you a voter of Drogheda?—I am.

1094. Did you come down to vote on the day of the polling?—I did.

1095. For whom?—For Sir Leopold McClintock.

1096. By what train did you come down?—By the train that left Dublin at a quarter before 10, I think.

1097. Were you one of the escorted party?—I was.

1098. Were you beaten on that occasion. Tell us what occurred to you?—I was passing down James-street with an escort, and I was struck by two or three stones slightly. Then I got a very severe blow on the side of my head, which is just barely getting well now, and I was knocked down and stunned very much. I had a friend with me, Mr. Barney, who is also a voter, and he fortunately was able to lift me up. My head was so giddy that I had great difficulty in walking, but he held me up, and we went on till we got on to the bridge. Then there was a rush back of the cavalry, and we were all thrown back, and I was, amongst others, thrown into a place called the Bull Ring. So we made an attempt to get into one house or two, and we did not succeed.

1099. And why did you not succeed?—They would not let us in; but at another house (I do not know whose), they were very kind, and let us in, I think through Father Matthews, but I do not know. He succeeded in getting us in. I felt very giddy, and I told the person as soon as I got in that I would like to get into bed, I felt so very uncomfortable. So they very kindly brought me upstairs and put me on a bed. I had a white handkerchief in my hand which I held to my head, and it was completely saturated with blood. The young woman of the house very kindly took my handkerchief away and got it washed, and nicely made it up to me; in fact, brought it to me again in the course of an hour quite clean, and, also, and in fact was very attentive all through.

1100. What became of you then?—I lay there, I think, three or four hours, up to nearly the time that the train was to start for Dublin; I attempted on some occasions to get up, but I did feel remarkably giddy, and I lay down again, and just lay quiet there for some hours. In the meantime I bled a good deal, and some medical gentleman was sent to me, who looked at the wound and put some little dressing on it; however, it bled until seven or eight o'clock that evening.

1101. By what train did you come up?—The train that arrives in Dublin, I think, about five o'clock; some time after three.

1102. Did you vote upon that occasion?—No.

1103. And each time that you raised yourself in bed you felt giddy?—I felt so giddy that I did not think I was in a state to get up.

1104. That you did not see the rest of the [illegible] which you could use your limbs?—I did not at all; I did not get up.

1105. You, as a medical man, are quite aware of what concussion of the brain is?—I am.

1106. Does that frequently cause giddiness?—It does.

1107. Did you continue ill for any length of time?—I was ill for some days, and I had a very eminent medical man in Dublin who attended me (Dr. Geoghegan). I continued ill for some days, and he would not allow me to move at all.

1108. Are you thoroughly recovered yet?—I am tolerably well now, but my head is quite sore yet, and what I call numb; not the feeling that I originally had in it.

1109. Did you see anything happen to Colonel Fitzclarence?—Well, I did not exactly see. He held me coming down the road by the right shoulder trying to keep up with us, for he was very feeble. I did all I could to help him along, but about the bridge he was knocked down, I think, and I saw no more of him.

Cross-examined by Mr. Fallon.

1110. I believe you were one of the gentlemen that made an affidavit, that you would not for any consideration come back to Drogheda to give evidence, in consequence of what you anticipated there?—Yes.

1111. Are you not very agreeably surprised?—Certainly, very much at present; for I did not think it was possible, from what I saw that day.

1112. When you were in this house, do you remember being waited upon by some gentleman who offered you an escort if you wished to vote?—There was somebody that did make an offer of the kind. I do not know who he was.

1113. I think what you said, by way of answer to it was, that there was no use in your going?—Very likely I did say that.

1114. That you at that time knew that Sir Leopold McClintock had no chance?—I do not say that.

1115. Did you use the words, "It was no use"?—I think very likely I did.

1116. Did you not use these words in addition, "There is no use in going, as Brodigan has made a hack fight"?—I said no such thing.

1117. Of course, when you came into the town at that time, you heard the state of the poll?—I did not.

1118. At that time you had no idea how the election was going?—No.

1119. What reason did you give for not voting?—Because I felt so very unwell, I was so giddy, that when I attempted to rise up in the bed, I found that I was obliged to lie back again.

1120. Some others of the gentlemen that were there went and voted, I think?—I do not know; the gentleman that came with me would not go; Mr. Barney, of North Frederick-street, Dublin.

1121. Is he here?—He is not, I believe; I do not see him.

[The Witness withdrew.

WILLIAM MORRIS REED, Esq., sworn; Examined by Mr. *Pinder*.

1122. You are a stipendiary magistrate?—I am.

1123. Were you here in that capacity on the day of the polling, in Drogheda?—I was.

1124. When did you first go out into the town in that capacity on that day?—At about a quarter to eight.

1125. Did you observe anything peculiar then, when you went out, in the state of the town?—No, nothing peculiar at that hour.

1126. When did you first go up to the railway station?—At about half-past eight.

1127. Did you observe anything then?—Yes.

1128. What?—I had a party of constabulary, 13 men and a sub-inspector with me; and when we got to the foot of Shop-street, there was a row there, and two men had taken refuge in the electric telegraph office, and I saw the crowd endeavouring to break in the door.

1129. Where is the electric telegraph office?—It is at the very end of the quay at this side of the bridge; it is a corner house. I ran to the door to prevent their forcing it in, and brought the police with me, and pushed the crowd on one side, and two men came out and claimed my protection. I asked them what they wanted; they merely said they wanted their lives protected. I told them I was going up to the railway station on duty, and that if they considered they required my protection there, I would take them there; and I did do so. The men had both of them lost their hats at the time, and one of them was cut and bleeding.

1130. Do you know who these men were?—I do not know; I think I could identify both of them, but I never saw them before or since.

1131. When you came up to the station what did you observe then?—Shortly after arriving there a very large mob collected, not a dense mob, but a scattered mob, all armed with bludgeons and pieces of iron hoops straightened out about two feet or two and a half feet long.

1132. Did you observe among them any persons of a better class than the mob?—No, I cannot say that I did.

1133. What occurred next at the station?—When the first train came in some gentlemen came down by it; one of those gentlemen whom I did not know at the time, but I know now, came up and told me he was a magistrate of two counties, and asked me if I was a magistrate, and I said I was the magistrate on duty there. He asked me to give him and his friends who were voters, protection down to the Town-hall; I told him I had recently come from there, and that with the small force I had at my disposal, namely, 30 constabulary, it would not be a safe experiment to take them down.

1134. At what o'clock was this?—About half-past nine; I told him if he wished to go I would go with him, but that it was a very dangerous thing to attempt, and that I would send a requisition to Captain Talbot, my brother magistrate, for further help, and I did do so; I sent for infantry and cavalry, and they both arrived shortly afterwards with Captain Talbot, who then considered that even the force at our disposal then was not sufficient to protect the parties to the Town-hall; and we sent a further requisition for more infantry.

1135-6. At that time how many infantry and cavalry had you?—At that time we had 20 infantry, 16 hussars, and 30 policemen, and the sub-inspector and the officers.

1137. That is 66 of all arms?—Yes; Captain Talbot then sent for a further augmentation, and we got 40 more infantry of the 6th Regiment. On the arrival of the next train, about half-past 11 o'clock, or shortly after half-past 11 o'clock, the party was formed to go into the town. The voters or gentlemen who said they were voters, numbering about 25 to 30, were placed between two files of infantry; the cavalry, the hussars, were placed four at each side of those files of infantry, and the remainder at the head of the party; and Captain Talbot being with Colonel Knox, who was in command of the cavalry; I brought up the rear of the whole party with the 30 constabulary; the moment after we left the railway premises, the moment we got outside of the railway gate, the stone-throwing commenced, but it was not very bad until we got to the narrow portion of that street which I believe they call James's-street; it is at right angles to the Bull Ring; there the stone-throwing became excessive; not only stones, but bottles and pieces of iron, and sticks were thrown at us. Then when we got on to the Bull Ring it was, if possible, worse; and almost opposite the police barracks on the Bull Ring two old gentlemen that I was walking with (they were the last of the party of voters, and to my right), were each of them knocked down; the outside man of the two was knocked down first; he fell backwards; and then the next man to me was knocked down, and he fell forwards. Seeing that, and also seeing the temper of the mob, I considered it would be perfectly unsafe to leave those two old gentlemen in the hands of the mob, and I ran forward at once to Captain Talbot, who was at the head of the column, and I told him what had occurred, and said we must make some provision for their safety; but when I got to the front I saw a scene, of which I had no anticipation whatever. When I was at the rear I found a large mob collected in front armed with bludgeons, pelting stones, and I said to Captain Talbot, "I must read the Riot Act." He said, "Yes, do." I then ran out between Captain Knox's and Captain Talbot's horses' heads, and I there read the Riot Act, the stone throwing men making demonstrations with bludgeons; I tapped Captain Knox on the left shoulder, and I said, "Captain Knox, charge them with the cavalry." Almost at the same moment the men with the bludgeons rushed forward and bludgeoned the cavalry horses on their heads.

1138. What followed upon that?—The effect of that was to knock the horses back. They fell back upon the infantry, who were utterly disorganized in consequence—the leading files of the infantry. I ran back behind the horses' backs, and that brought me to the left front of the infantry. I then waved my stick over my head, and I called out to Captain Dunne, who was in command of the infantry, to charge the mob with the bayonet. Then the mob got right on amongst the soldiers, whose organization was broken, and there was a regular stand-up fight between members of the mob and the troops. I saw Captain Dunne struck with something, and

knocked

W. M. Reed, Esq.

18 January 1869.

knocked half round towards me, falling towards the ground. I did not see him come to the ground; but I saw two men of the 9th Foot on the ground at the same moment, and I saw one of the bayonets of the 9th within an inch or two of a man's head. I then fell back a little along the left file of the infantry, and found the front ranks of the infantry in open order,—in fact, all disorganised. The next thing was, that two shots were fired almost instantaneously, and the effect of those shots upon the mob was to make them run in every direction. I never saw a greater stampede. The next thing was a charge of cavalry up Shop-street. The next thing was for us all to get up to the top of Shop-street the best way that we could. That was empty at the time, but there were stones being thrown from windows as we passed up.

1139. Had you any more duty to perform then?—Yes; the next thing was, that I went up with the troops to the gaol. Two men were handed over to the civil power.

1140. Mr. Justice *Keogh*.] You have been a military man, I presume?—Never.

1141. Did you see any persons urging on the crowd, or taking any sort of a leading part in the matter, guiding or directing?—No; I could not point out any person as a leader.

1142. Did you see any clergymen amongst the crowd?—I saw a Roman Catholic clergyman on the left of the window as we were coming down, before we got into James's-street, and, thinking he would have influence with the people, I went to him and told him to check the stone-throwing, and I must say he used every possible exertion to do so, holding up his hands to the crowd, and telling them to throw no stones.

1143. Do you happen to know who that gentleman was?—I would know him again. I did not know him at all. I am a perfect stranger in Drogheda.

1144. You have been in court for some time?—No; I only just came in previously to my being called.

1145. It is creditable to that gentleman, and, therefore, you had better look round and see if you see him in court?—I only see one Roman Catholic clergyman in the gallery, and I do not think he is the gentleman.

1146. Then, look round. It is creditable to the Roman Catholic clergyman, and it should be known?—I see two, now. I may be mistaken, but I do not think either of them was the gentleman. The front gentleman of the two is not unlike the clergyman. I should not say it was he, though.

1147. Mr. *Heron*.] Will you look at the Roman Catholic clergymen in court?—After looking round I only see two Roman Catholic clergymen here; and it was not that gentleman, nor was it this gentleman. I think (pointing to persons in court). Certainly this is very like the gentleman, but I would not undertake to identify him.

1148. Mr. Justice *Keogh*.] What was the time covered by the whole of this occurrence, from the time you left the station until the termination of the charge of cavalry, which appears to have been the closing scene of the whole?—I think we left the station at about a quarter to twelve, and I think it must have been about five minutes past twelve, or, perhaps, a little more, when we arrived at this court.

1149. There was no further rioting?—There was no further rioting during the day that I am aware of.

1150. You say you saw the cavalry horses bludgeoned. Do you mean by that that they absolutely struck the heads of the horses?—I saw the horses' heads struck, and I was driven back with the horses, and behind the horses.

1151. Were you mounted?—No, on foot.

1152. Had the hussars their swords drawn at that time?—They had no swords drawn from the time we left the station; when we got to the head of the bridge they had not been drawn.

1153. When they charged had they their sabres drawn?—I am under the impression that they had, but I am not positive.

Cross-examined by Mr. *Heron*.

1154. During the day before that, or immediately afterwards, did you see other Roman Catholic clergymen endeavouring to pacify the mob?—No; that was the only Roman Catholic clergyman that I saw, and he was acting upon my suggestion.

[The Witness withdrew.

Mr. JOHN DEVINE, sworn; Examined by Mr. *McDonogh*.

Mr. J. Devine.

1155. WHERE do you live?—About a mile from Drogheda.

1156. Are you a voter for the town of Drogheda?—Yes.

1157. Did you come to the railway station on the day of the polling?—I did, from Balbriggan.

1158. Were you in company with Mr. Hamilton?—No.

1159. Did you see Mr. Hamilton at the station that day?—I did.

1160. Had you promised to vote for any of the candidates?—I promised to vote for M'Clintock.

1161. When you came to the station, will you tell us, if you please, what occurred to you?—Why, I was afraid of my life.

1162. Tell us the facts that made you afraid of your life?—Why, the mob.

1163. Well, tell me all about it?—I declare I was afraid of being killed; only for that, I would vote.

1164. For whom?—For Mr. McClintock.

1165. Do you know Mr. Whitworth?—Well, I know him by eyesight.

1166. Did you see him there that day?—I did.

1167. Do you know a Mr. Clinton?—Yes, well.

1168. Did you see him there that day?—I did.

1169. Will you tell us what occurred, either with the mob or with those gentlemen?—Mr. Clinton asked me, would I vote for Mr. Whitworth, and I said nothing to him. Then Mr. Whitworth came up a short time after, and he asked for whom I would vote; and I told him I would vote for no one. Then I just walked on one side; and as I was going, Mr. Hamilton, he was afraid that I would be killed, and he told me to go back to Balbriggan again for safety. I went into the wrong carriage, and I came out again. Then, after a while at the station-house, I was dragged through the mob.

1170. How many persons do you suppose there were?—I think there were about 30; I could not tell you.

1171. When

1171. Where were you dragged to?—I was not dragged, but I was put on a jaunting car nicely. I went to Mr. Whitworth's tallyrooms.

1172. Before you were put on the jaunting car had you spoken to Mr. Hamilton?—Yes.

1173. Did you see him?—I did.

1174. Did you take hold of him, or did he take hold of you?—I left Mr. Hamilton; he just sent his man with me for safety, for fear I would be killed; he is a good gentleman.

1175. But how did they take you out of the station?—There they came up and dragged me.

1176. Was Mr. Whitworth present?—I did not see Mr. Whitworth at that time.

1177. Had you seen him shortly before that?—Before that I did see him, and Mr. Clinton too.

1178. Did you see Mr. Clinton at the time they were taking you away?—No.

1179. When they took you out of the station where did they put you?——

Mr. *Heron* objected to leading questions.

1180. Mr. *McDonogh* (to the *Witness*).] What did they do with you?—I was brought down to the town.

1181. How?—They dragged me.

1182. To put you on a car?—Yes.

1183. Where did they take you?—To Mr. Whitworth's tally-rooms.

1184. What became of you then?—I was kept there for a good while.

1185. Did anybody apply to you to vote?—No; indeed, sir, they did not.

1186. What became of you; did you go to the voting?—No.

1187. How long did they keep you in the tally-room?—Not long.

1188. What did they do with you, then?—Why, I might go home then.

1189. Did you go home?—I did.

1190. How?—Walking.

1191. Did you walk the whole way to your own house?—Yes. No; I beg your pardon, we hired a car.

1192. Then you drove home?—Yes.

1193. And you did not vote at all?—No.

Cross-examined by Mr. *Palles*.

1194. I believe you are a Roman Catholic?—Yes.

1195. Who is your landlord?—Mr. Cooper.

1196. How much land do you hold from him?—Very nearly 30 acres.

1197. At what rent?—Well, it is about a guinea an acre.

1198. What tenancy have you; is it a tenancy from year to year?—Yes.

1199. Who is the agent of your landlord?—Mr. Hamilton.

1200. Do you know that gentleman (*pointing to a person in the court*)?—I do.

1201. Did you ever see him before?—I did.

1202. Putting lease out of the question, and putting religion out of the question, whom would you have wished to vote for?——

Mr. *McDonogh* objected to the question.

1203. Mr. *Palles* (to the *Witness*).] Suppose you had a lease for ever, and your landlord had no power over you, whom would you have wished to vote for?——

Mr. Justice *Keogh* ruled that the question could not be put.

1204. Mr. *Palles* (to the *Witness*.] Did you tell that gentleman there that you were forced to vote against your conscience, as you had no lease?—It was my free will to go to Balbriggan.

1205. Did you use those words; I will try and bring your recollection to it?—Yes, you may.

1206. Do you remember meeting that gentleman (*pointing to a person in the court*) at the station the day you were going to Drogheda?—I do, but not the day I was going to Drogheda.

1207. What day was it?—A couple of days before, perhaps.

1208. On that occasion did you say anything like this: that you wished to vote for Mr. Whitworth, but that you were forced to vote against your conscience as you had no lease?—I forget.

1209. Will you say that you did not; you forgot?—I do.

1210. When did you go to Balbriggan?—On Tuesday.

1211. When you were speaking to that gentleman did you cry?—For what will I cry?

1212. I ask you the fact; did you cry?—No.

1213. I must ask you these questions because perhaps there may be a contradiction of your answer; did you or did you not?—No; I did not cry.

1214. Had you ever a vote before at the Drogheda election?—Yes.

1215. Whom did you vote for then?——

Mr. *McDonogh* objected to this question as being wholly irrelevant.

Mr. Justice *Keogh* overruled the objection.

1216. Mr. *Palles* (to the *Witness*).] Did you vote at the previous election?—I forget that.

1217. You forget; think now?—I voted for Whitworth.

1218. You told me a moment ago that you forgot for whom you voted at the last election; is that true? When you used those words, "I forget," did you not know and remember that you voted for Mr. Whitworth?—I do remember it.

1219. When you said that you forgot for whom you voted, did you know that you had voted for Mr. Whitworth?—I voted for Mr. Whitworth.

1220. Mr. Justice *Keogh*.] That is not what you are asked; you are asked, do you recollect for whom you voted, when you said you had forgotten?—I did forget it.

1221. Mr. *Palles*.] Why did you vote against Mr. Whitworth at this election if you voted for Mr. Whitworth at the last?—Because I got a letter from Mr. Hamilton.

1222. Have you that letter here?—Mr. Hamilton has it.

1223. If you had not got the letter from Mr. Hamilton you would have voted for Mr. Whitworth?—I would vote for no one; neither Brodigan nor Whitworth.

1224. You voted against Brodigan at the last election when you voted for Mr. Whitworth?—Yes.

1225. If you got no letter from Mr. Hamilton why would you not vote for Mr. Whitworth, as you did before?—I would vote for none of them.

1226. What was it changed your mind?—I thought there was very little good in both of them.

Mr. J. Devine.

16 January 1869.

Mr. J. D[illegible]. — 16 January 1869.

1227. And was that the reason you changed your mind?—Yes.

1228. When did you go to Balbriggan?—On Tuesday it was.

1229. Where did you remain the Tuesday night?—I forget; in a decent house.

1230. In Balbriggan?—Yes.

1231. Where did you remain on the Wednesday?—I suppose in Dublin; I went to Dublin, and I might have come back.

1232. Where did you remain on Thursday night?—At Balbriggan, I think.

1233. Are you certain?—I am certain.

1234. Was it in the house of a man of the name of Clinton you stopped in Balbriggan?—I do not know.

1235. Do you know Mr. Hodgens?—Yes, well.

1236. Who is he?—He is a rent-warden of Mr Hamilton's.

1237. Did you see him upon the Tuesday, Wednesday, Thursday, or Friday?—No.

1238. Who paid your railway fare from Balbriggan to Drogheda?—Mr. Hodgens paid it.

1239. Who gave you money to pay your fare back from Drogheda to Balbriggan?—Mr. Hodgens.

1240. Who paid your fare from Dublin to Balbriggan?—The money we had going up.

1241. They paid it all?—All myself got was very little.

1242. Was any one else with you?—Let every one speak for himself.

1243. Who else was with you?—Usher and McDonald.

1244. Mr. Hodgens paid for you all?—I suppose he did; he paid me half-a-sovereign.

1245. Why did you go to Dublin?—Because we thought it to be as good as to be in Balbriggan; to see the sport, as we were never at Dublin before.

1246. What sport was it that you were to see in Dublin?—The election.

1247. And was it for that purpose that Mr. Hodgens sent you to Dublin?—No, he did not send us at all; it was our own pleasure.

1248. Where did you stop in Dublin?—No place at all; we came back again to Balbriggan.

1249. I thought you said that you stopped Wednesday night in Dublin?—No, I did not tell you that at all.

1250. So that you must have stopped three nights in Balbriggan?—Yes.

1251. Do you know Emerson's?—No.

1252. Did you pay anything for your lodgings in Balbriggan?—No, we did not.

1253. Did you pay anything for your food in Balbriggan?—No.

1254. Who was to pay for that?—I do not know who was to pay for it.

1255. Now that your memory has been a little bit refreshed, perhaps now you remember what you said to Father Langdale?—No, I do not.

1256. Is it not a fact that you were forced to vote?—It was my own pleasure.

1257. Were you forced to vote?—For whom?

1258. For Sir Leopold McClintock?—No.

1259. You would have wished to vote for McClintock?—I would have voted for McClintock only I was afraid.

1260. Did you know what politics he had?—Indeed I do not know much of them.

1261. Did you know either of their politics?—I did not.

1262. Why would you prefer to vote for McClintock in preference to Whitworth, when you knew neither of their politics?—I had a good regard.

1263. Were you afraid of being put out if you did not vote for him?—No, I was not.

Re-examined by Mr. *McDonogh*.

1264. You told that gentleman that you would have voted for McClintock only you were afraid?—Yes.

1265. Of whom were you afraid?—Of the mob.

1266. Now, on the former occasion that you voted for that gentleman, Mr. Whitworth, when Mr. Brodigan and he were contesting, did Mr. Hodgens, the bailiff of Mr. Hamilton, canvass you for Mr. Whitworth?—Yes.

1267. Did you vote, to oblige Mr. Hodgens, for Mr. Whitworth?—Well, I did.

1268. Can you read?—I can, badly.

1269. Is that the letter which you got from Mr. Hodgens (*showing a letter to the Witness*)?—That is the last letter, I believe.

1270. It is the same; at all events we will read it:

"Balbriggan, 9th Nov. 1868.

"DEAR SIR,—Sir Leopold McClintock, one of the greatest men of the kingdom, will be member for Drogheda. You will oblige me and Mr. Cooper very much by voting for him.

"Yours truly,
"*Henry Alexander Hamilton.*"

Was it of your own free will that you voted for Sir Leopold McClintock?—Yes.

1271. Did Mr. Hamilton threaten you in any other way?—I did not see Mr. Hamilton at all.

1272. Did Mr. Hodgens threaten you in any way?—No.

1273. Mr. *Pallas* (*through the Court*.) Did you see Mr. Clinton, and did Mr. Clinton ask you for whom would you vote, and did you say, "I would wish ——"

Mr. *McDonogh* objected to the question.

Mr. *Pallas* supported the question.

1274. Mr. *Pallas* (*through the Court*.) Did you meet, when you were brought down on the car, Mr. Clinton at the tally-room on the stairs or in the room, and did you say to him you would rather not vote, and did Mr. Clinton say to you, "Very well, do not." Or did any conversation of that kind occur?—No; Mr. Clinton came up to the station-house, and Mr. Hamilton was with me, and he rushed in, Mr. Clinton did, and he asked me to vote for Mr. Whitworth, and I didn't give him any answer at all, either yes or no. Then Mr. Whitworth came in a few minutes after, and asked for whom I would vote, and I said I would vote for no one.

1275. When you were taken away on the car, and brought to Mr. Whitworth's tally-room, did you see Mr. Clinton after that?—No.

[The Witness withdrew.

Mr. John Usher, sworn; Examined by Mr. *Ryland*.

1276. Are you an elector of Drogheda?—Yes.

1277. And a voter?—Yes.

1278. Where were you on the morning of the polling day; were you in Drogheda the night before?—No, I was in Balbriggan.

1279. When did you come into Drogheda?—I came in that morning.

1280. By train?—Yes.

1281. At what hour about did you get to Drogheda?—It was nearly up to ten o'clock.

1282. Who was with you, do you know, at the time?—Mr. McDonald.

1283. Who else?—Mr. Hamilton.

1284. Who else?—I cannot remember any more.

1285. Were you at the station for any length of time?—I was.

1286. Did you see any persons there; did anything happen while you were there?—Yes.

1287. Do you know Mr. Clinton?—Yes.

1288. Do you know Mr. Whitworth?—Yes.

1289. Did you see either of those gentlemen there?—Yes, I saw both, I think.

1290. Did they do or say anything that you can tell us?—He was down at the station himself. He came down and asked who I voted for? I made no answer at the time; it was Whitworth; then he went away, and we walked about for fifteen or twenty minutes; then he came back again. I saw rioting about the place at the railway; he asked me who I would vote for, and I said I would vote for him sooner than be killed.

1291. Had you promised to vote for any of the candidates before?—Yes, I had.

1292. For whom?—For McClintock.

1293. Did you intend that morning when you were coming by train to vote for McClintock?—I did.

1294. When you said to him that you would vote for Whitworth, what occurred?—The mob got round and shoved me off; they put me on a car.

1295. What was done to you then?—They brought me up to the tally-room; they brought me into the tally-room; Mr. Whitworth followed me and told me he did not want me to vote at all.

1296. Did you vote?—I did not.

1297. What did you do after that?—I remained there for about an hour, and I came out and went home.

1298. Did you vote at all?—I did not.

1299. Would you have voted for McClintock, but for the rioting you saw at the station that morning?—Yes, I should have voted for McClintock.

Cross-examined by Mr. *Heron*.

1300. You are a tenant on the Coope estate?—Yes.

1301. And Mr. Hamilton is your agent?—Yes.

1302. How many acres have you?—About 60 or 62.

1303. What rent do you pay per acre?—Guinea an acre.

1304. You have no lease, but you are a tenant from year to year?—Yes.

1305. Had you before that promised to Mr. Whitworth that you would vote for him?—I told Mr. Whitworth when he asked me to vote; I said, "If my landlord is pleased I will vote for you, if not, I must go with my landlord."

Mr. J. Usher.

9th January 1869.

1306. How long before was that?—A few months; I suppose four or six weeks.

1307. Do you swear before his Lordship that you did not promise Mr. Whitworth who is here to vote for him?—I told him as I told you now; "If my landlord is pleased I will vote for you, if not, I must go with my landlord."

1308. Did you say I must go with my landlord?—Yes.

1309. Did you get half-a-sovereign also?—I did.

1310. When?—The day before I left home.

1311. Where?—I got it at my own place.

1312. Who gave it to you?—Mr. Hudson.

1313. Is Mr. Hudson a stranger?—No, he is the rent warden.

1314. You have known him a long time?—Yes.

1315. What did he tell you to do with the half-sovereign?—He told me to do nothing with it.

1316. Where did he tell you to go to with the half-sovereign?—He told me to go to no place; he gave it to me.

1317. Gave it to you for what?—He gave it to me for expenses to bring me from Balbriggan.

1318. Did he tell you what house to go to?—No.

1319. Did you go by accident into a house?—I did.

1320. Did you pay anything for your lodging in that house?—Not a halfpenny.

1321. Did you know the house you were going to?—No.

1322. And you do not know it now?—I know the house, but I do not know the name.

1323. You do not know the name of the people?—No.

1324. Did you go into the house by accident?—No, I did not.

1325. Who told you to go to the house?—Mr. Hudson.

1326. Which house did he tell you to go to? I do not know what is the name of the house.

1327. Answer now before his Lordship, where did Mr. Hudson tell you to go to?—I cannot tell the name of the house.

1328. Where did Hudson tell you to go to?—He told me to go to a lodging-house; I cannot tell the name.

1329. Did you know beforehand what lodging-house you were to go to?—No.

1330. Did you go into the first that occurred to you?—I did.

1331. Did you and Davies go by accident into the same house; did you travel with Davies?—I did.

1332. And McDonald?—Yes.

1333. And the three of you went into the same house?—Yes.

1334. And you paid nothing for meat and drink?—No.

1335. Did you get any more money?—I got another half-sovereign going home.

1336. From whom?—From Mr. Hudson.

1337. Where

Mr. J. Usher.

16 January 1869.

1337. Where did he pay you that?—In Balbriggan.

1338. Who paid your railway fare?—I cannot tell.

1339. You did not pay any railway fare?—No.

1340. Did Davies and McDonald also get a separate half-sovereign?—They did.

1341. Did you not vote for Whitworth in 1865?—I did.

1342. Do you know anything about politics?—Not much.

1343. Did you know that McClintock was a Tory, and that Whitworth was a Liberal?—I knew there was a difference between them.

1344. Did you know which was which; did you know which was Tory, and which was Liberal?—I did.

1345. Which were they?—Whitworth was for the Liberals, and a good man in the town of Drogheda for the poor.

1346. And that McClintock was what?—I never knew him until I saw him in the street.

1347. Did you get a letter from Mr. Hamilton?—Yes.

1348. Have you that letter, or did he take it away from you to-day?—It is here.

1349. Show me the letter?—(*The same was handed in to the learned Counsel.*)

1350. When did Hamilton take the letter from you?—I sent it to him on Wednesday.

1351. "Balbriggan, 9th November 1868.—Dear Sir,—Sir Leopold McClintock, one of the greatest men in the kingdom, will be Member for Drogheda. You will oblige me and Mr. Cooper very much by voting for him.—Yours truly, Alexander Hamilton." Had you ever heard of McClintock until you got that letter?—I heard he was coming in for Drogheda.

1352. Had you ever heard of *him* before you heard he was coming in for Drogheda?—Never.

1353. You told his Lordship that Mr. Whitworth finally told you that he did not want you to vote at all?—Yes.

1354. Where was it that he told you that?—In the tally-room.

1355. Had you said anything to him before that?—Not one ha'porth.

1356. Do you mean to say that he came up and told you that he did not want you to vote?—He came into the tally-room and said, "I do not want you to vote at all."

1357. What did you do then?—Remained there for half an hour, and came out and went home.

1358. You were not molested in any way by any crowd?—No.

1359. Where was the tally-room which you were in with Mr. Whitworth?—In Lawrence-street.

1360. How long were you there?—About an hour.

1361. Was that the first time Mr. Whitworth came up to you?—It was.

1362. Was that before or after you heard the shot?—Before I heard the shot.

1363. Before you heard about the shot being fired?—Yes.

1364. It must have been before 12 o'clock?—Yes, it was before 12 o'clock.

1365. Was McDonald with you then?—No, he was not with us that day.

1366. Was McDonald with you that day in the tally-room?—No.

1367. Were you alone with your party?—Yes.

1368. Do you remember Semple coming with you from Balbriggan?—Yes.

1369. Do you remember Semple coming down before you?—I met him in the train.

Re-examined by Mr. *Ryland*.

1370. You were asked whether you voted for Whitworth on a former election?—Yes.

1371. Were you canvassed by anyone?—No.

1372. By whom?—Mr. Hamilton.

1373. Mr. *Heron*.] Did you see Mr. Whitworth after the election?—I did.

1374. Did you tell him if you were put on the table, and told the truth, that you would not vote out of your farm?—No.

1375. What did you say to Mr. Whitworth when you saw him?—I told him that I could not go against my landlord.

1376. Did he speak about your evidence "on the table;" did you use the words "on the table;" did you say, "I cannot go against my landlord on the table"?—

1377. Mr. Justice *Keogh*.] Were you speaking in confidence to Mr. Whitworth at that time; whatever you were saying, did you expect it would be brought up to-day?—I was afraid it would.

1378. When you were speaking to him, did you understand that you were speaking confidentially to him?—Yes.

Mr. Justice *Keogh*.] Then the question ought not to be put.

1379. Mr. *Ryland*.] You told that gentleman that you voted for Mr. Whitworth at a former election?—Yes.

1380. Were you canvassed by your landlord, or anyone connected with the property, to vote for Mr. Whitworth?—At the last election?

1381. Yes, the last election?—Yes, I was.

1382. Who did you vote for?—Mr. Hamilton.

1383. Mr. Justice *Keogh*.] Did you vote at all at the last election?—No, I did not vote.

[The Witness withdrew.

Mr. JAMES CAHILL, sworn; Examined by Mr. *McDonogh*.

Mr. J. Cahill.

1384. Where do you live?—At Pitcher Hill.

1385. Is that in the town of Drogheda?—The borough of Drogheda.

1386. Had you promised at the last election to vote for anybody?—I told the landlord I would vote for him if he would protect me.

1387. What is the name of your landlord?—Mr. Smith.

1388. Had he canvassed you for Sir Leopold McClintock?—He asked me to vote for McClintock.

1389. Was it then you told him that you would if he would protect you?—Yes; I told him and I told Mr. Cooper; he called along with Mr. McClintock at my house, and I told him I would vote for him if he would protect me.

1390. Who

Mr. J. Cahill.

10 June 1857.

1390. What did you say about Mr. Cooper?—Mr. Cooper was with McClintock when he asked me for my vote, and I told Mr. Smith I would vote for him if he would protect me.

1391. Were those two gentlemen with you at the same time, or on two different times?—No; at one time.

1392. Did you intend to vote for Sir Leopold McClintock?—I did, if I was protected down to the poll; but I would not venture to come down to the poll unless I was protected.

1393. On the morning of the polling-day, before daylight, did anything occur?—The mob rapped at the door; my wife opened the door; I was in bed; I was not well, and she told them I was in bed; I cannot say what she said; I was in bed and was not well.

1394. Was there anything done to the door?—Not a ha'porth.

1395. At a subsequent time did any other mob come?—About 10 o'clock another mob came and rapped at the door, and they hailed groans and came so far as that, and they wanted me to go to vote, and my son-in-law said I should not; they were there a long time; I do not know what they said, but they went away; it was not very long after till Father Matthews came, and he opened the door and walked into the room where I was and asked me to vote; I said I would vote for the landlord. Father Matthews said, "Vote according to your conscience." I went to the door; he linked my arm and helped me up on the car; I was not very well able to go on the car; a grey horse was standing at the door with a car and another respectable man, a farmer; I had knowledge of him, but I do not know his name; he was with the priest, and I went down with them.

1396. Mr. Justice *Keogh*.] They put you on the car and you came down?—Yes.

1397. Mr. *McDonogh*.] Where?—They brought me up to a place, and they told me to say, "Whitworth" when I was asked.

1398. Who told you that?—They never told me who to vote for once after.

1399. Who told you to say "Whitworth"?—Father Matthews, the priest.

1400. Did he accompany you on the car?—He was on the car with me.

1401. What next happened to you?—Nothing at all.

1402. Did you come up to vote?—Yes, I voted for Mr. Whitworth; he brought me back again and put me on the car again; the man left me at home at my own house.

1403. Mr. Justice *Keogh*.] For whom did you vote?—Mr. Whitworth.

1404. Was that according to your wish that you voted for Mr. Whitworth?—I said I would vote for the landlord if I was protected, and then when I was not protected I voted the other way; I did not vote in Drogheda before, and had not a vote.

Cross-examined by Mr. *Heron*.

1405. Before this had you promised Father Matthews to vote for Whitworth?—No; he never mentioned Mr. Whitworth's name in his life.

[The Witness withdrew.

THOMAS MCKENNA, sworn; Examined by Mr. *Plunkett*.

T. McKenna.

1406. ARE you an elector of the Borough of Drogheda?—Yes.

1407. Do you know Mr. Brodigan?—Yes.

1408. Mr. *Plunkett* (to the *Witness*).] You were on Mr. Brodigan's committee, were you not?—Yes.

1409. And you know a great number of the Catholic electors of Drogheda?—I did.

1410. Did you canvass at all with Mr. Brodigan?—I canvassed five or six days in company with Mr. Brodigan and his committee.

1411. From your knowledge of the voters of the town of Drogheda, and from the canvass that you made for Mr. Brodigan, can you say whether a great number of voters had promised Mr. Brodigan?—The first day I went out with the canvassers?

1412. Had he asked whether there were many promises for Mr. Brodigan?—Yes; a vast majority in the places I went to with him. We went into the house of a Mr. Farrell, at the head of King-street, and he refused, and to the residence of a man named Pentony, who refused also; then we went to John Byrne.

1413. Mr. Justice *Keogh*.] "The vast majority of those canvassed," was your expression?—Yes; that day.

1414. Mr. *Plunkett*.] Do you know, as a matter of fact, how those men voted afterwards?—Yes, of course; I was sent out afterwards on the Thursday.

1415. Mr. Justice *Keogh*.] Cannot you answer the question; do you know how the men voted afterwards?—I was not at the polling place; I cannot swear how they voted; I know they did not keep their promises from the result afterwards.

1416. Mr. *Plunkett*.] Did you vote for Mr. Brodigan yourself?—No.

1417. Who did you vote for?—I did not venture into the town; I did not vote at all on that day. I was attacked by mobs, and threatened in an extraordinary way.

1418. Just explain how that was?—I live in North Road, and I have property in one lane, and there were two miniature coffins put up at the gate in the lane where I had stables and a barn, and place for cattle; the morning of the 20th, the day of polling, I went early, intending to go to Mr. Brodigan's committee, and I was set upon by a fearless mob, who attacked me with stones, pokers, hammers, and used violent language; they said they would set fire to the place if I dared to vote as an Orange Catholic against the Church; against the old religion. They said, "Be hanged for me;" that they would burn down the stables, and that they did in a most emphatic and violent way. They rushed up quite close to me with large stones in their hands, and all that.

1419. Were there any persons amongst them who threatened you, except the mob?—No.

1420. It was altogether the mob?—Yes.

1421. In point of fact, you did not vote?—No; and on the Monday, my Lord, Sunday was the 15th, and certain things took place on that day; everything was tranquil until then.

1422. What took place on the Monday?—On the Monday I saw that the reign of terror had commenced. I was walking along here, and a ferocious

T. McEnery.

10 January 1869.

ferocious mob rushed forward and attacked and shook me, and pushed and drove me, and they nearly threw me on the floor, except but for the police coming up and saving me. Mr. Gerrill came just in time to save me, and Mr. Latimer, one of Mr. Whitworth's best supporters, was blandly smiling on the crowd and encouraging them from Shop-street out here.

1422. Mr. *Heron.*] "He blandly smiled"?—Yes; I wondered at it——

Mr. *Latimer.*] That is not true, my Lord.

Mr. Justice *Keogh.*] Who says that?

Mr. *Latimer.*] Me.

Mr. Justice *Keogh.*] If you interrupt the Court by making observations on the evidence given here, I shall at once have you committed to gaol for contempt of court.

Mr. *Latimer.*] I beg your pardon, my Lord.

Mr. Justice *Keogh.*] I do not commit you now, because I suppose you are ignorant of the consequences of your behaviour.

Witness.] I was surprised at him doing so, because he was a near neighbour and friend of mine before; I also complained to the policeman Gammon at the moment.

1424. Mr. Justice *Keogh.*] Is he a police constable in the town of Drogheda?—Yes; and the men who attacked me were in the employment chiefly of Mr. Whitworth's committee, and I think some of the sheriff's men.

1425. Mr. *Plunkett.*] You said before you went into that description, that before the violence commenced, some things occurred; what things occurred, I ask you now. You say everything was quiet, and then some things occurred, and then there was violence; what things?——

1426. Mr. Justice *Keogh.*] What do you allude to; you say certain things occurred on the Saturday; what were those things?—The addresses to the people on Sunday against the ascendancy candidates; I would rather not speak about it.

1427. Mr. *Plunkett.*] Who delivered the addresses?—The Catholic clergymen; those that I heard were not of an inflammatory character at all, I must say. I was with Mr. Brodigan and his supporters on the day of nomination at the court-house, and I was a witness of the terrific scene that occurred here; there, whilst we were waiting in the street, I saw a number of persons through the court door was closed; I saw a number of persons inside through the window looking out.

1428. Mr. Justice *Keogh.*] Was that before you came in?—Yes, it was 10 minutes before 10 o'clock; we were not admitted until the clock struck 10.

1429. But do you say you saw persons inside?—Yes, looking out.

1430. Before the court was open?—Yes; there were a number of persons in the court house previously to that public opening; I heard a fearful groaning and boisterous clamour outside, and saw a missile, it was an egg, thrown at the McClintock party; it seemed to be aimed at Sir Leopold McClintock; we got into the place then, and when the door was opened a tumultuous rush took place, magistrates, clergymen, cask carriers, and labouring men, all classes pushed and drove in together in the crowd, a thing that never took place within the last 40 years to my memory before; since 1830 there was no such mode of admitting the people previously, and the rowdies at the place here; I was standing there then (*describing the scene*), a number were all standing with their backs to the gallery and round here, and what are called roughs were up here at this place, and some standing there along the ledge; Mr. McDonald and his brother jumped up when that lot in, and he appeared to me to act in some capacity like a fugleman or mob leader.

1431. Who did?—Mr. McDonald; from the time he got on the spot, the place was one terrific scene of uproar; he was gesticulating and waving his hat, and flourishing; the Rev. Mr. Macarthy stood there, and two or three persons and labourers stood close to that pillar; Mr. Town Councillor Byrne and the Mayor of Drogheda, and an active member of Whitworth's committee rushed up and drove in my nose with his fist on the spot.

1432. Mr. *Plunkett.*] Who did that?—Mr. Byrne, the Town Councillor, he was Mayor of the town at one time; it is a few years ago.

1433. Mr. Justice *Keogh.*] You say he was a member of Mr. Whitworth's committee?—Yes, and he was round canvassing in the town.

1434. What did he do to you?—He punched my nose in with his fist, and two or three days afterwards he apologised and said he hoped I would drop it; and I said I would.

1435. Was that in the court-house?—In the court-house about the time that the sheriff was standing there with some paper in his hand, but you could hear nothing he said; at the same time, I saw Mr. Carty, an aged magistrate, struggling through the hostile crowd, and trying to push his way forward, driving through them; I saw several respectable citizens jostled about in the presence of the sheriff, without his affording them the slightest protection, nor did he take any measure, whatever, to have order in the court, or to afford any protection to the citizens, either to the candidates, or seconders, or supporters; I was at all the elections since 1826, and I heard the speakers here; order was preserved, and the speakers allowed to address the candidates and their movers and seconders, until Mr. Whitworth's party commenced to fill the place with paid mobs; and since then all order and freedom of elections has gone, and that to the knowledge of every man in court who is present.

1436. Mr. *Plunkett.*] On the day after the nomination did you proceed to canvass for Mr. Brodigan, or attempt to do so?—No, I tell you I was at the committee-room on Friday, and heard the speeches made there.

1437. Mr. Brodigan's?—Yes, Mr. Brodigan's.

1438. On the Thursday, that is the day after the nomination, did you proceed about the town at all with Mr. Patrick Turner?—No; he is the sheriff; sure he did not accompany me on that day; I heard one of Mr. Brodigan's speakers out of the window.

1439. Did you, after the nomination, canvass at all for Mr. Brodigan?—No, I did not venture at all; I did not venture down the town at all.

1440. After the nomination?—No, nor this far into the centre of the town.

1441. Did you on either party on Tuesday before the nomination attempt to canvass; between Sunday and Wednesday did you attempt to canvass for Mr. Brodigan?—I think I was engaged

engaged all the time canvassing the lists of the voters with Mr. Simpson and Mr. Atkinson and some others; but not on those days I did not.

1442. You have already told us you did not vote yourself on the polling day?—No, I did not vote; there is another circumstance I must mention——

Mr. Heron stated that he objected to the Witness making a speech.

1443. Mr. Plunkett.] What does the circumstance which you wish to mention relate to?——

Mr. Heron objected to the question.

1444. Mr. Plunkett (to the Witness).] Do you know Mr. Hill?—Yes, he is an eminent merchant in the town.

1445. Do you know of his having taken part in the canvassing for this election; did you see him taking any part in the canvassing for this election?—No, I did not; I do not recollect that.

1446. Do you know, of your own knowledge, anything of mobs being hired in the borough of Drogheda?—Yes, upon one occasion, in Mr. Brodigan's room I saw 30 tickets given to a party to form a mob.

1447. Mr. Justice Keogh.] In Mr. Brodigan's room?—Yes.

1448. Mr. Plunkett.] Do you know, of your own knowledge, anything of the hiring of mobs by any of the other candidates?—No.

1449. Mr. Heron.] Did you see it?—No, I did not.

1450. Mr. Plunkett.] Did you on the night before the election go round for the purpose of bringing any of Brodigan's supporters up to the poll?—Yes, I did; the district was assigned to me and Patrick Tuman.

1451. Now tell us all about that, whatever you saw on that occasion yourself, when you went round with Patrick Tuman in your district?—I went to the house of a good many voters with Mr. Tuman on Thursday, who I had known to have promised to vote for Mr. Brodigan.

1452. Had those persons promised to vote for Mr. Brodigan?—Yes.

1453. When you went to them to bring them up, as you say, the night before the election, did they consent to come?——

Mr. Heron objected that the names were not in the list, and there was no evidence to be given of a person not named in the list.

1454. Mr. Plunkett (to the Witness).] Did these men, in point of fact, come up with you?——

Mr. Heron objected to the question.

1455. Mr. Plunkett (to the Witness).] Can you tell the names of any persons who had promised to vote for Mr. Brodigan; they did not come up with you?—Mr. Charles Barron; he said ——

1456. You cannot say what he said; anyone else?—Peter O'Neill and Mr. Thomas Owens.

1457. Anyone else?—Peter Matthews; I cannot say whether they voted or not, because they did not come in with us. I was not present in the booth.

Cross-examined by Mr. Pallas.

1458. How many people were there altogether in Mr. Brodigan's mob?—I cannot say.

1459. Give it as far as you are able?—I saw 30 tickets given.

1460. I mean the entire number that constituted his mob on the day of the polling; about 800, is it?—I have not the slightest idea.

1461. About 200?—I am not aware, the mob having been hired only on one occasion; I was present when tickets were given out.

1462. You cannot say that?—No; they would not let me know it, because I objected to the mob being hired at all; I protested in committee against it.

1463. Mr. Justice Keogh.] Was that at the last election or any former election?—The last election.

1464. You say you saw the mob hired in Mr. Brodigan's committee-room at the last election?—Yes, and I protested against employing the mob at all.

1465. Mr. Pallas.] You know that the mob consisted of a great many more persons than the 30 you know of?—No, there were 30 in the street present when I saw them go out of the house.

1466. You intend to tell his lordship that Mr. Brodigan's mob only consisted of 30 persons?—Upon that day it did not consist of 30 persons.

1467. On the day of the polling it did not consist of 30 persons?—No.

1468. On the day of the poll do you mean to say that Mr. Brodigan's mob did not consist of 30 persons?—No.

1469. I believe the election before the last you voted for Mr. Whitworth?—Yes.

1470. Mr. Brodigan was the only other candidate?—Yes.

1471. On this occasion you changed your mind, and preferred Mr. Brodigan to Mr. Whitworth?—Yes.

1472. You were aware, were you not, that Mr. Whitworth was on the grand jury in Manchester that found the bills against the Fenian prisoners; did you ever hear that?—I heard that. I had no objection to him on that account.

1473. I am not asking you what you yourself think, but you knew he did?—Yes. I read it in the papers.

1474. During the course of the election did you frequently hear Mr. Whitworth called the Manchester butcher?—I heard Dr. Waters denounce him that way (he does not belong to Drogheda), in reference to his having been at the Manchester trial.

1475. There was a Mr. Waters brought down in the interest of Mr. Brodigan?—I think he was brought from Dundalk.

1476. I only ask you as to the address of Mr. Waters, from Mr. Brodigan's committee-room?—I say I do not recollect the word "butcher."

1477. Whatever he said, he said something in reference to it?—His whole speech consisted in the denunciation of Mr. Whitworth on that account.

1478. That denunciation was from Mr. Brodigan's committee-room?—It was.

1479. How long did that speech last?—He made three or four speeches; it was very distressing to me to hear him talk at all.

1480. He made three or four speeches?—Yes.

1481. Upon what days were the speeches?—During the week of the election.

1482. And the day before the polling?—Yes.

1483. Were any of them on the day of the polling?—I cannot say.

T. McKenna.

16 January, 1869.

1484. How

T. McKenna.

14 January 1869.

1484. How long did the speeches occupy; a quarter of an hour?—One of them longer.

1485. Half-an-hour?—I do not think he could speak for half-an-hour.

1486. What evening was it when his speech, which was rather the longest, was delivered?—He spoke on Wednesday and Thursday evenings.

1487. I dare say he spoke on some other evening's as well?—He spoke in the day-time, as well.

1488. In fact, Mr. Waters was in the habit of denouncing Mr. Whitworth, in consequence of the Manchester matter, from Mr. Brodigan's committee-room?—He was.

1489. I believe there were large mobs usually assembled opposite the committee-room, where Mr. Waters was so speaking?—Yes; there was a crowd of people.

1490. Did you ever hear any other person make speeches of a similar character to Mr. Waters, or use similar expressions?—No; I think not so forcible as he.

1491. Perhaps more politely, but conveying the same idea?—He is the person who harped on the Manchester affair. I did not hear any other speaker do so.

1492. Did not you hear any of the other speakers refer to the Manchester affair?—They were speaking of Whitworth's nationality, and that he was an Englishman and a Saxon.

1493. Did you ever hear Connor denounce him for the Manchester affair?—I heard Connor attack his father in a most abominable way.

1494. From Mr. Brodigan's committee-room?—Yes.

1495. Did not he refer to the Manchester affair?—He did not refer much to it.

1496. Three or four words, such as "Manchester butcher," and "hangman;" did you hear him use those expressions?—Not "butcher," but I think he called him the "Manchester hangman," when he was speaking of Mr. Whitworth out of the window.

1497. Did you hear him denounce the people who were in the interest of Mr. Whitworth in his speeches from Brodigan's committee-room?—His speeches were very vulgar and low.

1498. Especially anything connected with Mr. Whitworth?—He denounced his father.

1499. Did you hear the expression "Manchester butcher" frequently shouted by the mob at the court-house on the nomination day?—No; you could hear nothing on that day.

1500. Were the mob outside shouting "Manchester butcher"?—No.

1501. You heard the mobs in the street shouting "Manchester butcher" frequently, did you not, or "hangman"?—No; the tables were turned completely from the Sunday during that week, by the mobs, in Mr. Whitworth's favour.

1502. Is it not the fact that his denunciation continued down to the Friday?—Yes; but without any evening effort by Dr. Waters, who was talking upon two evenings.

1503. Did you yourself ever use that expression, "Manchester butcher," or "hangman"?—No, but I did in another sense.

1504. Tell me first the words you used, and then the sense?—A Protestant gentleman in town called me in and showed me a report of the Evangelical Alliance, and he showed me Mr. Whitworth's name as a contributor to what the Catholics call the soup system; he was connected with the Band of Hope, the Evangelical Alliance, and things of that sort. They talked of his inconsistency in upholding these things in England when he was upholding other things in Drogheda. I said, "Manchester souper," because I had heard it in Drogheda.

1505. In addition to "Manchester souper," did not you refer, one way or another, to his finding the bill in Manchester?—No.

1506. Do you swear that?—I had no sympathy with it at all.

1507. I ask, did you in any way allude to it in conversation or speaking?—No, I think not.

1508. You think not; will you swear you did not more than once?—I referred frequently to the "Manchester souper," but not to the "Manchester butcher." I never applied such an epithet to Mr. Whitworth.

1509. Nor "Manchester hangman," nor allude to his finding the bill?—It was spoken of repeatedly to me. That matter was alluded to by Mr. John Morton.

1510. Will you swear just now; one word will do. No; did you ever speak or denounce Mr. Whitworth as the "Manchester butcher" or the "Manchester hangman"?—I swear I did not.

1511. Or alluded to Mr. Whitworth having found those bills?—I do not think I did.

1512. You are not so certain; did you see the town placarded with placards denouncing Mr. Whitworth as the "Manchester butcher"?—Yes.

1513. Did you see this (*handing a placard to the Witness*)?—Yes.

1514. There were other placards in addition?—Yes.

1515. Were there any other placards that had your name at the bottom of them?—Yes, which I will explain. The conducting agent, Mr. Healy, has stated this. I stood up in the committee and I objected emphatically to issuing such placards. I denounced them forcibly, whereupon Mr. Healy stood up and said, in the presence of Mr. Brodigan, the members of the committee, and the chairman, "I endorse every word of the condemnation uttered by Mr. McKenna."

1516. Mr. Healy was the conducting agent of Mr. Brodigan?—Yes; I objected entirely to it.

1517. Was not that placard issued from Mr. Brodigan's committee-room?—With my knowledge it was not.

1518. Do not you know that it was issued from Mr. Brodigan's committee-room?—I heard some say it was. I never saw that placard in Brodigan's place.

1519. Did you hear it discussed in Brodigan's committee-room, whether those placards should be issued or not?—Not more than I have described now; my own condemnation of them.

1520. Were not you overruled?—All persons agreed that I was right.

1521. Were not you overruled, and were they not issued?—They were issued notwithstanding.

1522. That is one of them (*handing a placard to the Witness*)?—Yes.

1523. In addition to that placard, was there another placard denouncing Mr. Whitworth in the same manner, published by Mr. Brodigan's committee?—No, not to my knowledge.

1524. Not to your knowledge?—No.

1525. You never saw one?—No.

1526. Directly or indirectly; that is the only placard you ever saw denouncing Mr. Whitworth?—I did not say that. I saw them on the walls.

1527. Was there a placard that had your name

to it?—There was, but it was a proper placard. A letter addressed to the electors and non-electors of Drogheda. I have that placard here.

1528. Give it to me now?—Here it is (*handing the same to the learned Counsel*).

1529. It denounces mobs and all that; the demoralization and drunkenness which Mr. Whitworth has caused by his distributing money among the people?—Certainly it does.

1530. Mr. Justice *Keogh*.] "That Ireland never trusted a Saxon but she was betrayed"?—That is true; I believe it firmly.

1531. Did you think that expression would make the Fenian mob more conciliatory towards Mr. Whitworth.

Mr. *McDonogh* objected to the question.

Mr. Justice *Keogh* ruled that the question could not be put.

1532. Mr. *Fallon*.] Who signed this?—I wrote every word of it except one word.

1533. What is that word?—The word is "cordially," and the word I wrote was "candidly."

1534. As you wrote that, perhaps you made some speeches against Mr. Whitworth and in favour of Mr. Brodigan?—Yes, I attended five or six speeches every night.

1535. And you made speeches, in addition, to the mob?—No, I could not catch the ear of the mob; I was cursed on that occasion.

1536. You did not make speeches to the mob?—I do not call it a speech; a few words.

1537. I ask you whether in this courthouse you did not use expressions similar to this: "Mr. Whitworth is a man who executed your countrymen in Manchester"?—No, I used no such words.

[The Witness withdrew.

Mr. JOHN CLARKE, sworn; Examined by Mr. *McDonogh*.

1538. WHERE do you reside?—James-street.

1539. Are you a voter of Drogheda?—Yes.

1540. On the occasion of the last election had you promised to vote for any of the candidates?—I promised to vote for Mr. Brodigan on certain conditions.

1541. What was the condition?—

Mr. *Heron* objected to the examination, the witness's name not being in the list furnished to his clients.

Mr. Justice *Keogh* ruled that questions might be asked as to general intimidation, but that the rule, with reference to the furnishing of lists, must be adhered to.

1542. Mr. *McDonogh*.] Do you know Father Matthews?—I do, perfectly well.

1543. Did you meet him upon the occasion of the polling day or the day before?—I did not.

1544. Did you meet him on an occasion antecedent to the election; to the polling?—I met him one day at my own door, and he asked me who I was going to vote for. I said I would vote for Mr Brodigan if I thought he would; if not, I would vote for Mr. McClintock.

1545. What did Father Matthews say to that?—He said he would trample me and Mr. Brodigan under his feet, if it was required.

1546. Was there any other expression used by Father Matthews on that occasion?—No, there was not; I walked away from the gentleman.

1547. Did any mobs come into your house?—Yes, there was a mob all round, and they attacked a party by the name of Ray; the mob said to me that if I voted for Mr. Brodigan or McClintock it would be the last I ever voted for.

1548. Was that after the expressions from Father Matthews to you?—It was four days before the election Mr. Matthews spoke to me.

1549. On what day was it that the mob said this to you?—On the day of the polling.

1550. Did you see any persons beaten on that day?—I saw they came and attacked the Rays and beat them.

1551. Tell his Lordship who you saw beaten?—I saw them beat a man of the name of James Ray and a man of the name of Edward Ray; I saw them beaten.

1552. When was that?—The morning of the poll.

1553. Where was it?—One hundred or 200 yards from where I live, in James-street.

1554. About what hour?—I could not say; it was before 10 o'clock; I could not swear what hour it was.

1555. Mr. Justice *Keogh*.] You have not stated whether these men were electors; were James and Edward Ray voters?—Yes, they were voters, I think, Sir.

1556. Mr *Heron*.] You think so; do you know whether they were or not?—I saw them on the list of voters.

1557. Mr. *McDonogh*.] Do you know a person of the name of Connor; did you see anything done to his windows?—No, I did not.

1558. Did you see Father Gavan at any time?—I saw Father Gavan go up the road that morning.

1559. Do you know a person of the name of Kearns?—Yes.

1560. You know his place?—Yes, I know Mr. Kearns, the brewer.

1561. Did you see anything come to his windows?—No, I did not.

1562. When was it that you saw Father Gavan?—They said there were 400 or 500 Orangemen coming down in a train; there was a mob of people going up the road; he was going up. I cannot say whether he was quieting them or encouraging them; I could not tell, for I was not going to run the danger of my life by getting up among them.

1563. Now, we must fix the place where you were at the time; where were you?—I was standing at the corner of old Mangan's public-house; I stood inside the door.

1564. What did you see pass?—I saw a whole crowd of people with sticks; crowds of women with stones in their aprons, and boys and girls.

1565. What did you hear about the Orangemen?—I heard the crowd saying they would be down by the next train.

1566. Where was Father Gavan when the crowd was going up with sticks and stones?—He might be going down to his home, for what I know.

1567. Where

Mr. J. Clarke. 16 January 1869.

1567. Where was he?—On the road, going up with the mob.

1568. Was it in the direction of the railway?—It was in the direction of his own house and the direction of the railway too.

1569. Can you fix the hour when it was that the mob passed?—I cannot give the hour at all for you.

Cross-examined by Mr. *Hamill.*

1570. Tell me, did you vote?—Yes.

1571. For whom did you vote?—For Mr. Brodigan.

1572. You voted quietly, and went home quietly?—Yes; I voted after the mass was over.

1573. Mr. *McDonogh.*] Did the mob pursue you this morning?—They did; I went out with two or three others to accompany Mr. Brodigan's voters from the country, and the mob pursued us, and some of them ran across the fields and across the gardens; there were five or six of us.

[The Witness withdrew.

Mr. John O'Dare, sworn; Examined by Mr. *Ryland.*

Mr. J. O'Dare.

1574. Are you an elector of Drogheda?—Yes.

Mr. *Heron* objected that the Witness was not on the list furnished to his clients.

Mr. *Ryland* stated that he only intended to examine the Witness as to general intimidation.

1575. Mr. *Ryland.*] Do you recollect the evening before the poll?—I do.

1576. Were you in your house that evening?—I was, the whole day, and kept my door locked and barred.

1577. Did any people come to your house?—They did; a party, between eight and nine o'clock at night.

1578. Were there many in that party?—To the best of my knowledge, there was 50.

1579. What took place when they came to the house?—My wife said she would open the door; I said, not; and they knocked they would beat it in; and for the third time they arrived; they said they would get in. I said I would remove, or go on the roof for protection. I went up on the roof, for further protection. My wife says, "You are going to be killed." I said, "Do not attempt opening the door; I will suffer my death before I leave the house." She got her hands round me, and cried out, and began to cry.

1580. What occurred at the door?—"I will open the door," says she.

1581. What was done at the door?—They insisted to get in; I went then out to the garden, and hid myself.

1582. Is that at the back of the house?—Yes; out of the back door.

1583. Did you hear the mob shouting out anything?—Yes.

1584. What did they shout out?—They shouted out as "tear him out of the house;" and then the door was opened by my wife; and I was hiding in the garden, and they entered the house, and the mob cried out, "He is on the roof." "No," says my wife; "there is the house; search it." With that she held a candle to them.

1585. Mr. *Heron.*] Did you hear all this?—I did. She held a candle to them; the mob cried out, "He is on the roof." My wife said, "Here is the ladder; go on the roof"; and I know no more about the mob.

1586. Was your door damaged on that occasion?—Yes, it was all broken down, the next morning.

1587. Mr. *Ryland.*] Was the damage done that night?—No.

1588. The following morning tell us what happened?—The following morning John Martin (I have the names in my pocket). I was lying in bed, before eight o'clock.

1589. When were you subpœnaed to come here?—A week, last Monday or Tuesday.

1590. Were you asked to give a statement of your evidence?—

Mr. Justice *Keogh* stated that he could not allow this course of examination to be pursued.

1591. Mr. *Ryland.*] Did you see any violence, the following day?—I did. A party came the next morning, before eight o'clock.

1592. I do not want to ask their names; but what did they do?—There came a party, before eight o'clock, and said to me, "You will come out of that." I asked them whether they were coming into my house, and the door locked on them. I said, I was very angry at my wife letting them in; but a lot of people did come, the house was full in a minute. The first came in the bed-room to me, and said, "Come up out of that." "What do you want"? says I. "We want you to come and vote for Mr. Whitworth." "Now, just go out of the house," says I, "you are breaking the law." "We are not," says a man, named Martin.

1593. Do not asked the names?—"We are not," says he; "but I am the man," says he, "who will make you become out of that, in a few minutes"; and then the mob began to catch stones; and I cried out to my daughter, "Shut it as quick as you can"; for I was lying just over the door, where the stones came in. She shut the door, and they kicked away, and kicked away. The window was next to it; that got smashed by some of the mob; but there were no windows where I was lying.

1594. What happened to you after that; did you leave your house after that?—No, not the whole day.

1595. Did you vote that day?—I did.

1596. Mr. Justice *Keogh.*] For whom did you vote?—For Mr. Whitworth.

Cross-examined by Mr. *Heron.*

1597. Did you want any money for voting for any one?—No.

1598. You never asked money from any one in your life for voting?—Not about the election.

1599. Nor any one to you?—They did.

1600. Who?—One of the parties of the mob. They said I would be going down every night, getting money; and I knew nothing about it.

[The Witness withdrew.

JAMES RAY, sworn; Examined by Mr. *Plunket*.

J. Ray.

16 January 1869.

1601. ARE you an elector of the borough of Drogheda?—Yes.

1602. Did you leave your house on the day of polling?—Yes.

1603. Were you alone, or was any one with you?—My uncle.

1604. What is his name?—Edward Ray.

1605. Tell his Lordship what occurred when you left your house on that morning?—We proceeded down to vote for M'Clintock; we were assailed by a party of men on the road.

1606. What o'clock was it in the morning?—About half-past eight.

1607. Were these men a mob, or were they people whom you knew?—I knew some of them as being workers in Mr. Chadwick's mill; they were living just beside us.

1608. These were mill-workers?—Yes.

1609. Except the persons who worked in the mills, were there any persons there whom you knew?—There was.

1610. Who?—There was a clergyman there that I knew.

1611. What is his name?—The Rev. Mr. Gavan.

1612. When this crowd met you with whom Mr. Gavan was, did you hear him say anything to them?—I did.

1613. What was it he said?—You have a holiday, and you know how to enjoy it.

1614. What happened then?—Stone-throwing commenced then; we both linked together.

1615. What did you do?—We got out of the way as quick as we could.

1616. Did you succeed in getting out of the way?—I succeeded in coming down, and then the parties that were throwing stones turned back. I was coming to the entrance of the town. They were principally composed of girls and boys and mill-workers.

1617. You say your uncle was with you; did you see anything happen to him?—I did.

1618. What?—When we came over the town, nearly opposite James-street, we met a man there, and he told us to go back or we would catch it.

1619. What happened; never mind what he said?—I proceeded further and my uncle was attacked, and the stick pulled from him, the hats knocked off both our heads, and he was knocked down on his knees by the mob of men, women, and boys as they were.

1620. After that where did you go, or what did you do?—We lost both our hats, and I dragged him on his knees from a place they call the Old Hill in James-street till we came over to the public-house of a man of the name of Farry; I dragged him in there on his knees, and the mob kicking and beating him, and the same with me, the whole time.

1621. Did you succeed in getting to the polling-booths at all yourself?—Yes.

1622. How did you get there?—When I got into the house, the man of the house said he could not keep us, or the house would be pulled down.

Mr. *Heron* objected to the Witness stating what the man said.

1623. Mr. *Plunket*.] Never mind what you said to him; when you left the court afterwards who was with you?—The high sheriff and Mr. Verdon got a car, brought us up to vote.

1624. What o'clock was it?—I should say 11 o'clock, because we were home about 12; he left us on the car too.

1625. How long were you in the court where you were shut up before the sheriff came; how long was it before the sheriff came?—I should say it was three-quarters of an hour; I am not very exact as to time.

Cross-examined by Mr. *Pollen*.

1626. Have you anything to say as to hiring any man for M'Clintock?—There came a man to write a list for him for 20 men for that day, and I wrote it for him.

1627. What is that man's name?—John Fehiley.

1628. What was the list?—For to go up to tally-rooms or the polling-booths to let the voters in.

1629. Did you see those men yourself?—I did.

1630. Give me their names?—I could give a good many names.

1631. Give as many as you can?—The two Brogans that swore on the inquest.

1632. Just give the names?—Hugh Brogan and Patrick Brogan, and John Fitzpatrick, Pat Docken and James Plunkett.

1633. Go on?—I cannot think of them, you go so quickly; a man of the name of Sheils, I do not know his christian name; I gave the list to the man; I cannot recollect.

1634. How much were the men to be paid?—I do not know.

1635. You did not hear that?—No.

1636. Who was to pay them?—The man I wrote the list for.

1637. I suppose in the interest of Sir Leopold?—I do not know.

1638. Those men were roughs?—They were labouring men.

1639. Had they sticks?—Not one.

1640. You saw them afterwards in the crowd?—I saw them coming down the town; they had not a stick in the world.

1641. Do you know of any other man being employed on Sir Leopold M'Clintock's part, except the 10 men?—I heard——

Mr. *McDonogh* objected to the Witness giving hearsay evidence.

1642. Mr. *Pollen*.] Did you write out any other list?—Yes.

1643. What other list?—The day of the nomination.

1644. What list did you write out on the day of the nomination?—Thirty-one.

1645. What is the name of the man for whom you wrote them out?—For Mr. Harvey.

1646. They were to act in the interest of Sir Leopold M'Clintock?—They were.

1647. In keeping order?—Yes, not to have them crowded, coming in here to the nomination.

1648. Were the 31 different from the other 20?—Some were and some were not.

1649. Did you write out any third list?—No.

1650. Did you see any other persons not included in those lists acting in the crowd for Sir Leopold M'Clintock?—No, not one of them.

1651. You were yourself a paid agent of Sir Leopold M'Clintock?—No.

1652. Were you acting gratuitously?—Yes.

1653. Was there any dispute about money by those men afterwards?—Not by me.

1654. Was there by any other person?—I heard there was.

1655. When did you first hear there was a dispute about money?—From some of the aforenamed parties.

1656. Before the poll was over did you hear of any dispute about money?—I heard nothing that day, because I was occupied.

[The Witness withdrew.

Mr. M'Donogh stated that he found John O'Dair was mentioned in his opening speech.

Mr. Justice Keogh stated that in that case he could be re-called and examined.

Mr. John O'Dair re-called; Examined by Mr. Ryland.

1657. Did you promise your vote at the last election to any one?—I did.

1658. To whom?—To M'Clintock.

1659. You told us that you voted for Mr. Whitworth afterwards; what was the reason you did so?—For the fear of my life, my family, and my property.

1660. You say that a number of persons came to your house and attacked you, and you were about telling us the names of some of them?—Yes.

1661. Now you may tell the names?—I have the names here in my pocket; when they came to my house I only took a few names down; one of them is John Martin, of Thomas-street.

1662. What is he by occupation?—He is a man that keeps a bookmaker's shop.

1663. What is the other name?—Pat Brougham. He keeps a bookmaker's shop in Lawrence Gate. Those are the remarks I took of the mob when they began to throw stones.

1664. Were they the first?—No, but they stated at the door, "We will make him bounce out of this again;" and then I told my daughter to lock the door.

[The Witness withdrew.

Patrick Boyle, sworn; Examined by Mr. M'Donogh.

1665. Do you know Mr. Kearns?—Yes.

1666. I believe you are in his employ?—Yes.

1667. I believe all your life you have been with the Kearns?—Yes, since I was 20 years of age.

1668. Are you a voter?—Yes.

1669. Did Mr. Kearns canvass you for Sir Leopold M'Clintock?—Yes.

1670. Did he ask you to vote for him?—Yes.

1671. What did you say to Mr. Kearns?—I told him that I would vote for Mr. M'Clintock.

1672. Did you go to the election?—No.

1673. What prevented your voting?—I was not able to come. I was afraid of getting out into the crowd; I did not come out at all; I stopped in the yard; I was frightened.

1674. Had any persons applied to you?—No.

1675. On the morning of the polling were you again applied to by Mr. Kearns?—Yes.

1676. To vote for Sir Leopold M'Clintock?—Yes.

1677. What did you say?—I told him I was afraid to come out.

[The Witness withdrew.

John Lowry, sworn; Examined by Mr. Plunkett.

1678. You came down on the morning of the polling day to Drogheda?—I did.

1679. What did you come down for?—I came down as poll clerk, or check clerk, or to serve in the booth till the clerk came, or whatever I might be appointed to when I would report myself.

1680. For whom?—For Sir Leopold M'Clintock.

1681. Do you know, of your own knowledge, any of the persons who were employed in the same way for the same person?—Oh yes, I knew several that were there.

1682. Were any of those persons Roman Catholics?—They were.

1683. When you arrived at Drogheda did you succeed in getting to the tally-room?—No, I had to shelter in the station and bridges in the road, and I was knocked down in the road, and I had a tallboard over my head, and I escaped thereby.

1684. Did you see at that time any persons who came down as clerks?—I did. I saw men on the road, and men with sticks beating them.

Cross-examined by Mr. Heron.

1685. How much were you to get for the day's work?—A guinea; the same as all the rest.

1686. The same as all the rest?—Yes.

1687. Who employed you?—A party of the name of Kennedy.

1688. In 47, Dame-street?—Yes.

1689. Were there about 50 of you there the night before?—No, I do not think there were 50.

1690. How many were there?—About 30.

[The Witness withdrew.

Mr. M'Donogh stated that that was his case.

Mr. Heron was heard to open the case on behalf of the sitting Member.

PATRICK TERNAN, Esq., sworn; Examined by Mr. *Pollen*.

P. Ternan, Esq.

16 January 1869.

1691. I BELIEVE you are at present High Sheriff of Drogheda?—Yes.

1692. And you were high sheriff at the time of the last election?—Yes.

1693. You remember the day of the nomination?—Yes.

1694. Do you remember whether, when the doors were opened the three candidates entered together in a body?—I cannot say. I was inside the court-house at the time; I cannot say that the three entered in a body, but very soon after the door opened Mr. Whitworth, Sir Leopold M'Clintock and his supporters and Mr. Whitworth's supporters also got in.

1695. Did you observe some of Sir Leopold M'Clintock's supporters enter nearly the first?—I did.

1696. Can you name any in particular?—Mr. Frederick Smith was up almost immediately beside me, one of the first.

1697. I need hardly ask you whether you did your utmost at the nomination to obtain a hearing for the candidates?—I did all in my power to do so.

1698. And I believe that there was equal difficulty in hearing any of the candidates, and any of the proposers and seconders?—Yes.

1699. At that nomination, with the exception of the noise which you heard, did you observe any actual violence as distinguished from noise?—There was a great deal of shoving and pushing about, and I observed one person strike at Mr. Cooper, of Cooper-hill.

1700. Was that the only blow that you observed during the nomination?—That was the only blow I saw during the nomination.

1701. Did you hear some opprobrious epithets used during the nomination?—There were cheers and counter cheers; I could not catch what the expressions were.

1702. I believe you had given instructions to the police to escort Sir Leopold M'Clintock to his committee-rooms?—I had.

1703. Did you yourself accompany him?—To the best of my recollection I did; I went up immediately after himself and his friends on leaving the court-house.

1704. Were you through the town the entire of that day of the nomination?—I remained here in the mayor's office some time afterwards, getting the poll-clerks sworn and deputy sheriffs, for, I think, about two hours, and then I walked through the town afterwards.

1705. Did you continue about the town during the greater part of that day?—I did until about seven or eight o'clock in the evening.

1706. Will you describe to his Lordship the state of the town when you were so passing through it?—I did not observe any violence except just in one instance. There were vast crowds through the streets, and I saw a crowd gathered together as it were, with some person in the centre, and I went over towards them, and immediately one man came out and walked away, and got away.

1707. With that exception you observed no violence?—None whatever on that day.

1708. Now I will come to the polling-day; that was the 20th day of November. At what hour were you in the town upon that morning?—I was in the town I think about seven o'clock in the morning.

1709. Where were you principally during the day?—Here in the vicinity of the polling-booths almost all the day.

1710. Will you tell his Lordship what violence if any, you observed during the day of polling?—At one time, I think about half-past nine or 10 o'clock, or so, I observed some voters coming down (I thought they were voters, and I believe they were) from Sir Leopold M'Clintock's committee-rooms, and as they turned the corner going into the polling-booth, I saw some sticks thrown at them; I at once ran up and got between the crowd and those voters, and called upon the people to desist, and just as I got there they had got into the polling-booth and the disturbance ceased.

1711. At about what hour of the day was that?—I cannot be quite certain, but I think it was about half-past nine o'clock or 10 in the morning.

1712. Do you remember getting some information that there were voters in Mr. Alexander King's house?—Yes.

1713. What did you do when you got that information?—I at once asked some of the police to accompany me down to that house. There was a body of police in Shop-street with a sub-inspector, and I asked them to accompany me down there, as I wanted to escort some voters up to one of the polling-booths. I got down to this house, and I saw those two voters there.

1714. Did they go with you to the booth?—On reflection I sent the police away again. I thought it just as well to do without them, and I had sent for a car, and got those two voters on a car, and I took them round up to the polling-booth in Lawrence-street, and they both voted for Sir Leopold M'Clintock.

1715. While they were with you, were they assaulted or obstructed in their progress?—Not in any way. I afterwards got them on the car again, and left them up very near the railway station; in fact, near their own residence in the Dublin-road.

1716. On their return to their residence were they either assaulted or obstructed?—No.

1717. I believe that you were present at the bridge when this unfortunate man was shot?—I was.

1718. Will you just tell us what you observed upon that occasion. I do not wish you to repeat everything which you saw, but state exactly what happened after the man was shot?—I had gone down the street with a view of going up to the railway station in company with two of the local magistrates, and I had told a man to keep a car in the street for me. When I went out I found that the car had gone away, so I said, "We will get a car down street, and as we walk down we shall meet one." As we turned into James's-street we saw the troops coming down from the railway station, and as they were entering the far end of James's-street I could observe some sticks and stones thrown at them from each side; that is to say, as those in front got into the street I could see sticks and stones coming as it were from the square on each side. There is rather a wide space as you enter the street, and I observed sticks and stones thrown at them there, not at those

those in front, but at those towards the centre of the escort. As I got up to the troops I found some men in front with sticks making a feint, as it were, to strike at the horses, and to prevent their coming on. I at once turned about in the centre of the street, and got between those men and the cavalry, and kept them off them as well as I could. There was a man on the pathway who observed what I was doing and the position I was in, and he came over to my assistance, and he took two of those men over to one side on the pathway, and after that there was, I may say, little or no obstruction in front until after the word "halt" had been called on the bridge, and the troops were standing there for some time.

1719. I believe you asked the resident magistrates if the troops might go on?—After the halt had occurred. The word "halt" was cried out behind. I was walking in front of the troops at the time, and when I heard the word "halt" I turned back, and I went to the stipendiary magistrate, Captain Talbot, who was on the extreme left next to Captain Knox; I asked him to get the men to come on at once, and not to remain there. He turned about in his saddle and called to those behind to come on. There was some answer made to him; I could not exactly catch what it was, but I found that they did then come on a few paces, and stopped again just as the bridge joined Shop-street. When I observed that they stopped again, I began to get more alarmed, and I went back to Captain Knox and I said, "For God's sake get your men to come on out of this; do not let them remain here; let us get those voters whom you are escorting up to the Tholsel; you are only inviting the crowd to collect and assail you by remaining here."

1720. I will not go into the question connected with that shot, but you remained there till after the shot was fired?—I did.

1721. After the shot was fired, we have heard the crowd fell back; is that so?—Yes.

1722. Did you remain there until the streets were nearly quiet, upon that occasion?—No.

1723. What was the next act which you did after the crowd fell back?—After the shot was fired I heard a second shot. The crowd had got past me; as the cavalry fell back they got past me, in between me and the cavalry, and I was under the apprehension that some more shots might be fired, and that I was in rather a dangerous position; and I went into Mr. Curtis's house, which is the third door from the bridge, on the left-hand side.

1724. Did you observe, or see there any voters who wished to poll; do you remember meeting a Mr. Jamieson?—I do; I was then going out into the street again. I do not know whether I met him exactly in the street or at the door. When I saw him first he was in company with a Mr. Collins. I took him upstairs into Mr. Curtis's, in company with Mr. Collins, and got him on to a sofa; and Mr. Curtis thought he was a bit frightened and faint, and got him a glass of sherry wine, and gave it to him. I told Mr. Jamieson to remain there until I would come back, and take him away after a little time.

1725. Did you afterwards return for him?—I did.

1726. In company with whom?—Mr. Whitworth.

1727. And anybody else; was Mr. Clinton with you?—I cannot say exactly. I chanced just to say to Mr. Whitworth that Mr. Jamieson was in a place, and that I must go down to get him out of it, and he at once said, "I will go along with you."

1728. And he accordingly accompanied you?—Yes.

1729. Did he accompany the gentleman to the booth?—He took Mr. Whitworth's arm, and I accompanied him too, and we came up there, and I believe he went into the booth and voted.

1730. Were you present at the meeting of the magistrates?—I was.

1731. Did that meeting take place before or after the occurrences which you have last mentioned?—Immediately afterwards I called a meeting of the magistrates.

1732. The gentlemen in charge of the military were there too?—They were.

1733. And I believe amongst other resolutions that were come to, it was thought that the military ought to be withdrawn from the streets?—That was the fact.

1734. Were the military immediately after that withdrawn from the streets?—They were; they were removed up towards the gaol.

1735. About what hour was that when they were removed?—I should say it would be about one o'clock, or so.

1736. After one o'clock, when the military were removed, did you continue in the streets, and about the booths, until the election was over?—I did.

1737. Do you remember going to the house of a man of the name of Maguire, in the Bull Ring?—I do.

1738. I believe you heard some report that there were voters there who wished to vote?—Yes.

1739. Were you accompanied by any gentleman; was Mr. Hammond with you?—Yes.

1740. And I think Mr. Bradwell?—Yes; I think so.

1741. The Rev. Thomas Matthews?—Yes, he was.

1742. Was Mr. Clinton there?—I think he was.

1743. Will you state what you observed on entering Maguire's house; did you find any voters there?—There were two or three voters there.

1744. Are you able to mention their names?—One of them was Mr. Ball; but I took his arm and brought him upstairs.

1745. Was Mr. Harris there?—I am not certain, but I think Mr. Harris was the other gentleman.

1746. What did you say to them?—I told them I had come there to escort them wherever they wished to go, either to Sir Leopold M'Clintock's committee-rooms, or to any of the polling-booths.

1747. And did any of the gentlemen accept that offer?—Yes; I took Mr. Ball up into the polling-booth which is in the top-room of this building, and I saw him vote there for Sir Leopold M'Clintock.

1748. Do you happen to remember whether you went to the tally-rooms before you went to the booth, or whether you went direct to the booth?—I went direct to the booth.

1749. Are you able to say whether any of the other gentlemen voted; for instance, did you go with Mr. Harris, or do you know who went with him?—I think it was Mr. Clinton went with him.

1750. But he went with some person to the booth?—He did.

1751. You do not remember the name of the third voter?—I do not.

1752. When

1752. When Mr. Ball had voted, did you conduct him back to any place?—Upon my word I do not remember whether I did or not.

1753. In bringing him from Maguire's to the polling booth, did you experience any obstruction?—No.

1754. Had the violence at that time partially or altogether subsided?—It had altogether subsided, I may say.

1755. About what hour was that?—I should say it would be about one or half-past one o'clock.

1756. Did you go there immediately after you left the meeting of the magistrates?—No, I first went to take up Mr. Jamieson immediately after the meeting of the magistrates, and after having brought up Mr. Jamieson, I then heard of this other gentleman and went back for him.

1757. Did you again go into another house for the purpose of conducting other voters?—Yes, I heard there were some other voters in Mr. Kelly's on the Bull Ring.

1758. Did any persons accompany you to Kelly's?—Yes, Mr. John Farrer.

1759. And Alderman Chadwick?—Yes, and Alderman Chadwick.

1760. How many electors did you find there?—I think it was either seven or eight.

1761. I think you found Colonel Fairclough there?—Yes, he was one of them.

1762. And Mr. Samuel Elkins?—Yes.

1763. And Mr. William Smith?—Yes.

1764. And Mr. Morton?—I do not know as to Mr. Morton; Mr. Matravedy was there too, as I think, and Mr. Vanhomrigh was there too; there were six or seven, at all events.

1765. What took place when you went into Kelly's house?—I at once told those gentlemen I had come there to escort them either to the polling booths, or in fact to any place they chose to go to.

1766. Did any of them avail themselves of your offer?—At first they were talking amongst themselves as to what they would do, and for some little time they did not decide upon what course they would adopt, and ultimately they all came away with us.

1767. Do you remember some of those going to Sir Leopold M'Clintock's committee rooms?—Yes.

1768. Those rooms are in Peter-street?—Yes.

1769. In passing to Sir Leopold M'Clintock's committee rooms, did you pass any of the polling booths?—We passed them all.

1770. Were you able to conduct them to Sir Leopold M'Clintock's committee-rooms, without any obstruction or violence?—Yes.

1771. Could they have voted without difficulty if they had been so inclined?—They could.

1772. Did you offer to protect them if they wished to vote?—I did.

1773. Did you hear in the course of that election up to five o'clock of any elector who wished to vote and had not voted?—

Mr. *M'Donogh* objected to the question.

1774. Mr. *Pallas* (to the *Witness*).] Did you know of any elector who wished to vote, and had not voted?—I did not, and if I had heard of any persons, I would at once have thought it my duty to have gone and escorted them, wherever they chose to go.

1775. Did you use your utmost exertions to find out if there was any person who wished to vote?—I did, because somewhat earlier in the day, I had gone up to Sir Leopold M'Clintock's committee-rooms and offered to go and escort any voters who wished to go up.

1776. Whom did you see upon that occasion; do you know the gentlemen who acted as Sir Leopold M'Clintock's counsel at the election?—I saw Mr Ryland for one, I think; Mr. Ryland came out, and I think Mr. Kay, and I think Mr. Mayne.

1777. Was this after the meeting of magistrates?—It was.

1778. What did you state to them?—I stated that I had come there to ascertain if they had any voters who wished to be escorted to the polling booths, and that if so, I would render them all the assistance in my power, and that I would do everything to take them without being molested in any way.

1779. Was any reply made to that statement of yours by any of the gentlemen?—When I went in first, I stated that I wished first to see Sir Leopold M'Clintock, and I think either Mr. Kay or Mr. Ryland, or Mr. Mayne came out; he went in as it were to let Sir Leopold M'Clintock know that I was there. I may mention that Mr. Whitworth and some other of his friends had followed me up, and they were on the landing just below me at the time.

1780. Then Mr. Kay went into the committee-room as if to make some enquiry?—One of the gentlemen did; I am not certain which of them.

1781. When he returned, what did he state?—I think he first asked us not to go in; that the floor was bad, and if so many of us went in, the floor might break down.

1782. How many people were with you when he said that?—

Mr. *M'Donogh* objected to the reception of this evidence.

Mr. Justice *Keogh* said that it appeared to him to be of no value.

1783. Mr. *Pallas* (to the *Witness*).] When Mr. Kay returned from the room, what did he say?—He stated then that they had closed the poll, because they had in fact given up endeavouring to poll any more.

1784. At that time were the streets in such a state that any person could have voted if he wished?—They were.

1785. Did you continue about the town up to five o'clock of the day of the election?—I continued up to seven o'clock in the evening.

1786. From the time the military were removed from the streets, up to the closing of the election at five o'clock, was there any difficulty to any person who wished to vote?—Not that I saw.

[The Witness withdrew

[Adjourned to Monday next,
at Ten o'clock.

PATRICK TERNAN, Esq., further Examined by Mr. *Pallas*.

P. Ternan, Esq.

18 January 1869.

1787. You stated on Saturday that before the doors were opened some persons were observed in the court-house; will you tell his lordship how that happened and what you did when you observed it?—I just wish to make a statement with reference to that. Captain Gardener had 170 police in front of the Tholsel under his command on the morning of the nomination. The instructions I gave him and the head constable, Coghlan, were that at 10 o'clock on the opening of the doors, they were first to admit the candidates and their friends; secondly, any electors who presented themselves, and if there chanced to be room after that in the Tholsel, that they then were to admit the general public; about 20 minutes before ten at which time the court was opened, I ordered 20 or 30 police inside the court-house lest anything might occur after the candidates were let in, and those 25 or 30 police and a magistrate, namely Mr. Patrick Matthews, the sub-sheriff, the court keeper, Devlin, who was to open the door, and myself, were the only persons inside the court-house previous to the admission of the candidates. Two of the polling booths were in this court-house, and three others within about 50 yards or so of the court-house, so that they were all in view of the court-house, and I spent the greater part of the day on Friday in the street in view of the polling booths, and whenever I saw it necessary at all or saw any of Sir Leopold McClintock's voters either come out of his committee-rooms or returning after voting, I walked beside them or behind them lest they might be molested in any way.

1788. During the entire election did you afford all the protection in your power to every person independently of party?—I did.

1789. And in all respects acted *bonâ fide* and impartially?—Yes.

1790. I think I asked you on Saturday whether a person could vote without difficulty in any of the booths from one o'clock to five?—Yes, I say so.

1791. You say that from personal observation?—Yes.

Cross-examined by Mr. *McDonogh*.

1792. You took all the precautions possible to maintain public tranquillity?—I consider so.

1793. I am sure you did; where was Mr. Cooper when he was struck?—He was passing out.

1794. By whom was he struck?—I do not know.

1795. Did you see the blow inflicted?—I saw one blow inflicted. The top of his hat was a little bit dented in, and the man was making a second blow against him, and I put up my arm and saved the second blow from him.

1796. Mr. Justice *Keogh*.] That was in the court-house?—That was in the court-house.

1797. Was that on the day of the nomination?—That was on the day of the nomination.

1798. Mr. *McDonogh*.] Notwithstanding all those precautions which you have indicated?—Yes.

1799. Did you see that a vast mob had assembled outside?—I did.

1800. And you gave directions that first the candidates should be admitted, and then their friends, and then the general public?—No, that is not what I stated; the directions I gave was that, first the candidates and their friends should be admitted and then the electors; and, thirdly, if there was room in the Tholsel, the general public.

1801. And how was Mr. Gardener, the officer of police, to distinguish between the electors and non-electors?—He is a long time in Drogheda, and he ought to know.

1802. He ought to know every man?—I don't say that he ought to know every man.

1803. In consequence of what happened on that day, I believe you provided an escort to take Sir Leopold McClintock from the court-house?—As soon as I went out, Mr. Cairns and Sir Leopold McClintock were standing on the stairs. There were some of the parties passing and threatened them, and I stood at the foot of the stairs myself between them and those parties, and when the people had got out of the court I went down before Sir Leopold McClintock and Mr. Cairns and some others, and I thought it more prudent to tell constable Coghlan outside the door to provide an escort for them to the tally rooms.

1804. Having heard threats in the precincts of the court offered to Sir Leopold McClintock and his friends?—Not to his *friends*. I heard one man say something to Mr. Cairns that I did not like.

1805. Mr. Justice *Keogh*.] What was the remark that you didn't like?—I think he said something about "Yellow Cairns," or something of that sort, in a nasty way; that is the expression he made use of.

1806. Mr. *McDonogh*.] On the day of the polling itself, will you tell me at about what hour especially, just to fix the time, you went for the Hayes that were locked up in the house?—I cannot tell exactly, because I didn't look at my watch or a clock at the time; but I should imagine somewhere about 10, or half-past 10 o'clock.

1807. Or it might be a little earlier?—I do not think so. I think it was about 10 o'clock.

1808. Where were you when you received the information that those men were in the house?—Just outside the Tholsel here, in Shop-street.

1809. And that they could not dare to leave it?—I cannot exactly say. I was told they were in a house in John-street, and that they had been beaten, I believe.

1810. Have you a doubt of it?—Yes, that they had been beaten.

1811. And that they could not come to the poll?—They could not come to the poll.

1812. And you felt it your duty to go and take them out?—I did.

1813. Where

1813. Where did you leave them?—I took them to the booth in Lawrence-street, where they both voted for Sir Leopold M'Clintock, and I left them afterwards in their own house on the Dublin road, a little beyond the poorhouse.

1814. And so long as they were in your company, I venture to think they were not touched?—Not in any way.

1815. So I should suppose; you were an active supporter of Mr. Whitworth?—I cannot say that I was an active supporter of Mr. Whitworth.

1816. You were a supporter of his?—I was.

1817. At what hour did you vote?—I voted, I think, at about 10 o'clock myself.

1818. At what time did you see the voters of Sir Leopold M'Clintock with stones and sticks thrown at them?—It was before that.

1819. How long before that?—I don't think there were any stones thrown. It was sticks I saw thrown at them. I think it was sticks I stated on Saturday.

1820. How many voters were there?—I think, to the best of my opinion, there might be about six or eight.

1821. Where were they coming out of?—They came down from Sir Leopold M'Clintock's committee-room, and passed round the corner of the street, and they were going into the booth in Lawrence-street.

1822. Was it as they were entering the booth, or just before that the sticks were thrown?—A little before it.

1823. Did you see a clergyman there at that time?—I did not notice any clergyman.

1824. That was before the other?—To the best of my opinion it was before the other.

1825. I think you told us that you were going to the railway station before the transaction on the bridge?—Yes.

1826. You thought your personal presence was necessary there?—No, I did not hear of any disturbance having taken place at the railway.

1827. At what hour were you going thither?—I think something before 12 o'clock.

1828. And you had not heard of the beating of the men in the early morning, at eight o'clock?—No, I had not.

1829. Or of the blood flowing on the station?—No, I had not heard a word of the blood flowing on the station. I will tell you what was the fact. There were two magistrates up at the railway station; Mr. Hamney was there; and I had spoken previously to that of going up to the railway with Mr. Hamney, and he asked me not to go but to remain here.

1830. What took you to the railway station?—I thought it was a long time that these voters were coming down; and I made the remark that the escort was delaying a long time, and I thought I had best go up and see what was detaining them.

1831. Then you knew of the arrival of the voters?—I knew of the requisition of Sir Leopold M'Clintock in the morning asking for an escort.

1832. And you knew that no escort, either large or small, had gone there?—I did.

1833. And you thought there was delay there?—I did.

1834. It appears the second train had come in, and you saw the full escort accompanying the voters down to the bridge?—Yes.

1835. Were they on the bridge when you first saw them?—No.

1836. They were approaching it?—No; they were just entering the far end of James's-street when I first saw them. They were just approaching James's-street, at the end of the Dublin road.

1837. Is that the other side of the bridge?—Beyond the bridge.

1838. Towards the Dublin side?—Yes, towards the Dublin side; it is a good distance beyond the bridge. In fact, as I turned into James's-street with Mr. James Matthews and Mr. John Chadwick, both magistrates, I observed them about entering James's-street; they had not quite reached the far end of James's-street at the time we turned the corner into the near end of James's-street.

1839. Did you perceive the stone throwing then?—As those in front got into James's-street, I perceived there were sticks and stones thrown from each side, from what they call Mangan's corner, and also from the other side of the street.

1840. Did you see any soldiers dropping from their horses?—No.

1841. But you saw the party was then in peril?—I saw sticks and stones thrown.

1842. Mr. James Matthews and Mr. John Chadwick were both supporters, as well as yourself, of Mr. Whitworth?—They were, I believe.

1843. Did you see the Rev. Mr. Matthews then?—I cannot say that I did.

1844. When did you see him?—I do not know when I saw him.

1845. Did you not say on Saturday that you saw him in Maguire's house?—That was after the thing occurred altogether.

1846. Did you see the Rev. Mr. Govan that morning?—I cannot say that I did.

1847. Can you say you did not?—I do not know as to whether I saw him or not.

1848. Did you happen to see an old gentleman; did you know the name of the person who had a long flowing beard down to his waist?—No.

1849. Did you know Colonel Fairclough?—No, not until after I had seen him in Kelly's.

1850. You knew him then?—I knew him then.

1851. Was he the old gentleman who was beaten down?—I do not know.

1852. Was he bleeding profusely when you saw him?—When I saw him he had a cut on his forehead.

1853. Was it then that you saw the Rev. Mr. Matthews?—No.

1854. When was it?—It was previous to that.

1855. How soon was it before that?—I should say about half-an-hour or three-quarters of an hour before that.

1856. Now could you fix the hour for me exactly when you saw the escort entering James's-street?—I think it was about 10 o'clock, as near as I can tell you.

1857. How long after that did you see the Rev. Mr. Matthews?—I think about an hour afterwards.

1858. Then it was near one o'clock when you saw him?—About that.

1859. Who was it that was taken into Maguire's house?—I saw Mr. Ball there. I took Mr. Ball myself out of Maguire's house.

1860. At what hour did you take Mr. Ball out?

P. Fenelly, Esq.

18 January 1869.

P. Thomas, Esq.

18 January 1869.

out?—Almost immediately after seeing Mr. Matthews; I was going down to Shop-street, to that place when Mr. Matthews and some other persons came up, and then we went down together, and I think Mr. Hammond was with him too; Mr. Hammond was with me first; I don't know whether Mr. Clinton was or not; I cannot say.

1861. Did you see the mob pelting the horses with bludgeons?—When the cavalry——.

1862. Will you kindly answer me first, and then you may explain, if you think it needs an explanation?—My opinion is this——

1863. I do not ask your opinion at all?—Let me say then that when the horses became restive and began to swerve round, and did swerve round, there were sticks thrown at them.

1864. Although that is perfectly harmless, yet that is not the question; before the horses swerved did you see them pelting them on the head?—Well, I cannot say that I did.

1865. You cannot say that you did not?—I cannot say that I did.

1866. When the horses were swerving round, were there stones flying then?—There were.

1867. When the horses had turned round and went behind the infantry, did you see the state of things at that moment?—The next thing that I heard was a shot fired, and looking round I saw a man fall.

1868. You saw a man lying prostrate?—I did.

1869. He was carried round, I believe, until he was carried upon the door?—No.

1870. Did you see any of the voters at that moment?—As the cavalry opened out, I saw some gentlemen in the centre between them.

1871. And they had a pleasant prospect, those persons who came from Sligo to vote; they saw the dead man, and they saw Colonel Fairclough lying upon the ground; this did more whole board and ——— and might have upsetted him to some regard?—I suppose it was so.

1872. There is a respectable paper (as there are many respectable papers in this town) on the Liberal side, the "Argus," is there not?—There is.

1873. I may take it that according I find there touching the persons engaged in this election in ——— were you, upon the 23rd of September 1868, appointed one of the committee for conducting the election?—No.

1874. Were you present at that meeting?—I don't recollect as to the date. I will tell you what passed. Some months before the election, and before there was any Conservative candidate in the field, in fact, before Mr. Whitworth had canvassed at all, I got a circular, one day, from Mr. Henry Clinton, to attend a meeting in his house; I don't know the date of it.

1875. And you did attend?—I did attend.

1876. That was before August, you know; we heard the dates from my learned friend, Mr. Heron, the other day?—I don't know the date of it.

1877. September the 26th, Saturday; the "Drogheda Argus"; that is the meeting to which I wish to call your attention, if you please, held on the 23rd of September; did you not attend that meeting?—I don't know as to the date.

1878. In September did you not attend a meeting?—I don't know that it was in September or in August.

1879. Did you attend another meeting, after the one for which Mr. Clinton sent you, the circular, I mean the one when you took the second chair; do you remember that meeting?—I cannot say I do exactly.

1880. Do you remember a meeting at which you took the second chair?—Not exactly.

1881. Do you consider it substantially ——— your attending a meeting in Mr. Clinton's office.

1882. But did you not attend another meeting?—I don't know; I cannot exactly say. If you will mention some little particulars about it, perhaps they might be able to bring it to my recollection. All I can say is that up to the present time I never thought that I attended any other meeting but that one.

1883. The fairest way is to hand you the "Argus" paper, so that you may look for yourself (handing a newspaper to the Witness)?—I think that is the only meeting that I attended that is alluded to there.

1884. That meeting was held on the 23rd?—

1885. Mr. Justice Keogh.] Where was the meeting?—At Mr. Henry Clinton's office.

1886. Mr. M'Donogh.] You know these gentlemen, Patrick Tornan, justice of the peace and high sheriff; that is yourself?—Yes.

1887. John Chadwick, James D. Matthews, Clarke, Simmonds (I am not reading them all), Hughes, Gallagher, and so forth; and I believe you were all appointed on the committee?—Well, I don't think there was any committee appointed.

1888. I will refresh your memory; will you be kind enough to read this favourite newspaper (handing a newspaper to the Witness)?—

Mr. Heron objected to this mode of cross-examination.

Mr. Justice **Keogh overruled the objection.**

Witness.—I see it is moved, "That the independent electors now present do form a working committee;" I see that that is so.

1889. Mr. Justice Keogh.] Was the working committee formed?—There is a resolution there to that effect.

1890. Mr. M'Donogh.] Were you not present, and did you not take the second chair?—I don't think I did.

1891. But you were there?—I was there.

1892. Have you a doubt now that the gentlemen present were appointed a working committee?—I know that at the meeting I attended there was some talk about going out to canvass.

1893. That is generally the result of appointing a committee?—Yes.

1894. And, accordingly, you all did go out to canvass?—No, I never did.

1895. Your holding the office of high sheriff, abstained from canvassing?—Yes.

1896. You saw them on their canvass?—I saw Mr. Whitworth a few days afterwards.

1897. Who went with him?—I don't know exactly.

1898. Was Mr. James Matthews with him?—Not when I saw him.

1899. Did you ever see him with him?—I often saw him with him, but I don't know that I ever saw him canvassing with him.

1900. Was Mr. Clinton present at the meeting I spoke of?—He was.

1901. Were you at the great meeting in November 1868?—When did that take place? (A newspaper was handed to the Witness.) I didn't attend that meeting at all.

1902. That

1902. Then I will not trouble you at all about it. I believe that you are a gentleman extensively engaged in trade?—Pretty much so.

1903. A fine establishment, I am told, it is; where is it?—On the quay.

1904. Is it a mill?—Yes.

1905. You have a great number of porters and workers in your establishment?—Not a great number.

1906. How many?—I dare say about 17 to 20 are employed in it altogether.

1907. On the day of the polling, were they out?—All I can say is that my establishment worked the whole day of the polling.

1908. Were they out?—I don't know, of my own knowledge, whether they were or were not; if they were they were out with my sanction or my leave.

[The Witness withdrew.

PATRICK KELLY, re-called; Cross-examined by Mr. *Heron*.

1909. Do you know a person named Thornton?—I do.

1910. James Thornton?—Yes.

1911. Had you any conversation with him about voting?—No; but he came to my house.

1912. Did he speak to you about voting?—He did, and another man with him.

1913. Did you ask him to get you 20 *l.* for your vote?—Not to my recollection; but he showed up his hand, with five fingers, to me.

1914. Did you use the expression "Twenty"?—Not to my recollection.

1915. Did you use the phrase that you wanted to get money for your vote?—I might say that may be, but I never asked for money.

1916. Did you say that you expected to be paid for your vote?—Not to my recollection.

Re-examined by Mr. *M'Donogh*.

1917. Who is this Mr. Thornton?—He was a publican in the Bull Ring.

1918. Is he a supporter of Mr. Whitworth's?—Well, I heard he was.

1919. And when he held up the five fingers, what did you understand him to mean?—I cannot tell.

1920. Could you tell us the day he came to you?—The day of the polling.

1921. How soon before was it that you were in the hands of the mob, when the Rev. Mr. Matthews told them to "hold the rascal"?—It was after that.

1922. Was it after you went away and refused to vote?—Yes; in my own house, just after leaving the streets.

1923. It was after leaving the streets and going home that he came to you?—Yes.

Mr. *M'Donogh* proposed to examine the Witness as to what had recently occurred to him.

Mr. *Justice Keogh* said that anything that had occurred since had better be stated by affidavit, and informed the Witness that he might depend upon the protection of the Court.

[The Witness withdrew.

BENJAMIN WHITWORTH, Esquire, a Member of the House of Commons, sworn; Examined by Mr. *Heron*.

1924. I BELIEVE you were first returned for Drogheda at the general election of 1865?—I was.

1925. Had you been previously residing in Drogheda, and were you the proprietor of a mill here?—I commenced building a mill here in 1861. I had resided here for eight or nine years, commencing in 1854 or 1855.

1926. At the recent election do you remember issuing your address, about the 4th of August?—I cannot speak as to the exact date, but it would be somewhere about that.

1927. It would be early in August?—It was in the beginning of August, I believe.

1928. You had stood on the Liberal side in 1865?—I had.

1929. And you expressed those opinions while you were Member for Drogheda during 1866, 1867, and 1868?—I did.

1930. Did you stand in the same interest in 1868?—I did.

1931. You have also property, and carry on business in Manchester?—I do.

1932. Do you remember going on your canvass for the present election?—I do.

1933. Do you remember at about what date you commenced to canvass from house to house, and to conduct a personal canvass?—I think it was in October.

1934. Was that about the 23rd of October?—Somewhere about that.

1935. Did you in the course of your canvass experience obstruction?—Very great.

Mr. *M'Donogh* objected to this evidence.

Mr. *Justice Keogh* ruled that evidence as to the state and condition of the town was legitimate.

1936. Mr. *Heron* (to the *Witness*).] I believe you have been on the Manchester grand jury?—I was on the grand jury on the trial of the Fenian prisoners there.

1937. Now, during your canvass, what was the nature of the obstruction which you received?—There was a mob who kept following me, and several prominent men in that mob always got before me into the doors during my canvass, and cried out "The Manchester hangman! the Manchester butcher"!

1938. Did that continue for some time?—It continued for two or three days.

1939. I ask you shortly, were you finally obliged to discontinue what I may call a public canvass of the town?—I was.

1940. And did you then yourself proceed occasionally without any public canvass of the town?—I did.

1941. At the previous election of 1865, had there been between yourself and Mr. Brodigan a public canvass of the town, going from house to house with your supporters?—There had.

1942. You

R. Whitworth, Esq., M.P.

18 January 1869.

1942. You said you were finally obliged to discontinue a public canvass?—I did.

1943. During this time, when you were going on with your canvass, where were you residing in Drogheda?—At "Simcock's Hotel."

1944. I believe you have not a residence in Drogheda?—I have not.

1945. What rooms had you engaged in "Simcock's Hotel"?—I engaged a back sitting-room and a bed-room adjoining.

1946. Had you any other rooms engaged in the hotel during the entire time?—I had not at any time.

1947. Were those the rooms that you had been in the habit of engaging at "Simcock's Hotel" when you came to Drogheda?—Invariably.

1948. I mean irrespective of election times?—Invariably the same, at election times or other times.

1949. How long was it before the nomination day that you had been obliged to discontinue a public canvass of the town?—I should think it would be about the 1st of November, as near as I can recollect.

1950. You remember Sir Leopold M'Clintock making his appearance as a candidate, as has been stated, on or about the 11th of November?—I do.

1951. Up to that time, had any one addressed the electors except Mr. Brodigan?—No.

1952. Mr. Brodigan's address and canvass was on the Liberal side?—It was.

1953. I may say, on the extreme Liberal side?—It was.

1954. And it had been the same in 1865, when he was a candidate?—It had.

1955. I come now to the Thursday evening, the statement of the speeches; you heard the names of the reverend gentlemen mentioned, Father Gavin and Father M'Kee, as having made speeches?—I did.

1956. Had those gentlemen canvassed with you, or had they declined to canvass with you?—I never asked them myself, but I understood——

1957. Never mind what you understood. Had, in fact, Father Gavin and Father M'Kee canvassed with you?—No, they had not.

1958. Did you receive from a supporter of yours a message from Mr. Gavin and Mr. M'Kee declining to canvass with you?——

Mr. *M'Donogh* objected to the question.

Mr. Justice *Keogh* overruled the objection.

1959. Mr. *Heron* (to the *Witness*).] Did you hear Mr. Biggar give evidence on Saturday?—I did.

1960. Before I come to that, do you remember that Thursday evening?—I do.

1961. Where were you during that Thursday evening?—The great portion of that evening I was in my own private sitting-room.

1962. Will you state where that private sitting room is situated in reference to the room from the balcony or verandah from which it is stated speeches were made?—It is immediately at the back of it; the verandah and coffee-room are in front, and my sitting-room is the next, and the bed-room behind that again.

1963. Had you engaged, or did you, in fact, pay for the use of the coffee-room?—I did not.

1964. Did you hear the reporter, M. Macnabe, read out from his note the speeches delivered by Mr. M'Kee and Mr. Gavin and Dr. Murphy?—I did.

1965. Did you hear the speech of either Mr. McKee or Mr. Gavin?—I heard Mr. Gavin speak at the end of the meeting.

1966. Did you hear any of the other speakers?—I heard Dr. Murphy say a few words.

1967. "Rev. Dr. Murphy.—Up to this moment the greatest peace had existed amongst the people; he trusted the same quietude would mark the proceedings up to the hour of closing the poll next day, and a glorious victory would be theirs." Did you hear him say something to that effect?—I cannot say that I remember the exact words.

1968. The whole of the speech before that is, "The Rev Dr. Murphy next addressed the meeting, and said they had arrived at a very important crisis in the history of their land; the worldly Catholic Member, Mr. Brodigan, and Orange emissaries from hell, had come amongst them; at this critical juncture he advised the people to be faithful in following the advice of their clergy, secular and regular, and the Catholic traitors and Orange demons would be soon routed from Drogheda (great cheering)." Did you hear the phrase uttered by any one of throwing the Orangemen into the Boyne?—I did not.

1969. Were you present, or did you hear any priest saying anything about meeting the Orangemen on the Boyne Bridge and hurling them into the Boyne?—I did not.

1970. Is it true, as we were led to infer from the evidence of Mr. Biggar, that you were present when those speeches were made?—I was not present when those speeches were made which you have described.

1971. You heard him give evidence about those two phrases on Saturday last?—I did.

1972. When did you yourself come out, as it were, from your own room to do anything about the meeting?—I came out; the committee told me that the crowd would not disperse unless I said a word or two to them.

1973. Then you came out?—Then I came out, and Father Gavin spoke a few words to them after I came out.

1974. What were those words that he spoke to them after you came out?—I really cannot say. I think that was a fair report, as far as I recollect it.

1975. That was Dr. Murphy's speech?—I think the speech that was taken down by the shorthand writer was, so far as I can recollect it, a fair report of Father Gavin's speech. I did not take particular notice of it.

1976. Mr. Justice *Keogh*.] You apply that observation to Father Gavin's speech, and you think it was a fair report?—I do.

1977. Mr. *Heron*.] What did you yourself then say?—I told them that I hoped that they would keep the peace, that any man who broke the peace was not a friend but an enemy; that it was the last expiring effort of the Orange party in Drogheda, who came to take advantage of what they considered a division in the Liberal ranks; that the only chance that they had was a petition against my return; that my victory was certain. And I then said, "Now I trust you will all go home and be as quiet as you usually are in Drogheda."

1978. Were you directly or indirectly on that or any other occasion a party to any act of violence towards electors or non-electors, or any persons?—Of course I had an altercation with Mr. Hamilton.

1979. Never

B. Whitworth, Esq., M.P.

13 January 1869.

1979. Never mind about that; what I mean is this; did you, directly or indirectly, and as the petition charges, organise any violence or attack against any human being?—Certainly not.

1980. Directly or indirectly did you authorise any human being to intimidate any voter or any candidate?—I did not.

1981. I come now to the day of the nomination. As we have been told, the entrance to the court-house was that entrance by which we enter?—Yes.

1982. And that was the only entrance?—The only entrance.

1983. How long had you been waiting at the door with your friends?—I should think about 10 minutes.

1984. Was Sir Leopold McClintock there?—He was there before me.

1985. And also Mr. Brodigan?—Mr. Brodigan came a few minutes after.

1986. You were with a few of your friends on the steps, the police next, and the crowd outside?—Sir Leopold McClintock was on the top step, and I was next to him. I was just close to him, within a yard. Mr. Brodigan was, I should think, four or five yards lower down.

1987. Had you been introduced to Sir Leopold McClintock, and were you conversing on that day with him?—I was introduced to him on the steps by Mr. Mayne.

1988. Mr. Justice *Keogh*.] Was that on the nomination day?—On the nomination day. It was either Mr. Mayne or Mr. Cairnes; I forget which.

1989. Were you and Sir Leopold McClintock and Mr. Mayne, and the others, before you came in, all conversing together?—We were.

1990. It is said that an egg was thrown. Do you remember the occurrence of an egg being thrown?—I do well.

1991. Whom did the egg finally hit?—It hit the door, and fell on the head of Mr. John Bradwell, a friend of mine.

1992. Was he a supporter of yours?—He was.

1993. Was anything else thrown on that day?—I saw nothing else.

1994. The door was opened, and everybody rushed in?—The people who were immediately near it.

1995. How did they get in?—The candidates and their immediate friends came up these stairs.

1996. By which his Lordship comes on the bench?—Yes.

1997. Then you all got possession of the bench first?—We did.

1998. Were you on the bench before the mob got into the body of the court-house?—There was a regular rush; we all came in at once. I think we were rather longer in getting on to the bench than the mob were in getting here.

1999. Where were you standing?—I was standing about opposite this lamp (pointing to a lamp), and Sir Leopold McClintock immediately under me to the left.

2000. Had you any conversation with Sir Leopold McClintock?—I had.

2001. I suppose, as described, there was great uproar?—There was great uproar indeed. I thought it a most disgraceful uproar.

2002. Mr. Justice *Keogh*.] What do you mean when you say Sir Leopold McClintock was under you?—He is rather a little man. He stood under me.

2003. But he was on the same platform?—He was on the same floor.

2004. Mr. *Heron*.] Were you and Sir Leopold McClintock, while the uproar was going on, conversing of course as honourable opponents, and talking together in a friendly manner?—Yes we were.

2005. Had you and Sir Leopold McClintock then any discussion about the chances of the election?—We had.

2006. What passed between you?—I said, "I hope this will convince you of the necessity of the ballot."

2007. What did you mean by "this"?—The uproar and disturbance. He expressed dissent from that, and I said, "Well, now you have come here, and you have been completely deceived; you cannot poll more than 180 votes unless you buy them or the voters are coerced. Mr. Brodigan cannot poll more than 60 under any circumstances." He said, "You are quite mistaken, he will poll double that; we shall buy no votes."

2008. Was this while the high sheriff was either reading, or attempting to read, the writ?—It was during the proceedings. I did not hear the sheriff myself read it. My hat was knocked off, and I think it was half-an-hour before I could get it again. I think it was under Sir Leopold McClintock's feet.

2009. And considerably damaged?—It was; I never could wear it since.

2010. Now I go to the day of polling. The polling commenced, and I want to know when you first went up by the railway station?—I went up, I think, at about a quarter past 10.

2011. Had you received any message from the railway station to make you go up?—My friend, Mr. Garnan, of Dublin, came into the polling booth——

2012. Mr. *McDonogh*.] Never mind that; don't tell us what your friends said?—I will tell you why we went up to the railway station—

Mr. *McDonogh* objected to this evidence.

Mr. *Heron* argued against this objection.

Mr. Justice *Keogh* ruled that the Witness might be asked what was his business at the railway station.

2013. Mr. *Heron* (to the *Witness*).] What brought you up to the railway station?—I was informed that several voters——

Mr. *McDonogh* objected to the reception of this evidence.

Mr. Justice *Keogh* overruled the objection.

Witness.] I went up to the railway station and looked on to the station to see if there were any Conservative voters who wished to come down. I could see none except a few gentlemen that I knew, and I then came out of the door of the station again, and I was informed that three of my own supporters——

Mr. *McDonogh* objected to this evidence.

Mr. Justice *Keogh* overruled the objection.

Witness.] There were three supporters of mine who were detained——

Mr. *McDonogh* objected to this evidence.

2014. Mr. *Heron* (to the *Witness*).] Did you see the two men, Usher and Devine?—I did.

2015. Did you hear anything about Usher and Devine until you had gone up to the station?—I did not.

2016. Had you known Usher and Devine before?—I had.

2017. Had you known that they voted for you in 1865?—I had.

2018. When you saw them first, where did you see them standing?—I saw them standing against the wall with Mr. Hamilton, with his arms encircling them in this way (*describing the same*).

2019. Which wall?—The wall just to the left going into the station.

2020. Was it outside or inside the station?—Outside the station.

2021. Did you go up to Mr. Hamilton and the two men?—I went up to Usher, whom I knew intimately; I said to him, "For whom do you wish to vote, Usher"? He said, "For you." I said, "Come along, then." So I just got hold of him by the collar, and Mr. Hamilton got hold of him and detained him. I said, "You ought to be ashamed of yourself; it is a bad cause that requires such conduct as this." Then I got Usher away, and put him on to a car and returned.

2022. Did you strike Mr. Hamilton, as he swore you did?—I didn't strike him; I certainly just used my open hand in this way (*describing the same*) when he came to interfere with Usher when he was coming with me.

2023. Had you canvassed Usher for this election?—I had.

2024. What promise did he make to you?—He had promised to vote for me.

2025. How long before this election?—I should think two months before.

2026. Did Usher go away with you of his own free will?—He did.

2027. Did he get up on a car?—He got up on a car.

2028. Did he go away then?—Not immediately.

2029. Did you go back to where Devine was standing?—I did.

2030. How was Mr. Hamilton then in reference to Devine?—He was standing close to him.

2031. Now say what you said?—I said, "Who do you wish to vote for"? After some hesitation he said, "I don't wish to vote at all." I said, "Well, I have no more to say to you." And then I left him, and went down town.

2032. Did you leave him and Hamilton then behind you?—I did.

2033. Then did you get on the car with Mr. Clinton and Usher?—I did.

2034. Was there any one else?—There was either one or two, but I cannot remember who they were.

2035. Did you, after that, in any way whatever, interfere with Devine up at the station?—I never saw him after; not at the station.

2036. After that did you see Usher in your tally-room?—I did.

2037. What did you say to him about voting?—Devine and Usher were both together. I said, "Well, have you voted"? And they said, "No, we have not; we shall only give offence to our landlords if we do." I said, "Very well, I don't wish you to vote; we have got quite plenty without you."

2038. Did you ever catch Devine or touch him at all?—I never touched him in any way.

2039. Did you see the other man that has been mentioned, McDonagh?—I did not.

2040. You know nothing about him?—No.

2041. Except that you know that he had voted for you in 1865?—He did.

2042. You heard Dr. Boyd, I presume by mistake say that you were on horseback up at the station.

Mr. *McDonagh*.] He said he had heard Mr. Whitworth was on horseback.

Witness.] He said somebody was pointed out to him as Mr. Whitworth.

2043. Mr. *Heron*.] Were you on horseback for the last 25 or 30 years?—I was not.

2044. You were not on horseback on that day?—No.

2045. You heard Patrick Boyd's name mentioned, and John Odair's name mentioned?—I did.

2046. Did you ever canvass those people?—I never did.

2047. Had you anything, directly or indirectly, to say to any intimidation being practised on those men, or any knowledge of it?—Certainly not.

2048. I come now to the unfortunate occurrence at the bridge. At what hour did you leave the railway station?—At about, I think, 20 or 25 minutes past 10 o'clock.

2049. Then after that, did you remain in the town about the business of the election?—I did; I never was, I should think, 50 yards from the Tholsel.

2050. Where were you when in fact you heard anything about what had occurred at the bridge?—I was up in the Record Court.

2051. Was that a booth?—Yes.

2052. When you heard of anything having occurred, tell his Lordship what you did, and what you saw?—I heard a great noise; I went to the window, and saw cavalry rushing up the street. I at once went down and heard that those men had been shot. There was considerable excitement. After some time the high sheriff said that he had requested a number of the magistrates to meet upstairs, and would I go with them. I went up, and Colonel [illegible] was also there, and I think two of the stipendiary magistrates. After some discussion, I said, "Well, I think the best course would be to take the troops from the streets; I am confident that it would quiet the people more than anything else." After some discussion it was decided to do so, and that those two men who had fired should be taken and given up to the civil authorities. Immediately afterwards the troops were withdrawn from the streets; and everything continued as quiet almost as it is to-day.

2053. Did that continue until five o'clock?—It did.

2054. At what hour were the troops withdrawn?—I should think about one o'clock, or a little after; a quarter past one.

2055. Was this court-house and the neighbourhood of the place where the five booths were, from one o'clock to five o'clock, perfectly quiet?—From one o'clock to five o'clock, certainly perfectly quiet.

2056. You were of course working in the election, and going about from the courthouse to the

the different booths before the riot occurred?—Yes.

3057. What was the condition of the streets from eight o'clock in the morning until five o'clock in the evening, and with what exception of time?—I was there at eight o'clock or a little before, but with the exception of ten minutes or a quarter of an hour when this unfortunate disturbance occurred, there was perfect tranquillity. Of course there was a little cheering, and that when my supporters came up, and perhaps a "boo" or two when one or two mixed men came up to vote against me. But I never saw the slightest interference with any elector.

3058. Did you yourself go to any of the Conservative electors?—I did.

3059. After the rioting?—After the rioting.

3060. After the 12 o'clock riot?—Yes.

3061. Will you state what occurred then?—I understood that some parties were in houses near the Bull Ring, and I accompanied the sheriff, and I, think Mr. Chadwick, a magistrate, and Mr. John Bradwell, and we saw several of those men who had been in the escort. They seemed of course alarmed, and we at once offered to bring them up to the poll, and guaranteed their safety. I brought up Mr. Jamieson, who voted for Sir Leopold M'Clintock, and I took him back again to Mr. Cairns' Brewery, on the other side of the river. Then I brought up Mr. George Ball, of Dublin; Mr. Ball, while I was linking with him up the street, said, "If you wish I will vote for you." I said, "Well, Mr. Ball, whatever"——

Mr. *McDonogh* objected that this was not evidence.

Mr. *Justice Keogh* allowed the objection.

Witness.] He offered to vote for me——

3062. Mr. *Heron.*] Did Mr. Ball plump for Sir Leopold McClintock?—He did.

3063. Who else did you bring up?—Those were the only two that I brought up.

3064. Can you name the gentlemen whom you offered to bring up?—There was Dr. Brodd, and one or two others. I don't know their names at all.

3065. Did you go into the tally-rooms of Sir Leopold McClintock?—I did.

3066. Did you make the offer of protection there?—I did.

3067. What did you say?—I said that if they had any voters who wished to poll, if they would let me know where they were, I should be very glad to go and escort them to the polling.

3068. At what hour was that?—I should think it would be half past two o'clock.

3069. At what hour did you go to the houses you mentioned?—I should think about half past one or two o'clock.

3070. Did you enter the houses before you went to the committee-rooms?—I did.

3071. You heard Kelly examined?—I did.

3072. Do you remember going to the polling-booth in Peter-street, a little after one o'clock?—I cannot recollect the hour, but I recollect——

3073. Was it after the riot?—It was.

3074. Had you known before you went that Kelly was there at all?—I did not.

3075. Did you see in the hall the Rev. Mr. Powderley, and Mr. O'Donnell, who was described as a Christian Brother?—I did.

3076. Did you hear what they were saying to Kelly, and do you know what they were trying to do?—They were trying to persuade him to vote for me.

3077. Mr. *Justice Keogh.*] Where?—In the hall of the polling-booth in Peter-street; the polling-booth was upstairs, and this was on the ground-floor.

3078. Were there any other persons with him?—There were two or three others, but I really cannot recollect who they were.

3079. In Kelly's presence, then, did the reverend gentlemen say anything to you?—They said, "Do you speak to him, and he will vote for you." I went to Kelly, and I said, "Come, Kelly, you'll vote for me, won't you?" "No," he said, "I've made up my mind not to vote." "Well," I said, "I have made up my mind that I will ask no man to break his word;" and I then said to Mr. Powderly and Mr. O'Donnell, "Don't interfere with him." I had the number at the time polled. I said, "We don't want a vote at all; we can do very well without him, if he is unwilling."

3080. What was the number?—I cannot speak as to the number at that particular time.

3081. But had you then an immense majority?—Oh, an immense majority.

3082. Did you, in fact, there interfere in any way with the man?—Not at all. Those were the only words that I said to him.

3083. In your presence, on that day, was the expression attributed to Mr. O'Donnell used; "Let him go to hell, where he is always going," or anything to that effect?—There was not. I remember the expression used. Mr. O'Donnell said, "Won't you vote for your church, and your clergy, and your country." That is all that I heard.

3084. Now, as to numbers; did you ask any elector to break his promise?—I did not; I distinctly refused to ask any man who had promised.

3085. Did you do that more than once?—I did.

Mr. *Heron* stated that it appeared from the poll books that the numbers polled for Mr. Whitworth were 348; for Sir Leopold McClintock, 189; and for Mr. Brodigan, 80. He also produced the register, which showed that the constituency numbered 728.

Mr. Justice *Keogh* inquired whether the counsel for the Petitioner objected to this.

Mr. *McDonogh* raised no objection.

3086. Mr. *Heron* (to the *Witness*).] At the previous election in 1865, did you hear the sheriff declare the poll at your election?—I did.

3087. Do you remember now the numbers?—

Mr. *McDonogh* objected to the numbers at the election of 1865 being given, and stated that he had raised no objection to the last statement because he believed it to be totally irrelevant as evidence.

Mr. Justice *Keogh* said he did not see how the question of the poll of 1865 could affect this election.

Mr. *Heron* submitted that in the statement he had made he had followed the precedent in Election Committees of the House of Commons.

3088. Mr. *Heron* (to the *Witness*).] You

27. I having

B. Whitworth, Esq., M.P.

13 January 1869.

having been Member from 1868, do you know the constituency thoroughly?—I know it very well.

2089. Did you yourself canvass personally the vast majority of the constituents?—The great majority.

2090. Of the 199 unpolled, first of all give the entire number who had promised to vote for you, and the number who had promised, or who had said they would not vote at all?—The total number of pledges in my favour were about 325 before the election.

2091. Of the 198 unpolled, dividing them according to the Protestants and Catholics, what were the proportions?—108 Protestant voters remained unpolled, and 90 Catholics.

2092. That leaves only 198; can you account to his Lordship for the missing one?—There is one double entry.

2093. What is the name of the double entry?—Cahill.

2094. What are his two franchises?—He has two different franchises.

2095. Is he in two different wards?—No, he is in the same ward, I think.

2096. Of the 108 Protestants, how many had promised to vote for you?—Out of the 108 Protestants 11 had promised to vote for me, but abstained from voting; 12 had promised not to vote against me; two are dead; three were agents, and engaged by the sheriff, and could not vote: There were in England, Scotland, or abroad, 17. There were in Ireland above 25 miles away, 19, leaving 44 in the immediate neighbourhood who didn't vote.

2097. Of the 90 Roman Catholics, how many had promised to vote for you?—I cannot tell you exactly the number of the Roman Catholics.

2098. Can you not give the same comparison as regards them?—I cannot.

2099. Then 90 Roman Catholics did not vote?—Yes.

2100. On the morning of the polling day do you remember about the state of the poll at half-past ten and half-past eleven?—At half-past ten I think I had 198 polled. I am not so clear as to the exact numbers polled by the other two candidates.

2101. We will prove that by the tallies up of the polls at eleven o'clock how many had you?—At eleven o'clock I had 230.

2102. And the polling was going on during the hour before the shot was fired?—It was; the polling never was interrupted altogether, even for a minute.

2103. I believe you are an Independent?—I am.

2104. When you went out from the room on the day of the speechifying, the Thursday evening, was Mr. Gavin speaking?—No; Dr. Murphy was speaking.

2105. When you came back again who was speaking?—I remained till the close, perhaps five or six minutes.

2106. And then you spoke yourself?—Then I spoke a few words for about a minute and a-half.

Cross-examined by Mr. *McDonogh*.

2107. You told my learned friend, Mr. Heron, that you met with considerable obstruction in the course of your canvass?—I did.

2108. On what day did you commence the canvass?—I don't remember the exact date.

2109. How soon after that meeting in September that you heard you ask the high sheriff about?—It was very soon after that.

2110. You were present at the meeting, I suppose?—I was.

2111. You saw the sheriff there?—I saw the sheriff there.

2112. And you saw the Rev. Mr. Mardon there?—I don't think I did.

2113. Soon after that you commenced your canvass?—Yes.

2114. On what day were you obliged to discontinue the canvass?—I cannot speak to the exact date, but the first day we commenced canvassing West-street, and before we had got very far, this mob commenced their disturbance, rushing before me to every door, and crying out "The Manchester butcher! The Manchester hangman!" and some stones were thrown.

2115. And they were a violent and angry mob?—They were.

2116. Were they in the interest of Mr. Brodigan?—I cannot say.

2117. What do you think?—I think they were.

2118. Is it not a fact, as you heard your counsel say the other day, that Sir Leopold McClintock didn't make his appearance until the 11th of November?—So I believe.

2119. And Sir Leopold McClintock had nothing to say to this?—Certainly not.

2120. Finally you were obliged to give up and discontinue the canvass; you had not gotten the 325 pledges then, had you?—I had not.

2121. They were refused in many instances?—No doubt.

2122. Did they not say they would vote for Brodigan?—I don't think I met half a dozen during the whole of my canvass who said they would vote for Brodigan.

2123. But you did meet half a dozen?—Certainly not more.

2124. The others refused you?—Others refused to promise me.

2125. Mr. Brodigan's people were active?—They were.

2126. You heard Mr. McKenna examined?—Yes.

2127. A respectable man?—Well, there is a difference of opinion.

2128. So there is about everybody; what did you hear about the two ministers' coffins being placed opposite his door?—I never heard of that until he named it.

2129. Having given up on the 1st of November, how came you——?—I do not fix the 1st of November.

2130. Well, it was about that time; at all events, you and Mr. Brodigan were scarcely in the field when Sir Leopold McClintock made his appearance?—We were.

2131. Mr. Brodigan was then the popular man for the time?—Well, I don't think he was.

2132. When did you resume your canvass?—While I was in Drogheda I kept slipping out by stealth; Mr. Clinton and I used to say, "Well now, you go one way, and I'll go the other;" and we generally met at his house, and then went and canvassed for perhaps a quarter of an hour, or half an hour, and then came back again to keep this mob from following us.

2133. In fact, to escape them?—We did.

2134. That

2134. That was a private canvass, which you were enabled to carry on in that way?—Yes; we carried on the canvass in that way.

2135. When did the light of popularity again beam upon you?—When Sir Leopold McClintock came into the field.

2136. Then it was about the 11th of November?—Somewhere about that.

2137. Had you canvassed in company with any of the Roman Catholic clergy up to that time?—I had.

2138. When?—Pretty early in the canvass.

2139. Will you mention the names of the clergymen?—The Reverend Canon Tierney, and the Reverend Mr. Powderly, and the Reverend Father Smith, who doesn't reside in Drogheda; he canvassed with me in the country districts.

2140. Is the Reverend Mr. Powderly a gentleman located in the town?—He is.

2141. He is a Roman Catholic curate, I suppose?—He is.

2142. And well known in the town?—Very well.

2143. Although he was with you, do you mean to say that the mob exhibited this angry feeling towards you?—I do.

2144. Even in his presence?—Even in his presence.

2145. Mr. Smith was a country clergyman?—He was.

2146. And you canvassed the country with him?—I did.

2147. When did you get the accession of any other of the Catholic clergy?—I had no accession at all.

2148. None at all?—None at all.

2149. Did the Reverend James Matthews ever accompany you?—He did one day.

2150. When?—I think about three or four days before the polling.

2151. Had they stood aloof from you for some time?—Who?

2152. The Catholic clergy?—Two or three of them had.

2153. Had the Reverend Mr. McKee?—He had.

2154. Had the Reverend Dr. Murphy?—No.

2155. Was he with you all through?—He was always a friend of mine.

2156. Was the Reverend Mr. Murphy; there are two?—He never interfered at all; I saw him at one meeting, but he never canvassed with me to my knowledge at all; he did not take an active part.

2157. Mr. Justice *Keogh.*] Did Dr. Murphy canvass with you?—He did not; he is very infirm, and could not walk about.

2158. Mr. *McDonogh.*] It appears that you had the whole body of the Roman Catholic clergy with you afterwards?—I believe so.

2159. The Reverend Mr. Gavin?—Yes.

2160. Did he canvass with you?—He did not.

2161. Did he canvass for you?—I do not think he did; I don't know that he did.

2162. Did the Reverend Mr. Matthews canvass for you?—I believe he did not in my presence; I have been told so; I don't know from my own personal knowledge.

2163. Did not the Reverend Mr. Matthews tell you that he was successful in his canvass for you?—He told me that he had spoken to several men.

2164. And that they had promised for you?—Yes, he did.

2165. Did the Reverend Mr. Powderly tell you that he had got promises from people?—He told me in one or two instances that he had seen voters who were away when he had called upon them, and that he had succeeded in getting promises.

2166. When did you manage to get Mr. Brodigan out of the field?—We didn't get him out.

2167. Up to the time that the tide of that charming thing called popularity set in in your favour, when you were hooted in the streets, how many pledges had you got, do you think, good, bad, or indifferent?—The hooting began on the very first day of my canvass.

2168. But you then, by stealth, endeavoured to pursue it. Up to the time that the tide turned in your favour how many pledges had you got?—I cannot say.

2169. Can you say, as an honest man, that you got 50 pledges?—I can say that on the very first day I got between 70 and 80.

2170. Notwithstanding all the insults and refusals that you met with?—Exactly.

2171. Did your getting pledges then stop?—Certainly not; I got pledges every day that I went out; the fact is, that I met with very few opponents.

2172. Did you hear that Mr. Brodigan claimed that he had a vast majority?—I did; I had heard that before.

2173. Suppose this went on, and that Mr. Brodigan retained his hold, there was peril between you both, that if a Conservative stood he might slip in between you?—My firm conviction was——

2174. I am asking you as a matter of fact, and not your own opinion?—My firm opinion is, that if Sir Leopold McClintock had spent 10,000*l.* in bribery he could not have got in.

2175. Although you told him he had no chance unless he bribed?—I told him he had no chance of polling more than 150 votes unless he bribed.

2176. And you whispered that to him on the Bench?—We were chatting very comfortably together.

2177. That was a very interesting dialogue between the two candidates amongst the noise?—I told him exactly what I thought.

2178. But he entirely disagreed with you?—I don't think he did; he didn't express any dissent as to the number who would vote for him, though he dissented as to the number that would vote for Mr. Brodigan.

2179. But he said that he would not bribe?—Yes, he did.

2180. Do you remember when Mr. Brodigan became unpopular?—He was always unpopular.

2181. Pardon me for a moment; do not be too severe upon him; wasn't he the popular man when you were hooted?—Certainly not.

2182. When did you see that he and his friends went through the streets?—I did not see him.

2183. Nor his friends canvassing for him?—I may have seen him just pass, but I never saw him canvassing; I never went near them.

2184. Your mob finally extinguished his, did it not?—I don't know; I had no mob.

2185. Now, you are serious?—I am indeed, perfectly serious; you will find that I shall not equivocate in any way; I will tell you the plain honest truth.

2186. Now, I wish to know as to the locality of this dining-room at Simcocks's; first, there is what one witness called the verandah, or the balcony; then there is the room inside; you call it the coffee-room?—It is the public coffee-room.

2187. Then

B. Whitworth, Esq., M.P.

18 January 1869.

2187. Then there were folding doors between your sitting-room and it?—There were.

2188. And beyond that again was your bedroom?—Yes.

2189. Then the folding doors being open, the rooms were all *en suite*?—No doubt.

2190. And you had been long a resident at that hotel?—Ever since I came to Drogheda.

2191. How was it that the meeting of that evening was arranged?—I don't know; I was not a party to it.

2192. Who made that arrangement?—A considerable number.

2193. And you don't know how it was arranged?—No.

2194. And Mr. Clinton never told you?—He did not.

2195. Well, you were very glad to see them all?—Well, I was not.

2196. Did you in opening the proceedings, or at all, ask them to give three cheers for Father McKee?—I did not.

2197. Did you ask them to give three cheers for anybody?—I did not, except for "Old Ireland," at the close of my speech.

2198. Were the folding doors open that evening?—They were not during this election; Mrs. Simcocks, or Mr. Simcocks had lined the crevices with green baize, and with something to hinder the noise, or people hearing anything that might occur in one room from the other.

2199. Were you in quietude in your sitting-room on that evening?—I was a considerable portion of the evening; and another portion of the evening I was down in the sitting-room of Mrs. Simcocks, on the ground floor.

2200. When did you know the meeting was going on?—I could hear the cheering and noise the whole time.

2201. And you knew it was a meeting in your interest?—I supposed it was.

2202. Had you the slightest doubt about it?—I had not.

2203. And you went up into the room, did you not?—I went into my own room.

2204. But did you not go into the coffee-room?—I will tell you exactly what I did——

2205. First, do me the favour to tell me whether you went into the coffee-room?—They came and told me the crowd would not disperse unless I said a few words to them.

2206. Where were you then?—In my own sitting-room.

2207. Were you reading?—I was not; I was speaking to Mr. Chadwick, and I think my brother William; I believe those were the two gentlemen that were there.

2208. Who was it that brought you that message?—I really cannot say.

2209. Then you went in?—I went out on to the balcony; of course I passed through the room.

2210. Was there a clergyman next you when you went on the balcony?—Yes, Dr. Murphy.

2211. Was he on your left hand or right hand?—He was on my right hand, I think.

2212. Who was on your left?—I cannot say; I think Mr. James Duff Matthews.

2213. And you heard Mr. Gavin make his speech?—I did.

2214. And you heard the reporter recite it the other day?—I did.

2215. That was an accurate report?—I could not speak positively to it, but I should consider it a fair report.

2216. Did you hear him read the report of Dr. Murphy's speech?—I did.

2217. Was that a fair report?—Well, I think it was.

2218. Did you hear him read the report of the Rev. Father McKee's speech?—I did.

2219. Do you think that was a fair report?—I did not hear the speech.

2220. Did you hear any portion of it?—Yes.

2221. But you stood with a clergyman on one side and the counsel on the other?—Mr. Matthews, I believe, was next.

2222. That was your counsel?—Yes.

2223. Another great man stood between the clergyman, but you had a clergyman on one side and a barrister on the other?—Yes.

2224. Was Dr. Murphy speaking while you stood by his side?—He was; he was speaking when I went on to the balcony.

2225. Then if a gentleman swore here that whilst the speaking was going on he saw you standing beside a priest, it would be true?—It would be true at that time.

2226. Now you gave them "a touch of a speech," as Lord Eldon said?—I did.

2227. And you took care, in that "touch of a speech," to assure them that this was the last expiring effort of the Orange party?—I did.

2228. That was to tranquillise them, of course?—I do not know; I just told them exactly what I thought.

2229. Was it for the purpose of tranquillising them?—It was, I believe; I don't know that that particular sentence was, but the whole of my speech was.

2230. The general context?—Certainly it was.

2231. What did they cry out when you said it was the last expiring effort of the Orange party?—They cheered.

2232. Do you remember their crying out, "Yes, Father, we will meet them in the morning"?—I do not.

2233. And after assuring them that victory was certain, and that it was the last effort of the Orange party, you told them to go home quietly?—I did.

2234. And as a commentary on that act, they broke Mr. Moore's windows?—They broke the windows in Simcocks' Hotel, too, at the very time.

2235. What an impartial mob! Now, with respect to your not riding, I am sure nobody will contradict that; does your brother ride on horseback?—I never saw him; I don't think he does.

2236. Are there two gentlemen of the name in the town besides yourself?—There are two.

2237. Does neither of them mount a horse?—I never heard of their so doing; I hear they have no horse.

2238. They are not afraid of that noble sport, horsemanship, I hope?—I don't know.

2239. Now, may I ask you, did you hear anything said in addition to what you and Mr. Gavin and Mr. Murphy may have said to the people about the Orangemen that were expected from Dublin?—I heard nothing except what Dr. Murphy and Father Gavin said.

2240. Upon that subject?—Upon any subject.

2241. Did you hear either of them say that the

the Orangemen were to be down in the morning?—Father Gavin said so.

2242. *Mr. Justice Keogh.*] Was that from the balcony?—Yes.

2243. Were you present when Father Gavin spoke?—I was; he said that an Orange mob would come to butcher the Catholics of Drogheda.

2244. Did he not say, upon the word of a priest, that 500 Orange ruffians were coming to butcher the people?—He said something to that effect; I cannot say exactly what the words were.

2245. Now, do you remember their saying, "Yes, Father, we will meet them in the morning"?—No, I do not; and I don't think such words were used at all.

2246. How soon after that was it that you made use of the expression that it was the last effort of the expiring Orange faction?—It was just at the close of the meeting.

2247. Did you, on the morning of the polling, take any step to prevent a collision between the supposed Orangemen and the mob?—I never feared any; I never had any idea of a collision.

2248. You did not do it?—I did not.

2249. Where did you first hear, if you ever heard, that Father Gavin was there in the early morning?—I never heard it until I heard it proved in evidence here.

2250. Is Father Gavin here?—Yes, he is.

2251. You were attending to the polling in the morning?—Yes, I was.

2252. As time is of some importance, and as you were not quite clear about the 1st of November, I will ask at what hour you reached the tholsel yourself?—On that morning?

2253. On the day of the polling?—I think it would be about a quarter past ten o'clock, perhaps ten minutes past.

2254. Did you then learn anything of the violence which had occurred there?—I did not.

2255. It was then you saw Devine, the voter?—I did, and Usher.

2256. Was there a large mob then outside?—There were, I should think, 100 or 150.

2257. Did you see whether they had sticks and stones?—Some of them had sticks; I saw no stones at all.

2258. Did you lay your hand upon Mr. Hamilton?—I did, as I have described.

2259. Well, I want you to describe it fully; did you see that Devine had him by the hand at the time?—Devine was not touching him at the time that I had my altercation with him.

2260. Did you see Devine at any time holding the hand of Mr. Hamilton?—I did not.

2261. Was Mr. Hamilton near Devine when you had the altercation with Mr. Hamilton?—Usher was between Hamilton and Devine.

2262. What made you lay your hand upon Hamilton?—I pushed him with my hand when he came to interfere with Usher going along with me after he said, "I want to vote for you."

2263. When you first asked Usher to vote for you wasn't he silent?—I think he was for a moment.

2264. And you repeated it?—I did.

2265. Did Mr. Hamilton then approach him and Devine?—He was close to him at the time, because he had his arms encircling him at first.

2266. And in order to enable you to take Usher away, you put your hand upon Mr. Hamilton?—I asked Usher, as I said before, "Usher, whom do you wish to vote for?" After some little hesitation, which, of course, in the presence of his agent, he naturally felt, he said, "I want to vote for you." "Well," I said, "come along." Then Mr. Hamilton got hold of him, and forcibly prevented him from coming; and I then said, "You ought to be ashamed of yourself for such conduct, it is a bad cause that requires such work as this." I just shoved him again with my open hand, and Usher walked out.

2267. And then you say you shoved him again with your open hand?—I pushed him again; I did not say "shoved."

2268. I beg your pardon, you did. Having pushed him again, you got Usher away?—I did; he came away.

2269. Did you leave Mr. Clinton behind you?—I did not.

2270. Did you make any effort to take Devine?—I did not.

2271. Will you swear that?—I do, most positively.

2272. Was the car yours upon which Usher was taken away?—I don't know whose car it was.

2273. Had you cars engaged?—I had not.

2274. Had your committee?—I believe not.

2275. I am not asking you what you believe?—I tell you I had no cars hired, and I don't believe any were hired.

2276. How soon after that did you meet Devine and Usher at the Tholsel?—I didn't meet them at the Tholsel; I met them at my tally-room at, I should think, about half-past eleven o'clock.

2277. And it was then that you said you did not want them?—I asked them, "Have you voted?" and they said, "No, we have not; we don't want to offend our landlord." "Well," I said, "never mind voting, I have got quite plenty without."

2278. I suppose you thought you had the election nearly won then?—I was sure.

2279. Were you perfectly sure?—I was as sure as I can be of anything that is not an absolute certainty.

2280. However, you were quite sure, I presume, that at twelve o'clock, or a little after half-past twelve o'clock, when the man was shot, there was no doubt whatever you had a majority then?—None whatever.

2281. Then after the time of the riot, from one till five o'clock, you know there was security in Drogheda?—It was quite as quiet as one could wish it to be.

2282. But at the close of the rioting, and when the man was shot, the election was in your favour, virtually?—No doubt.

2283. And could not be retrieved?—It could not be retrieved under any possibility.

2284. You had received but 325 pledges, and you had 334 at a certain point of time, as you stated to my learned friend?—Yes, at eleven o'clock.

2285. After the rioting had ceased, by the death of the man; then, at about one o'clock, was there a meeting of the magistrates?—I think about one o'clock, or a little before, perhaps.

2286. And then it was utterly irretrievable that any man could win the election?—Except myself.

B. Whitworth, Esq. M.P.

18 January 1869.

B. Whitworth, Esq., M.P.

18 January 1869.

2287. In fact your success was indubitable, and was complete, when the rioting was over?—It was, and before.

2288. Do you not think it was as great a mockery as ever was enacted, for you and your friends, after you had triumphantly won the election, and the rioting was over, to go round to the poor voters belonging to Sir Leopold McClintock and tender your services?—I can swear this, that I should have been very glad to have brought up any of Sir Leopold McClintock's voters at any time of the day; that my success was as certain, in my own mind, as anything in the world could be.

2289. What state or condition was Ball in; was he bleeding?—I don't think he was.

2290. Was he weak?—He is naturally weak; he is an old man, and he is a weak man.

2291. Was he tottering?—No, he was not tottering.

2292. Was he leaning upon you?—He did lean upon me, no doubt.

2293. Had you known him before?—I had not.

2294. You never saw him before?—Not that I am aware of.

2295. Had he known you?—He had known me by reputation.

2296. He knew that he was speaking to Mr. Whitworth?—Yes.

2297. You had never canvassed him?—I had not.

2298. You had never seen him before?—I had not.

2299. Was he weak after being beaten?—I do not know that he was weak.

2300. Do you think that one of the voters escaped being beaten who were escorted?—I think so.

2301. Do you mean to tell me that this man, whom you had never seen before, and never canvassed, while he was walking arm-in-arm with you, said he would vote for you?—He did; he had promised, through his agent, to vote for me.

2302. Did you see him vote for Sir Leopold McClintock when you brought him up?—I did.

2303. Sir Leopold McClintock's clerks and people had been all withdrawn at that time, had they not?—No, they had not, that I was aware of.

2304. About how many thousand did the mob consist of that day?—Where?

2305. In this town, where the firing took place, and the man was killed?—I was upstairs when that occurrence took place, very much to my surprise. I had no idea there was any rioting going on.

2306. You did not hear of the way in which the voters were treated when they came in in the morning; sticks and stones being thrown at them?—Not a word.

2307. The high sheriff did not tell you?—He did not.

2308. You did not know of the house being locked up after the Bay's had been beaten?—I did not.

2309. How many hundreds of people are employed in your factory?—I should think about 600.

2310. How many women are there?—I should think there would be one-half.

2311. Of those 600?—I should think so.

2312. Did you hear the priest say, "Boys, you have a holiday, and you know how to use it?"—I did not.

2313. Did you give them a holiday?—I did not.

2314. Were they out?—They were, on the nomination day.

2315. Did they form a portion of the assemblage which ornamented the room?—Not that I am aware of.

2316. But they were out on that day; you let them all out?—They would not work. We told them they must work, but they would not work; it is a very great loss.

2317. Did you pay them for that day?—We did not.

2318. Were they out the next day?—Which next day?

2319. The interval between?—Certainly not.

2320. Were they out on the polling day?—They were, part of the day; we started the engine, as I have heard from my brother; my brother consigned me as to it. It is a serious loss; a loss of 30*l.* or 40*l.* a day, every day the mill stops, and it gets them into idle habits. They will not come, even after the election is over. They started the engine at about six o'clock, but at half-past seven a message was sent to my brothers' house to say that he was wanted down at the mill. They there told him that they would not work on that day, and, of course, he could not compel them to work.

2321. And they all left?—They did; the engine was stopped, and they left.

2322. The starting of the engine was not a make-believe, any more than the going about with those voters?—It was not.

2323. But at all events, starting at six o'clock, it was stopped at half-past seven?—Somewhere about that time.

2324. And the whole 600 men and women walked out?—There are very few men employed at our mill.

2325. But they are stalwart boys, are they not?—The majority of them are 15 or 16 years of age.

2326. And the women?—They are young; they are young girls.

2327. And they wear aprons, I suppose?—I cannot say.

2328. Fit to carry stones?—I cannot say.

2329. And did you pay them for that day?—No.

2330. Did your brother?—He did not. I only know from what I have been told.

2331. Do you know Mr. Thomas Owens?—I do.

2332. He was an active supporter of yours?—He was a supporter of mine.

2333. Did he pay a mob?—I do not know.

2334. Is he in this town?—He resides in the town.

2335. Do you not know that they got 5*s.* a-piece?—I do not.

2336. Do you know John Odair?—I never saw him till I saw him in this chair the other day.

2337. Do you know Mr. Martin, of Thomas-street?—Yes.

2338. He is an active supporter of yours?—I believe he voted for me.

2339. And canvassed for you?—Not that I am aware of.

2340. Did he not tell you so?—He may have done;

B. Whitworth, Esq., M.P.

18 January 1869.

done; I dare say he may have said, "I have spoken to Bennigan."

2341. Do you know **Mr. Bennigan, of** Laurence-gate?—I do not.

2342. Is Mr. Martin in this town?—Not that I am aware of; I do not know.

2343. Is he not here now?—I do not know.

2344. He lives in the town?—He does; there are several Martins.

2345. What is his business?—I think he is a shopkeeper.

2346. He is a huckster, is he not?—He is a huckster.

2347. Did you hear **Odair say that Martin** and Bennigan came to **his house with a mob, and that the door was battered in with the** stones?—I did not.

2348. Were you here?—I was, but **I do not** remember hearing him say that.

2349. Did you know that Odair had hidden in the garden?—I did not; I never knew anything of him. I never knew who Odair was till I saw him in this chair.

2350. You saw that man Kelly, the baker?—Yes.

2351. At about what hour was it that you saw him, when he was addressed by a clergyman?—I should think about half-past one o'clock, as near as I can speak.

2352. That was after the dreadful riot at the bridge, and the death of the man?—It was.

2353. Was it the Rev. Mr. Powderley that addressed him, and asked him to vote for his Church?—I think not; I think it was Mr. O'Donnell.

2354. The Christian Brother?—I think so.

2355. Did you hear him say, "It is not my Church that is concerned in this election"?—I did not.

2356. Did you catch any words to that effect?—I did not.

2357. Showing that the man knew the question was the disestablishment of the Protestant Church?—I did not.

2358. After they had spoken to him, as you say, in the manner you have told us, was it true that they said, "Ask him yourself, and he will vote for you"?—It was.

2359. Which of them was that?—I think it was Father Powderley, but I am not very clear.

2360. **You did ask him?—I did.**

2361. If the election were so completely won, no matter what the violence was, no matter what the intimidation was, why did you press the man to vote for you, if you were so sure?—I did it because I was asked to do it.

2362. By the clergyman?—Yes.

2363. Did you speak to Father **Matthews** about him?—I did not.

2364. Do you know now that it was Father Matthews that had him kept by the mob until the father ascertained that he had not voted?—I do not.

2365. Did you hear Kelly state that?—I heard him say something of the sort.

2366. Did you make any apology to the owner of the hotel for the use of his sportsman on that night?—Certainly not.

2367. You are an old familiar customer?—It was not my business to do so.

2368. You did not meddle with the matter at all?—I did not.

2369. How many thousand pounds has the election cost you?—This election?

2370. Yes?—I have paid 700 *l*. How much of that has been spent I do not know. Of course I have paid fees to my counsel on this trial; 600 *l*. or 700 *l*. is all that I have spent.

2371. That is all that you have spent?—It is; and I said that I was quite sure that no such amount as that would be required. That remark was occasioned by my brother wishing to say that he had paid 500 *l*. into the Bank of Ireland to the credit of the election agent, for election expenses.

2372. Who is he?—Mr. Campbell.

2373. And then there was another 100 *l*.?—The other 100 *l*. was before that.

2374. How much do you believe it will cost you?—I expect I shall have some returned. Mr. Clinton says, "I can return you some of it; I do not think it will be all wanted."

Re-examined by Mr. *Hore*.

2375. How much did you pay for the last election in 1865?—Between 400 *l*. and 500 *l*. If I may be allowed to volunteer a statement, I will swear positively that if the election had depended upon illegal expenditure, I would not have done it.

[The Witness withdrew.

Mr. George Butterley, sworn; Examined by Mr. *Hamill*.

Mr. G. Butterley.

2376. You are the sub-sheriff, are you not?—Yes.

2377. Do you remember the morning of the polling?—I do.

2378. When the doors were opened can you tell who were the parties inside this place?—There was the high sheriff, the court keeper, I think some members of the constabulary, and myself, and a gentleman came in at that window, a magistrate.

2379. Were those the only persons in the place when the doors were opened?—Yes.

2380. Up to the time of what is called the riot did you observe any personal violence to any one in Drogheda upon that day?—No personal violence.

2381. Were the poll-booths open for any one to come forward to vote?—They were.

2382. After the riot, say from about half-past 10 o'clock up till 4 o'clock, when the booths closed, was there perfect liberty for any one to come to any of the polling-booths to vote?—Perfectly so.

2383. Did you canvass for Mr. Whitworth or take any part for him?—No, I did not.

2384. You remained independent?—Neutral, except voting.

Cross-examined by Mr. *Plunket*.

2385. On the day of the nomination were there any tickets distributed to the various candidates?—No.

2386. Was there any application made that there should be any such distribution to your knowledge?

knowledge?—Well, there was a good deal of——

2387. Who made the application?—Well, I think Mr. Brodigan did.

2388. Any person else?—And his agent, Mr. Healy, the solicitor.

2389. Any person else?—There may have been, but I am not so clear about anybody else.

2390. Do you know whether there was any application made on behalf of Sir Leopold McClintock for tickets?—There may have been, but I will not say.

2391. Were tickets given out?—No.

2392. Will you explain why they were refused; you were the person who was applied to, I presume, for tickets?—I was asked would tickets be issued.

2393. You took that as a requisition, I presume, that they should be?—Well perhaps I did. I said I would consult the high sheriff, and I did; and the high sheriff said he did not see the necessity.

2394. The advantage of it?—"The necessity," I think, or words to that effect.

2395. Were you asked a second time to give out these tickets for the nomination?—Indeed I was, more than twice.

2396. Did you make any promise about opening the door a little earlier so as to let people in quietly?—No, I did not.

2397. Did you make a promise that you would open the door at a quarter before 10 o'clock?—No.

2398. Do you happen to know yourself whether the sheriff made that promise?—I do not know, neither do I believe he did, from the conversation I had with him.

2399. You were asked just now whether you observed any violence on the day of the polling, before the affair of the bridge, and you said, no personal violence. What do you mean by "no personal violence"?—I did not see any person injured, that is, struck, or any assaults committed.

2400. Did you see any people about the streets at all?—Indeed I did.

2401. Did you see any mobs about the streets?—I did.

2402. Were they in rather an excited state?—They were.

2403. Were any of them in an intoxicated state?—With liquor?

2404. Yes?—No.

2405. Were they in rather a friendly state?—No.

2406. In rather a quarrelsome state were they?—I cannot say that I saw any number of people under the influence of drink on that day at all. I beg your pardon, at the row at the bridge I did see one man, and he must have been in a fearful state of intoxication to act as he did. There may have been hundreds, but I did not happen to see them.

2407. What did this one man in Drogheda do who was in this state?—After the mob was shot at the bridge, I saw him rush over to attack the military a second time, and if I recollect right, he had a cudgel in his hand.

2408. And I suppose he was the only person there who had a cudgel in his hand?—Oh, hundreds had, as well as I recollect, but this one individual made himself remarkable to me. I was pretty convenient to him, and Mr. Brady, the pawnbroker in West Street, caught him and drove him back again.

2409. You are prepared to say that except the little incident of that man rushing forward, you saw no person that day under the influence of drink?—I think I saw them in the evening, but not up to that hour.

2410. Do you mean to say that after this rioting was over there was no more violence in the town at all?—The town was remarkably quiet, considering there was an election.

2411. Were there any crowds about?—There were, but it was remarkably quiet for an election.

2412. That was from one o'clock until five o'clock?—From one o'clock until the close of the poll.

[The Witness withdrew.

THOMAS GREEN, Esq., sworn; Examined by Mr. *Pallas*.

2413. WERE you mayor of this town during the last election?—Yes.

2414. Do you remember the day of the polling?—Yes.

2415. During the principal part of that day, where were you?—Principally in the court-house.

2416. Did you continue there until five o'clock?—No, not until five o'clock; I might have been here until about three o'clock.

2417. Up to the time you had left, was there any obstruction in the court-house as to voting? None.

2418. Was it free to everybody to vote as he wished?—Free to everybody.

2419. I suppose, being in the court-house, you saw nothing of this rioting?—No.

Cross-examined by Mr. *Ryland*.

2420. Were you on the committee of Mr. Whitworth?—I never was on a committee at all, but I was chairman of a meeting of his supporters. I never heard of a committee.

2421. Were you walking about before twelve o'clock on the day of the polling?—I was here nearly all the day.

2422. Were you outside the court-house or in the window?—In the window, in what they call the mayor's court.

2423. That commands a view, I believe, of both Lawrence-street and Peter-street?—It does.

2424. Did you see any mob of people in Lawrence-street, near the tally-rooms, on the morning of the polling, between eight o'clock and 12 o'clock, at any time?—Of course I saw several.

2425. Did you see sticks or stones flying in the air?—I did not see sticks and stones flying in the air, but I saw them in the hands of the people.

2426. Did you see the men with the sticks strike any people?—No.

2427. Did you see them rush at any people?—I might have seen it, but I did not; I saw no one struck.

2428. You

2428. You saw them rush after them with sticks as they were going to the tally-rooms?—I did.

2429. Did you see them flourishing the sticks?—Not to my knowledge.

2430. Had they the sticks raised above their heads?—They generally had them on a level with their arms or shoulders.

2431. So that you could see them plainly?—Certainly.

2432. Did you see green hatbands on any of these men?—I saw two or three, I think.

2433. Two or three, I think, with each mob?—No.

2434. Was there but one mob that you saw there?—I could not say whether there were mobs or one mob.

2435. Did you see a mob of people where there was not a man with a green hatband on?—Yes; I only saw three persons with green hatbands, small green ribbons.

2436. Were they the leaders?—I had no idea that they were the chief persons; I thought they only had the green on for safety to themselves going through the mob.

2437. You say you saw this mob in Lawrence-street; did you see any mob in Peter-street?—I did.

2438. Did you see them there rushing at the people as they went to the booth in Peter-street?—I saw them rushing up and down occasionally.

2439. Did you see the people coming down to the booths in Lawrence-street?—I saw them come from the committee-rooms down to the court-house, and to Lawrence-street, but I did not see anyone going from Shop-street.

2440. Did you see any persons rushing at them with sticks as they came down?—No, I did not see a single stick raised to strike anyone, or at least I did not see anyone struck by a stick.

2441. But did you see people rushing towards them; when they came out of the committee-rooms to vote did you see the mob rushing towards them?—I did, occasionally, but they were very generally protected; the sheriff was generally with them, and the two Mr. Chadwicks.

2442. And the police?—The police were stationary; they very seldom walked with them.

2443. Did you see any voters walking down that the mob did not rush towards them?—I cannot say.

2444. You did not see them?—I did not.

2445. Did you look down Shop-street at all?—No, I could not; there was no view from that place.

2446. Were you out at all during the day?—I suppose I might have been out during the day.

2447. At what hour?—I daresay it might have been, perhaps, near two o'clock.

2448. Were you out before one o'clock?—I think not.

2449. From eight o'clock to one o'clock, were you in this building?—No; I was not here, I suppose, until about half-past nine o'clock; that is the hour at which I used to hold my court.

2450. By what way did you come to this building?—From my own house.

2451. Where is your own house?—Near the viaduct; I think it was over the back lanes I came, and up Shop-street; I am not certain, really, but I think so.

2452. Did you see many people as you were coming at half-past nine o'clock?—There were not many in the streets then, as I thought.

2453. Did you see many people towards the bridge, and towards the quay, as you passed through Shop-street?—No; I did not see any people there at that time.

[The Witness withdrew.

BENJAMIN WHITWORTH, Esq., M.P., re-called; further Examined by Mr. *Heron*.

2454. HAD you, in fact, any committee?—I I had no committee.

Further cross-examined by Mr. *McDonogh*.

2455. Were you not present at the meeting in September, when those several gentlemen whose names you heard me mention to his Lordship, as stated in the "Argus," were in attendance?—I was.

2456. Was not the last resolution put then, "That the gentlemen now present do form a working committee"?—There was a resolution passed, but I certainly have no recollection of what that resolution was.

2457. That is the most you can say?—It is.

2458. Will you look at that paper (*handing a paper to the Witness*)?—"That the independent electors now present do form a working committee, with power to add to their number, for canvassing purposes." I have no recollection of that; I suppose it must have been so if it is in that paper; I have no recollection of any committee being formed; I was at the meeting, but I have no recollection of that resolution being passed.

2459. You will not deny that that resolution was passed?—I will deny that I have any recollection of it.

[The Witness withdrew.

R. Bergwall, Esq. 13 January 1869.

2467. And with the exception of the time that you were at the mills were the streets quiet, so far as you saw?—There was a great deal of excitement before the military were withdrawn from the streets, but when I returned from the gaol the streets were perfectly quiet.

2468. At what hour was it when you returned from the gaol?—At about three o'clock.

2469. At that time was there any difficulty in a person polling if he wished it?—Certainly not.

2470. Did the streets continue in that state as long as you were there?—I left the town at four o'clock.

2471. Were your mills working on that day?—One mill was working up to one o'clock, and the other mill worked up to the breakfast hour; and the engine was stopped after the breakfast hour, and was obliged to be stopped because the people were not coming in.

2472. Why was the mill that was worked up to one o'clock in the day stopped?—I was told——

2473. Mr. *McDonogh*.] Never mind what you were told?—Then I don't know any-thing about it.

2474. Mr. *Pollux*.] Who is in charge of that mill that worked till one o'clock; is Mr. Mason in your employment?—He is the manager over all the mills.

2475. Did you give permission to any of your work-people to be out on that day?—Quite the contrary; I gave most decided instructions to them to do all in their power to keep the mills working.

2476. Was there any pay stopped in consequence of the men being absent?—All those who were absent did not get their pay.

2477. I believe you from time to time escorted voters of Sir Leopold McClintock's?—I assisted in escorting them. I went down to the Bull Ring twice.

2478. Whenever you heard a voter was anxious to poll, did you offer an escort?—Yes, I was moving about the whole day.

Cross-examined by Mr. *McDonogh*.

2479. When did you begin to be escort for Sir Leopold McClintock's voters?—After the row.

2480. After the row you went to the gaol, I think?—No, not immediately; I escorted some voters first.

2481. At about what hour did you become escort for Sir Leopold McClintock's voters?—There was a meeting of the magistrates immediately after the row. After I attended that, I was told, when I came from the room up-stairs, that there were some voters in the Bull Ring who wished to vote, so I went down with some others.

2482. You, I believe, voted for Mr. Whitworth?—I did.

2483. And you were on his Committee?—No, I was not.

2484. Were you at the meeting?—No, I was not.

2485. At the time that you volunteered your services as an escort for your opponent's voters, or Mr. Whitworth's opponent's voters, may I ask you, did you believe that the election was virtually over?—Yes, I was quite sure of it.

2486. Are you the active member of the firm in managing the mills?—No.

2487. Who is?—Mr. Chadwick.

2488. In fact, the work-people did not come back after breakfast, and the water was running away; was that so?—No, the steam-engine was running away.

2489. The rotatory motion went on?—You can imagine that when an engine is intended to drive a hundred and twenty horse-power, and you have no power on it, it is very likely to run away.

2490. Well, the people would not come to work. How many hundreds of them were absent?—I cannot tell that.

2491. About how many?—I was told only about 70 came in after breakfast.

2492. You do not know how many hundreds were away, seven hundred or eight hundred?—Precisely.

[The Witness withdrew.

JAMES MATTHEWS, Esq., sworn; Examined by Mr. *Howe*.

J. Matthews, Esq.

2493. I BELIEVE you have been on the Commission of the Peace for about 35 years?—Yes.

2494. And you have been five times Mayor of Drogheda?—Yes.

2495. Were you in Drogheda on the 20th of November last?—I was.

2496. That was the day of the polling?—Yes.

2497. Do you remember driving up to the railway station?—I do.

2498. Did you drive your own phaeton?—I did.

2499. Did you see there Mr. Henry Alexander Hamilton?—Yes, he was there along with several others.

2500. Did you make any offer to Mr. Hamilton to bring him into the town?—I did.

2501. And to any of the other gentlemen?—Yes.

2502. How did you offer to bring them into the town?—In my phaeton.

2503. At what hour was it?—I suppose it was about 11 o'clock.

2504. That was for the purpose of bringing them up to the Tholsel here to vote?—Yes.

2505. You knew Mr. Hamilton and the other gentlemen came to vote for Sir Leopold McClintock?—Oh, of course.

2506. Were you about the town during the day until five o'clock?—No; I was about the town in the early part of the day, but not the latter part of the day; after the unfortunate occurrence, I went home.

2507. Except the unfortunate occurrence at the bridge, was there any rioting in the streets during the day?—I saw none except from the bridge up to the railway.

2508. That is, after the man was shot?—Yes, and before it.

2509. How long before it?—Well, perhaps a quarter of an hour.

2510. Before you drove up, had you been about the Tholsel and the polling booths here?—Yes.

2511. Was there any interruption whatever to the voting before the riot at the bridge?—None that I saw.

2512. Of course, I presume there was the ordinary excitement, cheering, and shouting?—There

There was cheering, and occasionally hooting, and all that, you know.

2513. But did you see any violence whatever? —I did not.

2514. Or any necessity for your interfering as a magistrate?—I did not.

2515. I need scarcely ask you whether you would have done so had it been necessary?—Most certainly.

2516. For either Conservative or Liberal voters?—Certainly.

2517. Did you, through the day, as far as you could as a magistrate, do your best to keep the peace?—Certainly.

Cross-examined by Mr. *McDonogh*.

2518. At what hour did you drive in from your country house?—Perhaps a very few minutes after eight o'clock.

2519. And then, I presume, you were in the immediate vicinity of the court-house?—Yes, a great part of the time.

2520. You did not see the violence offered to Sir Leopold McClintock's voters as they were coming to the booths?—Yes, I did with the military, but not otherwise; I saw no violence offered before that.

2521. You were not present when the high sheriff interfered to prevent the throw of stones? —No, I was not.

2522. And you did not see anything of the Boyle being beaten?—I did not.

2523. May I ask, had you heard of the injuries inflicted upon the people at the railway at about eight o'clock in the morning?—I had.

2524. Perhaps it was that that took you to the railway?—No, it was not; hearing that Mr. Hamilton was there, I went up. *J. M[illegible], Esq.*

2525. To offer your assistance?—Yes. 10 January 1869.

2526. You knew that the state of the town was at that time very bad?—I knew no such thing.

2527. And perhaps you thought it very good? —Well, I thought the usual excitement was going on at the election; I saw a great many elections at Drogheda a great deal worse than that.

2528. I should be sorry to think that there was anything worse, but do you think Mr. Hamilton required your protection?—I believe if Mr. Hamilton had walked down he would not have been molested.

2529. Did you think he required protection when you invited him to come into your phaeton? —I thought he was under apprehension of being assaulted.

2530. Who was the other gentleman?—Mr. St. George Smith.

2531. Those were the two gentlemen whom you invited?—Yes; I saw a great many gentlemen there; the Reverend Mr. Morton, whom I had not seen for a great many years.

2532. They having declined to go into the phaeton with you, did you drive down towards the town?—I did.

2533. Did you see the dreadful stone-throwing?—I saw nothing at all as I was coming down, and then I came here to the Tholsel.

2534. Then, were you here before the riot commenced?—I came down and returned with the sheriff and Mr. Chadwick.

[The Witness withdrew.

Mr. James Latimer, sworn; Examined by Mr. *Heron*.

Mr. J. Latimer.

2535. You heard Mr. McKenna's evidence on Saturday?—Yes.

2536. He is asked, "What took place on the Monday?" (*A.*) On the Monday I saw that the Reign of Terror had commenced. I was walking along here, and a ferocious mob rushed forward and attacked and struck me, and pushed and drove me, and they nearly threw me on the face, except for the police coming up and saving me. Mr. Gardener came first in time to save me, and Mr. Latimer, one of Mr. Whitworth's best supporters, was blandly smiling on the crowd, and encouraging them from Shop-street out here." Is that true?—It is not true.

2537. Is there any other person of your name in this town, or any person of the name who could be spoken of as a warm supporter of Mr. Whitworth's but yourself?—There is not.

2538. Will you tell his Lordship what occurred? —I was in Shop-street, standing talking to Mr. Eugene Clarke in his doorway on a matter of business, and Mr. McKenna turned out of West-street, round the corner of the Tholsel, into Shop-street, and a few women after him; I think a considerable number of women. They were using language that would indicate to me that it was owing to his own conduct, not at all in connexion with the election, that they were abusing him; I do not wish to go into the matter, because it is a private matter; I did not see it commence; I was not in the street with McKenna; neither by act nor motion, directly or indirectly, did I either encourage or do a single thing; Mr. Clarke and I drew into his shop when we saw them coming on.

Cross-examined by Mr. *McDonogh*.

2539. About how many women were there? —I cannot tell.

2540. About how many?—I should think there might be about 30 or 40.

2541. Might there be a hundred?—I cannot say; I drew a little into the shop with Mr. Clarke.

2542. Might there have been a hundred women?—Indeed there might; I will not pledge myself to the number.

2543. Did you not in your very first answers, say that there were a few women?—I only saw a few coming round the corner at first.

2544. Did you not then go on to say, "a considerable number of women"?—I will not bind myself to the number at all.

2545. Did you see any men amongst them?—Not that I remember.

2546. Did you see men following Mr. McKenna down the street?—Some may have been.

2547. They may have been; did you see a hundred men following him down the street?—I did not.

2548. Did you see many men following him down the street?—I do not remember many; there may have been some.

2549. You do not know in your conscience that there were?—I do not.

2550. What

2550. What do you believe?—The persons that I saw pulling at McKenna's hat were women.

2551. Did you see any men following him?—There may have been.

2552. Were there not?—I don't believe there were.

2553. Will you swear that you don't believe it?—I will swear I don't believe there were.

2554. Did you see them going down the street?—I did.

2555. Did you hear the shouting?—I didn't hear any shouting except afterwards.

2556. Did you hear them booing at him?—No. If you wish, I will tell you what the women said to him.

2557. I have no wish whatever about it; were there about a hundred women; did you smile?—Really I cannot tell.

2558. Did you hear the manner in which he described it; that he described it that you "blandly smiled"?—Yes, I did; I heard him say so.

2559. And you cannot say that you did not smile?—I cannot say that I did not, but I did not blandly smile.

[The Witness withdrew.

PATRICK MINELLA, sworn; Examined by Mr. *Fallon*.

2560. WHERE do you live?—24, Vicar's-street, Dublin.

2561. Do you remember the day before the polling of the Drogheda election?—I do.

2562. Do you remember meeting a man of the name of O'Rourke upon that day?—Yes.

2563. You and O'Rourke had a conversation?—Yes.

Mr. *McDonogh* submitted that this evidence was irrelevant.

2564. Mr. *Fallon* (to the *Witness*).] Did you speak to a man of the name of O'Rourke, on the day before the polling for the Drogheda election?—Yes.

2565. Did you and O'Rourke go to any place after that conversation?—47, Dame-street.

2566. Do you know a Mr. Kennedy?—I do.

2567. Did you see a Mr. Kennedy at 47, Dame-street?—I did.

2568. Will you state what took place, if anything, between you and Kennedy?

Mr. *McDonogh* objected to this as being recriminatory matter.

Mr. Justice *Keogh* considered that at present there was no ground for the objection.

2569. Mr. *Fallon* (to the *Witness*).] Is Mr. Kennedy in court?—He is.

2570. Will you point him out?—He is beyond, at the corner there in the window (*pointing to a person in court*).

2571. State what passed between you and Kennedy.

Mr. *McDonogh* objected to the question.

Mr. Justice *Keogh* overruled the objection.

Witness.] Mr. O'Rourke brought me up by the shoulder and says, "This is a stout lump of a chap that would not be afraid of a row." That is the way he introduced me, and he took down my name.

2572. Mr. *Fallon*.] Was there anything else that passed?—He told me on Saturday at 10 o'clock, that Mr. Hamilton would pay me 1 *l.* for coming down.

2573. When were you to go down?—The next morning at half-past four.

2574. Were there any other persons present on that occasion?—There were over 70 in the house.

2575. Was Kennedy employing these persons?—Taking down the names; he took down my name and read to the whole of us that we would be paid by Mr. Hamilton at 10 o'clock the next day, Saturday.

2576. What Mr. Hamilton was that?—The was the Member that was for the county of Dublin.

2577. You saw the 70 men that were being hired?—I cannot say that all of them were hired.

2578. Were some of them strong fellows?—They were.

2579. Like yourself?—Yes.

2580. Did you see Kennedy again that evening?—Yes, I did.

2581. Where?—In O'Connor's public-house.

2582. What were you doing there?—I was brought in to get drink.

2583. By whom?—Mr. Kennedy.

2584. Did you next morning, go by train to Drogheda?—I did.

2585. Did you see Kennedy?—I did.

2586. Did you see a great number of others there?—I did see them.

2587. Did others come after you?—Yes.

2588. How many altogether before the train left?—There were 60 that got tickets, and then there were four or five left behind.

2589. Had any of them any sticks or weapons with them?—I seen sticks in, too.

2590. Many?—In the side of the carriage that I was in there were 12 men, six on a side, and I could say there were about six sticks, and out of that there was one short one loaded.

2591. Had you yourself any?—No, I had no stick.

2592. Did you hear anything said by Kennedy about any weapons that the men had?—That they had them for to hide them going down the town.

2593. When did Kennedy say that?—I think it was at Laytown.

2594. Do you remember Kennedy saying anything in which the word "coward" was used at any time?—That we should have no cowardice about us.

2595. When was it that he said that?—I think it would be on the platform.

2596. Did you see any arms beside the sticks?—No.

2597. Kennedy, I believe, got the tickets, and then the party came down?—Yes; I was about the fifth that was served with a ticket, a single ticket.

2598. Do you remember when the train arrived at Drogheda?—I do.

2599. And the men getting out?—Yes.

2600. Were there girls and boys collected at the platform, or near it?—Sitting on the wall as you came down from the railway.

2601. Do you remember any words being used on that occasion about fighting?—I saw a few girls there and a few boys.

2602. Did you hear any of your party say anything of what you were to do when you got to Drogheda?—I did not know myself what I was for.

2603. Were you to act as poll-clerk?—I never heard a word of it.

2604. Do you know what a poll-clerk is?—He has to take the votes as they come in.

2605. When you got out of the train, did you see a girl struck by a person?—I did by one, for booing; she was hooting.

2606. Did he say anything when he struck her?—I forget now.

2607. Was she knocked down?—She was.

2608. Did you see a woman knocked down by a stone?—I did.

2609. Was that stone thrown by one of your party?—They were thrown at both sides.

2610. Did you see any men knocked down with sticks upon that occasion?—I saw one.

2611. When did you leave those 50 people?—This is what made me leave the town altogether. There was one man called Woodhouse, and he met some priest on the road, and he said, "If I had a revolver I would shoot that bloody papist priest. So I says, "I am in bad quarters," says I, "and I will get away."

2612. What was the Catholic clergyman doing when these expressions were used?—When the girls and the men began to pelt the stones at one another, he told them not to pelt any stones.

2613. And it was then that these expressions were used?—Yes.

2614. After that, before you left, did you see another girl knocked down?—I only saw the woman and the girl altogether.

2615. When did you leave Drogheda on that day?—I suppose it would be about half-past nine o'clock in the morning.

2616. And at about half-past eight o'clock, I suppose, you arrived?—Yes; I got into a house, and I stood there smoking a bit.

2617. Were you afterwards paid for coming down?—Yes, I was. On Saturday morning, after I had walked in from Drogheda, I went up to Mr. Kennedy, and I told him that I had to cut my old shoes up for walking home. "Well," he said, "we will not make you the same as the others; there is 5s.," he says, "on account." So the following Wednesday night I walked up, and he gave me a shilling. Then they were to be all paid on Friday, so I did not go on Friday, but I heard that they were paid, and I went up to Kennedy's own place, and he paid me 19s.

2618. All the men were to be paid the same?—No, but I was to get half-a-crown extra for walking home.

2619. Did you see a list of names with Kennedy of the persons who were brought down?—I did.

2620. Do you remember how many names there were on the list?—I know there were 60 came, but there might be a lot that were left behind.

2621. Did you see that list within the last week?—I saw it yesterday.

2622. In whose possession?—In Kennedy's.

2623. Is your name on that list?—It is.

2624. Do you remember the number of it on the list?—54.

2625. Is that the Mr. O'Rourke that you refer to (*pointing to a person in the Court*)?—That is the man that introduced me to Kennedy.

P. Hinelin.

18 January 1869.

Cross-examined by Mr. *M'Donogh*.

2626. Mr. O'Rourke keeps a public-house in James's-street?—Yes.

2627. What are you?—I am a dealer.

2628. In what?—In fish, such as oysters and shell-fish.

2629. You are not an Orangeman?—No.

2630. You are not one of the "bloody Orangemen?"—No.

2631. You did not come down to take the town of Drogheda by storm, did you?—Give and take, that was the name.

2632. You had no stick?—No.

2633. Were those small sticks, the size that you saw amongst all those men?—Some of them were big ones, and one loaded with lead.

2634. With a ferrule on it, as you would call it?—No, no ferrule; it was loaded in the head with lead.

2635. Did you see the attack that was made upon the men, when they came here?—It was nothing of any account.

2636. You did not see the blood flowing?—I saw blood.

2637. Did you see the shower of stones coming from the women?—Aye, and I saw them going back too.

2638. They went back as they came in?—Other stones, not the same that were thrown.

2639. Did you throw a stone?—Yes.

2640. You really did?—Yes.

2641. Were you struck with a stone?—Well, slightly, I was not hurt at all.

2642. Did you see any men amongst them?—No, they were all little girls. There were only two men with sticks at the cross of St. James's-street.

2643. You do not mean to say you threw a stone at the little girls?—I did at the women and girls.

2644. Did you see the men come in upon the station?—I did not go to the station; I did not go back to it.

2645. But did you not go to the station in the first instance?—From Dublin I did.

2646. Did you see the men break into the station?—No.

2647. Did you see any one in the station?—I did.

2648. Did you see them beating those men who came from Dublin?—No, not them.

2649. When did you see them doing it?—Give and take; I see them coming down with stones, I did not see them beating at all.

2650. Did you see them beaten with stones by the men?—Who beat with stones?

2651. The men that came down in your company?—I was told they were beaten, but I did not see them.

2652. Was blood flowing?—I saw the cuts, but I did not see the blood from them.

2653. Where was the priest?—There is a little gateway on the road as you come down from the station, and he was just there.

2654. And he was there when the train arrived?—Not at the train.

2655. Was he at the station?—I did not see him until I saw him where I tell you.

2656. How soon after you arrived at the station did

P. [illegible].

18 January 1869.

did you see him?—I saw him the very minute I came into the road.

2657. Do you know who he was?—No.

2658. Did you hear that his name was Father Gavan?—No.

2659. Would you know him again?—I might.

2660. Is he in this Court?—I do not know.

2661. Look about, look up in the gallery, is that the gentleman (*pointing to a person in the Court*)?—I am not sure; I think that is like the gentleman, that put up his hands, and told them not to be throwing any stones; I am not thoroughly sure about that.

2662. Did you see amongst those men that came down with you, one that had a wooden leg?—I did.

2663. Did you see another of them that wanted an arm?—Not with us, he did not come down.

2664. What was the wooden legged man's name?—Reeves, I believe.

2665. Did he sit in the carriage with you?—Not in the carriage with me.

[The Witness withdrew.

The Rev. JAMES POWDERLY, sworn: Examined by Mr. *Heron*.

Rev. *J. Powderly*.

2666. Are you one of the Roman Catholic curates of Drogheda?—Yes, I am curate of this town.

2667. Who is the parish priest?—The Very Rev. Dr. Tierney.

2668. How long have you been in Drogheda?—I am in my 16th year in Drogheda now.

2669. As Roman Catholic curate of this parish?—As Roman Catholic curate of this parish.

2670. You remember the day of polling at the last election?—I do.

2671. Did you hear a person named Kelly examined in Court on Saturday?—No.

2672. Did you see him here to-day in Court?—Yes, I saw him here to-day.

2673. Do you remember on the day of polling seeing Kelly in the hall leading to the booth?—I met a person said to be named Kelly, but I did not know him, otherwise, except that I heard his name was Kelly.

2674. Was he then in the booth in Peter-street?—Not in the booth; he was in the hall leading up to the booth.

2675. In Kelly's presence, were you asked whether you would go and speak to him?—I was walking in the street, and some person came to me and said there was some voter in Peter-street, and that if I would ask him to vote for Whitworth, he would probably do so; and I complied with the request.

2676. Did you go and see Kelly?—Yes.

2677. What did you say to him?—I asked him whether he would vote for Mr. Whitworth. I said that Mr. Whitworth had strong claims upon the people of Drogheda; that he was a Liberal, and would support the great Liberal party, who were now promising good measures for this country; and that it would be a great matter for us to return a man who would carry out our wishes, and support measures that might be brought forward in the Imperial Parliament for the benefit of Ireland.

2678. What did Kelly say?—Kelly said that he would rather not vote.

2679. Did he assign any reason for not voting?—I think I recollect him to say that he was afraid of his landlord.

2680. Was that all that occurred before Mr. Whitworth came up?—I do not know whether that occurred in the presence of Mr. Whitworth or not. I am not quite sure about the moment that Mr. Whitworth appeared or Mr. O'Donnell.

2681. Were you speaking to him before Mr. O'Donnell, the Christian brother, came?—I think I was speaking to him before Mr. O'Donnell came. I remember distinctly that I saw Mr. Whitworth and Mr. O'Donnell, and there were some others present, but I could not recollect at all who there were.

2682. From the time Mr. O'Donnell came up to Kelly, did you hear all that occurred?—I heard all that occurred while I was there, of course.

2683. Did Mr. O'Donnell say that Kelly would go to hell if he did not vote for Whitworth?—Certainly not in my hearing at all. I heard Mr. O'Donnell, I think, say to this person, who was supposed to be Kelly, "Won't you vote for your priests?" or "with your priests?" and he might, perhaps, have added the words, "for your country"; but I could not be so sure of that. That is all I heard Mr. O'Donnell say on that occasion.

2684. Do you remember Mr. Whitworth coming up and saying anything to him?—I remember Mr. Whitworth asking him, "Won't you vote for me, Kelly?" and he declined, and said he would not.

2685. What did Mr. Whitworth then say?—I think we left them there. Immediately after I said, "If this man does not wish to vote, we do not want the man." I was only there a few minutes altogether.

2686. Did Mr. O'Donnell say, "Let him alone; let him go to hell; he is always going there"?—Certainly not; I never heard him say such words.

2687. On the day of the polling, were you in and about the Tholsel and the different booths?—I was, frequently.

2688. Did you point out to the mob to attack an old gentleman with a long white beard who had voted for Sir Leopold McClintock?—Certainly not.

2689. On that day, or at any time during, or before, or after the election, did you excite the mob, or lead the mob, or in any way influence the mob, to commit personal violence upon any person?—Certainly not. On the contrary, I did everything in my power to prevent the mob doing any harm of any kind. I made no speech, I say remark, before the day of polling or on the day of polling, until after the man was said to be shot. When I heard that there was a man shot, I at once said it was time to draw the people, if possible, off the streets altogether, and to prevent any further disturbance or confusion; and I went to the nearest place at which I could address them publicly in the streets, and that was at Mr. Thomas Daly's, where the judges' lodgings are. There is a balcony, and I went there, and I knew when they saw a priest standing there they would come away from the soldiers. I may remark that.

that when I saw the soldiers, they seemed in a great excited state after coming up from the bridge. I saw only one of the soldiers bleeding a little from a wound on the side of the head, and I spoke to them for a moment, and I said, "If you can at all keep quiet here, do so." They were trembling with emotion, and in a most excited state, and seemed to have their guns ready to fire almost, and I was really afraid that some other accident might occur; and I begged them to have a little patience for a moment, and said that I would do everything in my power to withdraw the mob. So I went to Mr. Daly's window, and I told them that the state of the poll was now such that Mr. Whitworth was certain to be returned, and I said that I was very sorry to say that the victory now gained was not gained without some bloodshed; and in order that there might be no further accident, I begged of them to have one of their pastors who had been here so long with them, and to follow his advice, and that was, to disperse, and to go home as quickly and as quietly as they possibly could to their own houses. I then told them to go up to the Whitworth Hall, which is in Lawrence-street, some distance from the polling, in order to take them entirely from the streets, and that they would be addressed there by the clergy, and by other friends of Mr. Whitworth. This was merely to take them away from the place, and when we got there I repeated what I had said at Mr. Daly's window, and begged them then to go home quietly; and, in order to do this more effectually, I left the place and went down, before them, to the post-office, which is about half-way up Lawrence-street, and I stood in the centre of the street, and I told them, as they went back, that I would not allow anyone of them to pass; at least I requested them not to go down to the Tholsel any more, and I begged them to go home; and that if they lived in this side of the town, they could go to it; and if they lived in the other part of the town, they could go to it by a lane which is called Free School-lane, on the one side, and on the other side by the lane leading down to Shop-street, and across the bridge. Not more than one or two passed me, and those living in Lawrence-street, so they all dispersed; and afterwards the town remained perfectly quiet.

8690. Except on that occasion when you were walking before the crowd?—I brought them with me; they followed me at once.

8691. Except on that occasion, is it true that on that day you were in any way a leader of a mob?—Not of a mob in any manner.

8692. You walked up the street before them, telling them to come after you?—Yes; I told them publicly from the balcony of Mr. Daley's, to follow me, and to come up Lawrence-street.

8693. To take them away from the soldiers?—To take them away from the soldiers, and to make them disperse peaceably, and for no other object.

8694. Did you on that day lead on the mob at the station?—I was not at the railway station at all that day; I did not cross the bridge at all that day.

8695. Had you canvassed for Mr. Whitworth?—I had.

8696. When did you do so first?—Almost at the beginning of his canvass; the first time he went to see the voters that lived in the country, I went with him.

8697. Did you, on the day of the polling, do your best as a minister of peace, to preserve the peace?—Certainly, on all occasions.

Cross-examined by Mr. *McDonogh*.

8698. You canvassed for Mr. Whitworth, (as you had a perfect right to do), and went with him, I presume, on his canvass?—I did.

8699. And from the very commencement?—Not from the very commencement; it was about the commencement, certainly, but he had been canvassing a few days through the town before I went with him.

8700. And you reported to him the results of your canvassing as you went along?—Certainly.

8701. Upon this occasion in question, it appears that you saw this man Kelly; did you see the Rev. Mr. Matthews before you saw Kelly?—Mr. Matthews was not there at all to my recollection.

8702. Did it come to your knowledge that Mr. Matthews had had the man in custody?—I knew nothing whatever of it.

8703. Can you tell who the person was that said to you, "Do come and speak to the man to induce him to vote"?—I could not at all; I did not know the person at all.

8704. And did you canvass the man?—I asked him to vote for Mr. Whitworth, certainly.

8705. And then Mr. Whitworth joined you?—Yes.

8706. And then he canvassed the man?—Certainly.

8707. Did you hear anything said by anybody about his bread being taken?—Not a word at all that I recollect.

8708. You knew he was a baker?—I did not know what he was; I never knew anything of him at all, whatever.

8709. Did you hear Mr. O'Donnell, the Christian brother, say anything at all about his bread being taken?—I do not remember anything of it at all; it might have been said, but I have no recollection of it. Mr. O'Donnell may have been there after I left.

8710. Do you remember this expression; when he was asked to vote for his church, that did Kelly say, "This election has nothing to do with my church"?—I do not.

8711. Can you say whether or not; you can swear those words did not occur?—Everything I say, I am swearing.

8712. I know that, but there is a difference between swearing and positive affirmation; did those words occur in your hearing?—Certainly not.

8713. The man was very reluctant to vote?—The man was very reluctant to vote; consequently, I left him; I was not two or three minutes speaking to him; we did not want him, and I told him so.

8714. At what hour was that?—I do not recollect what hour.

8715. Was it after the man was shot?—I really could not decide; I heard some of the witnesses say it it was half-past one, but I cannot say myself, whether it was before or after the man was shot.

8716. You cannot tell me the hour?—I cannot indeed.

8717. The man was shot before one o'clock?—I heard so; I do not know from my own personal knowledge.

Rev. J. [illegible].

18 January 1869.

2718. But the dreadful event must have impressed itself on your mind?—Certainly.

2719. Are you able to say whether this conversation was after the shot had been fired?—I am not able to say, because I was in and out from half-past seven o'clock, or eight o'clock in the morning, throughout the entire day.

2720. Where were the soldiers when they were trembling with emotion and agitation?—Standing opposite the Thosel here, on the other side of the street, near Shop-street; they appeared to be very excited.

2721. And you very properly came to the determination of withdrawing the people?—Certainly.

2722. Lest some dreadful collision might ensue?—I did not know at the time what had occurred at the bridge; I was in West-street at the time.

2723. Surely you had heard of it?—I had heard of it, but I did not see it; I did not know the particulars of the man being shot.

2724. But you knew at the time that the man was killed?—Yes; at what time?

2725. At the time you saw the soldiers trembling with emotion?—Yes, that was about half past 12 o'clock or a quarter to 1 o'clock when the man was shot that I was aware of.

2726. And then you came to the determination of withdrawing the people?—Certainly.

2727. And making them all quiescent?—Yes.

2728. And sending them away?—Yes.

2729. And you did that to prevent any collision with the soldiers who had their guns in their hands?—They had, and I think they were at full cock and ready to fire if they got the least word of command.

2730. They were in that nervous state that if they were not assailed they would have fired?—I could not tell.

2731. But you were apprehensive of that?—Yes.

2732. The thing to be achieved was that you as a Christian minister should get the people out of the trouble?—Certainly.

2733. And then you went and addressed them from Daly's?—Certainly.

2734. And you had a powerful influence over them?—I got them all off; I knew the state of the poll at that time to be that Mr. Whitworth had such a majority that there was no possibility of any other result; I knew from the beginning there was no chance for Sir Leopold M'Clintock at any time.

2735. But you knew then the victory was won?—I did.

2736. And you announced it to the people?—Yes.

2737. And you knew, of course, the victory having been announced, that that was a tranquillizing statement coming from a gentleman in your position?—Certainly; it is generally called a victory when one succeeds in an election matter.

2738. I have no doubt of the truthfulness of your feeling, that you regretted that your victory had not been won without bloodshed?—I regretted that there had been bloodshed.

2739. And you so stated to the people?—Yes, I so stated to the people.

2740. And still acting with a determination of withdrawing the people and getting them out of the way, you, as it were, were at the head, and you knew they would follow you?—Some went before and some followed; I was in the middle of them sometimes.

2741. But you took up a position near them?—Yes.

2742. Then you separated them from the soldiers?—They were separated from the soldiers before this; I took them away from the soldiers up to the end of Lawrence-street, and the other clergymen that were there addressed them there, and then I went down before them in order to prevent their coming back.

2743. And accordingly you withdrew them?—Yes.

2744. You were out the night before at the [illegible] Hotel, were you?—I was.

2745. What brought you there?—I was just out to see what was going on, to see Mr. Whitworth; it was quite usual to be down there sometimes in the evening to see our friends.

2746. You were in the habit of going therefore into that coffee-room?—I was not.

2747. Where used you to go?—To Mr. Whitworth's sitting-room.

2748. And you saw him there on that occasion?—Very likely I did.

2749. But did you, or did you not?—Well, I should think I did.

2750. But did you not?—I think I did see him.

2751. Have you any doubt of it?—It is quite possible; I think that I saw him; I can say no more.

2752. Were you on the balcony when the speeches were made?—I was not on the balcony at all at any time.

2753. Did you make any speech?—I did not until after the man was shot; I was quite opposed to any speeches being made; I heard them speaking and saying that no speeches should be made. Some people were suggesting that it would be well to have some speeches made, and Mr. Clinton, Mr. Whitworth, and myself, came to the determination most distinctly that it was best that no speeches should be addressed to the mob.

2754. But you were overruled?—We were not overruled, because they came and acted for themselves.

2755. And you disapproved of the sentiments of those speeches?—Of some of them certainly.

2756. Did you hear Mr. [illegible], the reporter, give his evidence?—No, I did not.

2757. Did you hear the Rev. Father [illegible] make a speech?—I heard him saying a few words; I did not hear all his speech.

2758. Did you hear the Rev. Dr. Murphy?—I heard him saying a few words.

2759. Did you hear the Rev. Mr. M'[illegible]?—I heard him saying some, I did not hear the entire of his speech.

2760. Did you hear the 500 Orangemen from Dublin talked of?—I might have heard it, but I am not quite sure whether I heard it there, or whether I saw it in the papers a few days afterwards.

2761. But you disapproved of the sentiments you heard?—Of some, not of all.

2762. What sentiments did you disapprove of?—I disapproved of treating any person in an injurious manner, or of any words that would produce that effect.

2763. Do you remember their being said to meet them coming down in the morning; that was what you disapproved of, was it not?—I tell you

you I disapproved of everything that would lead to violence.

2764. Was that the sentiment that you particularly disapproved of, "Do not forget, boys, to come down in the morning, and hunt them into the Boyne"?—Of course, I could not approve of that.

2765. Did you hear this—"So we will, father, with sticks and stones"?—I did not.

2766. Did you express any disapprobation to the clergymen who used those words?—I told some of the gentlemen who were speaking that they should discontinue and say no more on that subject at all, and tell the people to go home quietly; and when I heard some of the clergymen that were speaking using language that I thought likely to lead to violence, I begged them to stop, and not to address such language to the people, and to retire after telling the people to go home quietly, and to disperse.

2767. Did you see Mr. Whitworth standing next to the Rev. Dr. Murphy on the balcony?—I did not.

2768. Did you hear a witness say here (it may have been a mistake) that an old woman, being asked what the name of the clergyman was that pointed out the voters as they left the polling, said that that was Mr. Powderly?—I was here on Saturday when a witness said that he saw a clergyman pointing to the mob when he saw an old man come down after voting for Sir Leopold McClintock, and giving them to understand that they should offer some violence towards him. He was asked then did he know who the clergyman was; he said he did not, but that he heard that it was the Rev. Mr. M'Kee. He was asked then, would he identify that clergyman again if he saw him; he said he was not sure, but he might; and he was asked to look round the court, and he saw me standing here, and he said, "I think that is the clergyman I saw."

2769. But he did express positively that you were the person?—He was not positive; he was quite wrong about it; I was not the person.

2770. Do you not think that you were one of the main causes of the dispersion of the crowd that day?—I contributed a good deal towards it. Rev. J. Powderly.

Re-examined by Mr. *Heron*. 26 January 1869.

2771. Did the Rev. Mr. M'Kee and Mr. O'Donnell assist you in dispersing the crowd?—Yes, I think they did; certainly they did; and the Rev. Mr. Glynn also, and Father Doyle.

2772. (Mr. Justice *Keogh*.) You say that you, when you heard some language which you thought was calculated to lead to violence, very properly interposed, and recommended that there should be no further address; can you recall what was the language that you apprehended would lead to violence?—I do not remember distinctly the words now, but it was something about the Orangemen coming from Dublin.

2773. Was there anything about throwing them into the Boyne?—I think I heard that.

2774. Did you hear any expression from the crowd in reply to that address?—I have been asked by Mr. M'Donogh if I heard the people in the crowd say, "We will beat them with sticks and stones on to-morrow morning."

2775. But did you hear any expressions from the crowd in answer, after those observations were made, of which you disapproved?—I cannot say exactly at what time it was, but I think I heard some one in the crowd say they would meet them.

2776. Was Mr. Whitworth there at the time?—I really cannot say; I am not quite sure whether, when I heard those remarks, I was standing amongst the crowd myself, or whether I might have been in the room.

2777. At all events you have no doubt that you did interpose to stop the use of language that you thought calculated to lead to violence?—Certainly; I endeavoured to make the gentlemen sit who were addressing the crowd.

2778. It is very creditable to you.

[The Witness withdrew.

The Reverend EDWARD O'DONNELL, sworn; Examined by Mr. *Hamill*.

Rev. E. O'Donnell.

2779. ARE you one of the Christian Brothers stationed in the town?—I am.

2780. Were you here on Saturday, or did you hear the evidence of Mr. M'Kenna delivered in this court?—I was here on Saturday, but I did not hear the evidence of Mr. M'Kenna.

2781. Did you afterwards hear it, or hear it spoken of?—I heard it spoken of.

2782. Did you canvass for Mr. Whitworth?—No.

2783. Were you here upon the day of the nomination?—I was.

2784. Will you let me read to you a passage from Mr. M'Kenna's evidence; he says that the people were in the gallery, "and some were standing along the ledge; Mr. O'Donnell, a Christian Brother, jumped up where that bar is, and he appeared to me to act in some capacity, like a fugleman or mob leader;" is there any truth in that?—I stood upon the bench, but I did not act in the capacity of fugleman or mob leader.

2785. Were you a mob leader?—Decidedly not.

2786. Then he says, "From the time Mr. O'Donnell stood on the spot the place was one terrific scene of uproar; he was gesticulating, and waving his hat and flourishing it." Just tell us what you did at the day of nomination?—I cheered for Mr. Whitworth, and waved my hat or my hand from time to time.

2787. Did you do that in any capacity at all as a mob leader, or as one desirous to guide or direct the crowd?—By no means; I was neither by accident nor by arrangement connected in any way except with the mob.

2788. Do you know a person named Kelly, a voter, or did you know him before that day?—No, not before that day; I saw him on the table to-day.

2789. Did you see that man upon the day of polling?—I did, though I would scarcely know him, other than that I saw him here to-day.

2790. Where did you see him?—At the hall; at the booth in Peter-street.

2791. Who was with you when you saw him?—Mr. Whitworth, and the Reverend Mr. Powderly, and some others.

2792. Just state to his Lordship what you said, and what was said in your presence, and what Kelly said, as you best recollect?—I heard the Reverend Mr. Powderly recommending him to

Rev. S. O'Donnell.

18 January 1869.

vote for Mr. Whitworth; Kelly said he had not his mind made up to vote at all; Mr. Powderly repeated what he had said at first; Kelly still refused; Father Powderly said that Mr. Whitworth's principles were known to be those of the great Liberal party; why would he not vote. Mr. Whitworth said, "Why will you not vote; you know my principles?" I heard that much, and then I added, "Vote with your priests, and for your country." I repeated those words perhaps twice, and then on seeing that he was still obstinate, and refused to vote at all, I said, "Let the fellow go, he doesn't intend to vote; it's useless to press him."

2793. Did you use the word "hell," or that "he is going to hell;" or that he was "about to go to hell, where he was always going," or words to the like effect?—I never used the word "hell" on the occasion, nor that "he was going to hell," nor anything whatever about "hell" or "damnation," as is attributed to me.

2794. Did you assist the Reverend Mr Powderly, the last witness, to calm the crowd, or take away the crowd after the occurrence at the bridge?—I did.

2795. And you did your best to quiet them?—Yes.

Cross-examined by Mr. *Plunket*.

2796. I have no doubt you did your best to quiet the mob at the bridge, and I believe you had some success with them?—I was not on the bridge at all upon that occasion.

2797. After the transaction, you asked the people to disperse?—Yes, I did my best.

2798. And you had some success with them, had you not?—Very considerable, I think.

2799. Until you and the other clergymen addressed them, they were very much excited?—They were excited.

2800. In fact, your addressing them with the other clergymen, had the effect of dispersing them and sending them home?—It sent vast numbers of them home.

2801. I suppose you came there on the nomination day, and supported Mr. Whitworth?—I came there to witness the proceedings.

2802. You are not a voter I suppose?—No.

2803. But you came there to witness the proceedings, and to take part in supporting the candidate you approved of?—I came there not intending to take any active part at all, but merely as a spectator; but I was interested in Mr. Whitworth's return.

2804. But being interested in it, your spirit entered into the spirit of the scene I suppose?—Just so.

2805. Had you not some influence with the mob that day?—Probably they respected me; I had the influence that any respectable person would have, and perhaps something more.

2806. On that occasion, when you saw the voter Kelly, you say that you said, "Let him go;" are you sure that you did not add words to this effect, "the way he is always going"?—I never repeated it.

2807. But did you say it?—I did not say it; I did not know Kelly, consequently I could not say "the way he is always going."

2808. I suppose that if a man of your religious persuasion was opposing the cause of which you approved, you would think he was going a bad way?—We were voting for a Protestant and Independent.

2809. But I speak of the cause?—That is merely a religious question.

2810. But you said, "At all events, let him go"?—It was useless to press him.

[The Witness withdrew.

The Reverend Thomas Matthews, sworn; Examined by Mr. *Pollen*.

Rev. T. Matthews.

2811. I believe you are the parish priest of one of the parishes in Drogheda?—Yes.

2812. How long have you been a clergyman in the town of Drogheda?—Better than 31 years.

2813. Do you know Clarke, who was examined on Saturday?—I do.

2814. Prior to the election, had you any conversation with Clarke, and did you make any promise to support Mr. Whitworth?—I did.

2815. About how long before the election?—It was several weeks; seven or eight weeks I dare say.

2816. Did he promise you that he would vote for Mr. Whitworth?—He said that he would promise to vote for Mr. Whitworth.

2817. Did you on that occasion say you would call upon Mr. Clarke, or did you meet him casually?—I met him casually; he lives close by me.

2818. Do you remember meeting him again on the day of the polling?—Not upon the day of the polling, but I met him some few days before.

2819. What passed upon that occasion?—It was a casual meeting; he was standing at his door, which is quite close by my residence, and having heard that he was going to the entertainment Mr. Brodigan was giving in the evening, eating and drinking, I began to suspect that he might not be firm in his first resolution; he mentioned also, himself that he was going there and getting the entertainments, and I said to him, "Clarke, I hope you will continue to support Mr. Whitworth," and he said, "I think I will support Mr. Brodigan;" and then I made an observation to the effect that Mr. Brodigan and himself were a very worthless pair.

2820. Did you make use of any expression to the effect that you would trample him and Brodigan under your feet?—Nothing of that sort whatever.

2821. Do you remember calling at Kelly's house upon the morning of the day of the polling?—I do.

2822. Did you see him?—His wife was in the shop; I stood just inside the door, and I think he descended the stairs from a room upstairs, and I said, "Kelly, will you come to vote for Mr. Whitworth?" and he answered and said, "Will you give me 20 *l*.?" Then I told him Mr. Whitworth gave no money; and then he said, "I will not vote without money;" and I said "That is impossible; I will call in another part of the day, and you will have your mind made up;" and I think he said as I retired, "If so, bring 100 *l*. with you."

2823. Did you afterwards, in the course of the day, see him in West-street?—Between 10 and 11 o'clock I came up to West-street, to see that all was going on quietly. Kelly was walking here close

close to the court, with three or four persons around him, who seemed to be parties acquainted with him, and I said, "Kelly, did you vote?" and he said, "I did vote for Whitworth:" "Take care, Kelly," said I. "I will inquire." Three persons were with him, who I thought were well known to himself, and were not like roughs or anything of that description; I went, and after a time, I made out the booth where Kelly should have voted, and I found he didn't vote; after a time, I met Kelly about the same place, with scarcely any person with him, and I said, "Kelly, you told a lie, you're a great rascal," or something of that kind; and they appeared to urge him to vote, and said he ought to; and after a time, I retired and left him there, but I didn't give him into the hands of the mob in any way.

2824. On the first occasion, before you went to the booth, did you use any expression, such as, "Hold him there, while I see whether he has voted?"—Nothing whatever of that tendency.

2825. And then, when you found he wouldn't vote, you left him?—I left him.

2826. When did you see him next upon that day?—I don't think I saw him that day after?—

2827. Do you remember seeing a man of the name of Cahill, on the day of the polling?—Yes, I called at his house.

2828. At what hour was that?—Somewhere about 11 o'clock, or perhaps a little before that.

2829. What took place upon that occasion?—I went to Cahill's house; seven weeks before, he had told me he would vote for Mr. Whitworth; I called in, and his wife was there, and his son-in-law and daughter, and I asked where was Cahill. They said he was down in the room; I went down and said to Cahill, "Will not you come to vote as you promised," and he said, "They are opposed to me here," meaning his family. With that we came towards the room door, that is the parlour door, quite close by the hall; and the son-in-law particularly said, "Oh, the landlord is here, he cannot go and vote." He said, "I think that he would be destroyed." I said, "Cahill, have you a lease?" "I have," he said, "a long lease;" and immediately after that his daughter came up and said, "You must go with the priest," and he came.

2830. Is that the substance, as well as you can remember, of everything that took place upon that occasion?—Those are the whole particulars.

2831. There was a witness of the name of Boyd, who was examined here; had he promised you to vote upon any occasion?—He had not.

2832. Do you remember after the shot was fired, some of the escorted party coming under your protection?—I was in my own house, and the escort came down; I went along with the escort, and endeavoured to pacify the people. Some little persons, boys and girls, were throwing stones in a small way, so as to let them drop upon the parties in the escort; and they came on to the bridge and met the people at the bridge, immediately the gun was shot, and the ranks were broken, and seven, eight, or nine parties whom I knew to be voters, claimed my protection. I gave them protection, and told them they would be quite safe, and I brought them with me, and I put them into Maguire's house; the other houses were closed on account of the crowd in the street. Dr. Brenden, as I found afterwards, had his head cut; he was, I think, the only party that received any injury, and the doctor was sent for to dress the wound, and he came after a little, and I said, "Now remain so, and I will go and get you to vote; I will see some of the authorities." I sent for the sheriff, and some of the other magistrates came with me, and I think six or seven came out; but Dr. Brenden by this time was in bed; he was an old man, and he was feeble.

2833. And any of them who wished to vote you saw were properly escorted?—Yes, I took the first, a Mr. Smith, and I think he voted for Sir Leopold M'Clintock, and the others did also.

2834. Before you gave them that protection, had you any communication with Mr. Whitworth at all?—None whatever.

2835. Were you about the town the greater part of the day of the polling?—Except when attending on those parties.

2836. Did you do everything in your power for the purpose of quieting the mob?—Everything as the other priests did.

2837. Did you see other priests in the streets upon the same day?—Yes; the Reverend Mr. Gavin was there doing everything to appease the people, and to prevent the throwing of stones.

2838. Was everything done by you during the disturbance to prevent throwing stones?—Certainly, because we knew firstly that it would be a means of injury to the people; and secondly, because we knew it was just what the opposite party would wish.

2839. Did you do anything whatever to excite clamour?—Certainly not.

Rev. T. Matthews.

18 January 1869.

Cross-examined by Mr. McDonogh.

2840. Was there a large number of persons present when you told this man he was a great rascal?—I think there might be six or seven, some few; I don't think they were near enough to hear us; they were about, and he was walking about by himself loosely, through the place.

2841. You are now speaking of Kelly?—Of course.

2842. And you had repeatedly tried to get him to vote for Mr. Whitworth?—Only on that morning; I might have once before; but I knew he was a character, from report and from my own observation, that would not vote without money.

2843. Did you not ask him to vote upon a former occasion?—Perhaps I did; I am not quite sure; but I had no idea that he would vote for anyone except upon this condition.

2844. Did you not state that you had canvassed him originally?—I don't think I stated that.

2845. Perhaps that applied to Clarke?—Just so.

2846. When you met him, you asked him if he had voted, and he said he had, for Mr. Whitworth?—Yes.

2847. How near was that to the voting booth?—I found the voting booth, afterwards, was in Peter-street, and this was two or three perches to the west of the court-house.

2848. Did you find him, when you came back, in the same place?—Not in the same place.

2849. But the people were about him still?—Only a very few.

2850. Do you mean, now, to represent to the Court that, when you went to ascertain whether he had voted, he was a free agent to go where he liked?—Perfectly so.

2851. And

Rev. T. Matthews.

18 January 1859.

2851. And you mean to represent that?—Perfectly.

2852. You didn't say, "Hold him, boys, while I try whether he voted"?—Certainly not.

2853. Nor anything to that effect?—Nor to that effect. There were some few persons near him of his own class, and I then said, "Kelly, you shouldn't have told a lie." I may have used the word "rascal"; I dare say I did.

2854. What did you do with him then?—I left him there to himself.

2855. You left him to his own devices?—Exactly.

2856. Did you see Father Brodeirey afterwards?—No; I think I saw him addressing the people.

2857. Did you see Kelly in the mob after you left him?—No.

2858. You did all you could to make him vote for Mr. Whitworth?—Just what I told you.

2859. You afterwards ascertained, of course, that he refused to vote at all?—He told me early he would not vote without money, and I thought he was looking about for money.

2860. Was it soon after that you went to Cahill and got him?—I didn't say the particular hour. I think Cahill was before that. I will not say that it was a casual meeting with Kelly here.

2861. At about what hour did you get Cahill to vote?—I think it was some short time after 10 o'clock.

2862. Had you been often at his house?—I think only once that day, and on a former occasion I was there once when I was on duty in the neighbourhood.

2863. When on duty in the neighbourhood you dropped in to get the vote for Mr. Whitworth?—Exactly.

2864. And on this occasion, notwithstanding the remonstrance of the son and of some of his family?—He made no remonstrance; he said they were opposed to him in the house, meaning some of his family; but the daughter came down and said he should vote. That, I think, was from his stating that he had a long lease, and that he had no apprehension of his landlord.

2865. Did you take him then and poll him?—No; he was an old man, and I walked out with him, and helped him up on the car.

2866. And then he voted for Mr. Whitworth?—Then he voted for Mr. Whitworth.

2867. At what hour?—I said at about half-past 10 o'clock, but I wouldn't be quite certain.

2868. He was one of the triumphant majority?—The majority was quite certain weeks before.

2869. And when Mr. Whitworth could not show himself in the street, it was quite certain?—That was in consequence, I believe, of a mob being hired against him.

2870. Brodigan's mob?—I think the other had a mob. I am quite sure of it, so far as observation could go. Sir Leopold McClintock was not known until the advanced part of November.

[The Witness withdrew.

The Reverend Henry McKee, sworn; Examined by Mr. Hore.

Rev. H. McKee.

2871. Are you one of the Catholic curates of Drogheda?—Yes.

2872. How long have you been in the town?—Nine years.

2873. You are also an elector of Drogheda, are you not?—Yes.

2874. Originally, did you canvass with Mr. Whitworth?—I never canvassed with him.

2875. Had you declined to do so?—Yes.

2876. When first did you go near Mr. Whitworth as a supporter of his?—When Sir Leopold McClintock appeared on the field.

2877. How soon was it after Sir Leopold McClintock came?—From the moment I saw him canvassing I knew he was in earnest; that was on the 14th of November.

2878. I believe the 14th of November was the day his address appeared in the newspapers?—It appeared three or four days previously; it was placarded through the town.

2879. On the day of polling, at what hour did you vote?—At half-past eight o'clock on the day of the polling.

2880. Did you remain about the town on the day of the polling?—I remained in the vicinity of the Tholsel, except that I was away for about 10 minutes, but came back again; I remained in the vicinity of the Tholsel till about half-past nine o'clock.

2881. Up to that time, had you seen any disturbance?—Not until half-past nine o'clock.

2882. What occurred then that you saw?—I saw the Hussars coming up Shop-street, brandishing their swords; I was then afraid there would be a collision between them and the people, as the street was crowded; I then, to create a diversion, went up Peter-street, and took off my hat, and the mob followed me.

2883. Away from the soldiers?—Away from the soldiers.

2884. Did you do that as a matter of precaution and a measure of peace?—Decidedly.

2885. You brought the crowd, you say, up Peter-street?—Yes.

2886. How far did you bring them away from the military; did you bring them completely away from that direction?—Undoubtedly; they followed me up to my own house in Fair-street, where I was going at the time.

2887. Is that your parochial residence?—It is.

2888. Did you then go in there?—Yes.

2889. Did you, after that, come out from your own house, until after you heard that the shot had been fired?—Shortly afterwards, I went into the reading-room of the St. Peter's Young Men's Society, which is next door to my own house, and I remained there reading the paper till shortly after 12 o'clock.

2890. After the shot was fired, did you use any efforts to keep the peace?—I used every effort.

2891. Where did you go after the shot was fired?—As soon as I heard of the man being shot, of which I heard a little after 12 o'clock, I went down to West-street, and I then saw the Reverend James Brodeirey addressing the crowd from Thomas Daly's windows; I went there to give him all the assistance in my power to preserve the peace.

2892. Did you yourself address the crowd there?—Not from Mr. Daly's.

2893. What did you do then?—Then it was suggested that it would be better to withdraw the crowd from the neighbourhood of the soldiers, and

Rev. H. McKee.
——
18 January 1869.

and I and Mr. O'Donnell, and the Reverend Father Glynn and others went down in the direction of the Whitworth Hall for the purpose of addressing them there, and in order to keep them away from the crowd; we then found that the windows would not open, and we went over to William Magee's ——, and from those steps Father Brosnahan addressed them, and I addressed a few words to them also; then Father Glynn and I came down to the Tholsel and found the crowd remaining there, and we thought it better to move them from it; Father Glynn then addressed them from the Tholsel steps, and told them not to interfere with the military; that only two men were criminals, and that we would see justice done in the case, and not to molest the soldiers, who were completely innocent of any part in the shooting: I said, "The two criminals are in custody; we will see them lodged in the gaol, and let no stone be thrown at the military:" and the people took my advice to the letter.

2894. Did you afterwards accompany the military?—I did.

2895. Where did you go?—I went first of all to make certain that the military would not be attacked even by a passing stone; I went with Mr. O'Donnell and Mr. Glynn in front of the military; we went up to the gaol, and then I remained there until I saw those two soldiers safely lodged in gaol; there was a good deal of time occupied in the gaol taking the depositions of the witnesses, &c. After all that was done, I and Father Gavin, and Father Glynn, and Mr. O'Donnell accompanied the military to Millmount Barracks, and parted with them there.

2896. After that, did you see the streets up to five o'clock?—That was about three o'clock; then I went home, and I saw nothing further.

2897 On the Thursday evening, you made a speech from the balcony?—Yes.

2898. Was that the only occasion on which there was any speechifying at which you were present?—I made a speech on Wednesday evening.

2899. But you spoke on the Thursday evening?—Yes.

2900. Have you been in court and heard the evidence given by the Reporter?—I was not present when he read my speech.

2901. Did you see the official short-hand writer's report?—I read the report, in the Conservative journal of this town, which he supplied to the paper.

2902. Can you give any explanation of that to his Lordship; first of all had you heard that an orange mob was coming down?—I had heard that evening——

Mr. M'Donogh objected that that was not evidence.

Witness.] On that occasion, as I had heard four or five of the speeches, I and my brother clergyman, the Reverend Thomas Murphy, went down that evening, at seven o'clock, to Simcocks's hotel, not for the purpose of making speeches at all ——

2903. Mr. M'Donogh.] Nobody asked you what you went there for.

2904, 2904. Mr. Heron.] You did not go down for the purpose of making a speech?—Certainly not.

2905. What led to the making of the speech, and what occurred?—The reports were quite general that 600 Orangemen were to come down the next day to Drogheda as an orange mob. It was suggested then that the people should be told of the Orange mob coming down, in order that they might not be taken unawares if those men were let quietly into the town. It was thought well that the people should know that those Orange men were to come in the next day to create a disturbance in the town. I was the second speaker on that occasion. I told him I knew well what an Orangeman was—that I was from the county of Armagh, where Orangeism had its first existence. I then told them that, with all their boasted loyalty, they were not loyal—that they were loyal so long as they got the loaves and fishes, but no longer. Then I said, that not long since, a Protestant minister of the north of Ireland stated that sooner than he would submit to any change from Parliamentary ascendancy, he would throw the Queen's crown into the Boyne. "Now," said I, "are you content to become slaves. It is reported that Orangemen are coming down to-morrow from Dublin to Drogheda; if they do come down, let them be hurled into the Boyne—let us be up at the train, and meet them, and give them a warm reception." That is the entire of the speech, at least substantially. I used the word "Boyne" in connexion with the expression of parson Flanigan. The parson said, he would kick the Queen's crown into the Boyne. Then said I, "Hurl them into the Boyne." As I have stated, I didn't leave my own premises from 10 o'clock till about a quarter past 12 o'clock. The man was then shot. I then went to Mr. Daly's. I was not then in the neighbourhood of the Tholsel at all. I therefore did not directly, or indirectly, point out any aged man with a long beard to any mob, to have him assaulted, as was stated by a Trinity College boy.

2906. On the day of the nomination, or the polling, or at any time during the election, did you point out any person to be assaulted by the mob?—No.

2907. Did you point out any person to be insulted by the mob?—Certainly not.

2908. Were you with the mob, or the crowd, at any time, except when you were bringing them away from the military, up towards Peter-street; were you with them upon any occasion during the day; you have already told us that, as a matter of precaution, you brought the people up Peter-street?—Yes; that was at half-past nine o'clock.

2909. Were you with a mob, or crowd, at any other time than that?—Not until the time I was leading the crowd from the Tholsel to Laurence-street; I was not across the bridge at all.

2910. Were you with the mob at any time except with the intention of preserving the peace?—I think not.

2911. Did you hiss or hoot any person or voter that day?—I did not, nor require it to be done.

Cross-examined by Mr. M'Donogh.

2912. May I ask you, do you indulge generally in historical observations?—Not often.

2913. On this occasion did you give them a touch of Cromwell. I will take the liberty of reading it:—"The Rev. Mr. M'Kee said, this would be a momentous contest; it was a contest against their deadly enemy. He was a North of Ireland man, a native of Ulster. He was born within a few miles of the Yellow Ford, where Hugh

Rev. H. M'Kee.

18 January 1859.

Hugh O'Neill gained a victory over the English. (Cheers). He had read of the persecutions which had occurred in Drogheda in bygone times. They had all heard of the butcher Cromwell, who gave glory to God for the numbers he had butchered in Drogheda in one day. (Hear, hear.) That church which stands at the head of Peter-street had a wooden steeple when Cromwell came to Drogheda, more than 200 years ago. Cromwell went first to Saint Mary's Church, where they had the other day to fight a battle over again. Cromwell was opposed there by the good priests, who mounted the walls to resist him, but they were beaten back, and fled for refuge to St. Peter's Church, which then belonged to the Catholics. (Hear, hear.) Their priests and nuns fled to Peter's Church for refuge, but Cromwell came with his invading army, and what did the butcher do? He found he could not force them to surrender, and he set fire to the steeple, and when they fled from the church he butchered them without the slightest mercy. When the Cromwellians gained the victory they robbed their forefathers of their property. Who are the party that are now coming forward to act a similar part? The descendants of Cromwell's soldiers, whose ancestors hung their forefathers at the Tholsel of Drogheda." That is your speech?—Yes.

2914. Then, "The Rev. Mr. M'Kee next stated that the present Bishop of Glasgow's father was flogged at Milltown, and that the father of Mr. Brodigan, the present member, went up to see the inhuman act performed. (Groans.) He (Mr. M'Kee) knew what an Orangeman was; he was sorry to say that Orangeism had its origin the county of Armagh. Orangemen say, they will be true to the Government as long as they give them places and emoluments; so long as they give them the loaves and fishes they will be loyal. (Hear, hear.) *A Voice:* 'Down with the Orangemen!' (Cheering.) Rev. Mr. *M'Kee:* "The Orangemen are loyal as long as they get everything in the country, as long as they feed on the vitals of the Catholics. (Cheers). A few months ago one of the ministers in the north of Ireland said, that sooner than they would submit to a change from Protestant ascendancy he would see the crown of the Queen thrown into the Boyne. (Cheers). Now, he asked them, were they to become slaves?" This is the application of all the historical learning?—Yes.

2915. "Were they to become slaves? (No, no.) The Orangemen of Dublin were on next day to come down to Drogheda. (Hear, hear.) If these men should come down let them hurl them into the Boyne (Vehement cheering.) Let the people meet them in the morning at the train, and give them a warm reception." That is the speech which you delivered on that occasion?—Substantially.

2916. You first gave the history, and then you pointed the moral, "to hurl them into the Boyne"?—No; the moral was to resist Orange ascendancy.

2917. You have told us, in a former part of your evidence, that you waived your hat, and called upon the people to follow you, and the people took your advice to the letter?—Yes, that was after the man was shot.

2918. This was a speech on the night before the man was shot?—Yes.

2919. Your power over the people was so great that they took your advice to the letter?—My power is shared by all the others. As one of the Catholic clergy, I am convinced I have a good share of influence.

2920. Now, you said that the people took your advice to the letter?—Yes.

2921. And you knew they would?—I did.

2922. And when you were addressing them in the language which I have just read, you knew your power over the people?—Yes.

2923. And you said what you meant?—Certainly.

2924. And you meant what you said?—I may have used exaggerated language, of course, on the occasion.

2925. Did you know that Father Gavin went up to the railway station the next morning?—I did not.

2926. Was Father Gavin present when you made that speech?—I could not say; I think he was. I don't recollect having seen him.

2927. Did the Rev. Mr. Brodie try to prevent any speeches being made?—He never spoke to me upon the matter, either directly or indirectly.

2928. Did you see any old gentleman voting for Sir Leopold McClintock in the booth, and afterwards raise your hand and point at him?—I did not; I was at no booth that day, except when recording my own vote.

2929. Did you stand at the door, and point at any voters, after voting?—Most decidedly not.

2930. Mr. Justice Keogh.] You have stated that that report of your speech is substantially correct?—Yes.

2931. You have also stated that you knew the people would take your advice to the letter?—I have said that they did take my advice; I addressed the crowd after the man was shot.

2932. I am not alluding to that; you said that the report of your speech the previous night was substantially correct?—Yes.

2933. You have also stated that you knew the people would take your advice to the letter?—I don't mean upon that occasion; I knew they would be well prepared to meet the Orangemen when they came into the town, and would resist them too, because I believe they were all armed with revolvers. I know what an Orangeman is.

2934. Did you know that the people would go to the railway station on the following morning after you made that speech?—I believed they would go.

2935. Did you know that they were there on the following morning?—I did not of my own knowledge.

2936. Did you believe they were there?—I concluded they would go there, after my remarks, undoubtedly.

2937. Did you take any step to go amongst them, and to see what would be the result of your remarks?—I did not, for I knew the police had heard my speech, and would be there to take every precaution. It was only a strong form of expression.

2938. You say that you knew they would be there?—I knew the people would be there, to meet the Orangemen coming down from Dublin in the morning; I knew that I expected they would be there.

2939. In consequence of your language?—Yes.

2940. Did it occur to you, that it would be right to try and prevent a collision?—I knew others would do it as well as I would. The railway station is not in my parish; I did not go in that direction.

2941. At

2941. At what hour did you record your vote? —At half past eight o'clock.

2942. Where did you go after that?—I went up to Mell, beyond Trinity-street, and came down with a voter who voted for Mr. Whitworth.

2943. In what place did he vote?—He voted in one of the polling booths in Lawrence-street.

2944. I thought you told me you were not in a polling booth, except to record your own vote? —Neither was I; he came on a car with me to the Tholsel, and he went into the polling booth and voted.

2945. Then after you recorded your own vote you came down again to the polling booth?—I recorded my vote at half past eight o'clock. I then went up and brought down this voter to the Tholsel; I remained there, outside in the street, till half past nine.

2946. Then it is a fact that after you had recorded your own vote, you did come back again to the polling booths?—Yes, after I recorded my vote, I then went and brought this voter down.

2947. And then you returned to the polling booth?—To the Tholsel.

2948. Then you were mistaken in saying that you didn't return to the polling booths after you had recorded your own vote?—I had not till after 10 o'clock.

2949. You expected the people would go up to meet the Orangemen, whom you also expected would be armed?—I believed they would be coming down by special train in the morning, not by the ordinary train; I believed they would be here by about seven o'clock, or so, that morning; and I heard they were come and gone at half-past 8. When I voted I heard that the Orangemen had come and were gone, and believing so, I then knew that there was no other cause for excitement whatever, and then I concluded that everything would be calm and tranquil for the remainder of the day, the Orangemen having gone back to Dublin.

2950. Did it occur to you to communicate that, if it was your belief, to the people whom you had addressed the previous evening?—They had all heard it; it was quite the opinion that they had come and gone.

2951. At what hour?—At half-past nine.

2952. Then, it is a fact which you now state, that at half past nine o'clock it was generally believed in the town, that the persons you call Orangemen, had come and had gone?—Yes; that was my impression.

2953. And that there was no danger of any collision with them?—Yes.

2954. And for that reason you returned to your own house?—Yes.

[The Witness withdrew

The Rev. THOMAS GAVIN, sworn; Examined by Mr Howell.

2955. Are you Curate in what is called St. Mary's parish?—I am.

2956. How long have you been a curate in Drogheda?—Going on for four years.

2957. Is your residence between James's-street and the railway station?—It is about half-way.

2958. I believe you made a speech upon the night of the Thursday preceding the election?—I did.

2959. That speech has been read, perhaps you have seen it?—Yes.

2960. Is there anything in that speech that you would like to answer upon?—It is all substantially true, with one exception.

2961. What is that?—Where it is mentioned that I said "you will meet them to-morrow," and I was interrupted, there was a shout, "We will." But then I said, "You will despise them," and then immediately after that I said, "I do not want people to treat these hirelings as they should be treated; but I want to show to what extent those in the interest of the Conservative party go to send Sir Leopold McClintock to perpetuate that badge of conquest and blot upon the English Constitution."

2962. Have the words, "We will despise them," been omitted from the report?—They were omitted from the report.

2963. On the morning of Friday, did you see persons near to you, or where you reside, upon the steps or roadway?—I saw about 40 or 50 girls.

2964. Did you see some men also?—I saw some that were about their business.

2965. Did you observe the girls throw stones at those men?—I did.

2966. When you saw that, what did you do? —I ran down as fast as I could; however, they began to pelt, but as soon as I got an opportunity I raised my hand, and I said, "For God's sake stop this." There were two men, and one of them came and seized me by the collar, and there was a screech made that I was going to be killed.

2967. Where did those two men come from?—One man turned out from among the party.

2968. Were they the people at whom the girls were throwing stones?—They belonged to the party.

2969. When those men caught you, what happened?—The girls ran and threw themselves between us, and I raised my hands over the heads of those men that I wanted to put away the sticks, and one of the men seeing that I was anxious to save them, said, "Why won't you take Father Gavin's speech."—So they pulled off the girls, and I said, "For God's sake let me out, and it will be all right."

2970. Did you succeed in protecting those men?—I did; I sent them with two or three respectable men up through the crowd.

2971. Do you remember when the escort was coming down the road, sometime about 12 o'clock? —I do.

2972. Do you recollect Mr. Reed, the magistrate, having spoken to you?—Yes.

2973. Are you the clergyman that he referred to in his examination?—I am.

2974. Did you, before he spoke to you at all, do your best to quiet the people?—Yes; if I got the world I could not do more.

2975. Did you speak to the people?—I spoke to the people from the Tholsel four times.

2976. To go back; did you speak to them before Mr. Reed spoke to you in James's-street?—Yes, and I took hold of the collar of one fellow, and I told him I would strike him with a stick if he took up one stone.

2977. Did you all through that do your best

Rev. T. Gavin. — 18 January 1869.

to keep the people quiet?—If I could get the world, I could do no more.

2978. Do you recollect stating to them afterwards, to the effect that the man who had raised a stick or threw a stone would be an enemy?—I stated it here, opposite Clarke's stores, from the steps, and I think Mr. James Matthews was present.

2979. You did all you could to keep the people quiet?—I did all I could; I could do no more.

2980. Did you canvass for Mr. Whitworth at all?—No, never.

2981. In point of fact, did you take any part in the canvassing?—I have not taken any part in any election at all, nor did I intend to take any part at all beyond recording my vote.

2982. Do you know a person of the name of Ray?—I know a person, an old Mr. Ray.

2983. Were you in court when James Ray, his nephew was being examined?—I was.

2984. Did you hear Ray say that he had been attacked by some mill-people, girls and boys, and that you said to them, "You have a holiday, boys, and you know how to enjoy it;" did you use those words, or anything of that kind?—Certainly not, nor anything of that kind more than that I did not see Mr. Ray the whole day.

Cross-examined by Mr. *McDonogh.*

2985. Those are words you would not use?—Which words?

2986. Just what you have negatived, "You have a holiday boys, and you know how to enjoy it"?—I would see no reason for using the word "holiday," because it was not a holiday.

2987. Do you know the meaning of the word?—I know what a holiday is; it is a vacant day.

2988. I know it is, too; we have no vacant days; but do you know the meaning of the language attributed to you?—Yes; I say that the meaning of it should be, that it was exciting the people to beat others.

2989. That is the meaning of it; that is what I understood by the language?—I think so.

2990. Having a remote resemblance to the more vulgar expression, "Do not mill his ears to the pump," do not you think so; now, I will take the liberty of reading the language you did use—"The Rev. Mr. Gavin now came forward amid loud cheers, he said, he knew by their voices that they proclaimed him a friend, not an enemy. (Cheers.) He knew by their voices that they believed he was prepared, as their forefathers were, to go to the block, lay down his head, and sacrifice his life for their interests. (Cheers.) When he last spoke to them, he told them that there was a crisis arrived at in reference to the three kingdoms." You had spoken in the early part of the evening?—No.

2991. Then I beg your pardon; I refer to another speech. "When he last spoke to them, he told them that there was a crisis arrived at in reference to the three kingdoms, England, Scotland, and Ireland, but particularly to Ireland. ('Down with the Orangemen.') He told them last evening that there was a question not only before the three kingdoms, but before all Europe; a question was brought before the people to decide, and that question was the disendowment and the disestablishment of the Protestant Church, which was generated and nurtured in lust and crime, while it was fattened on the spoliation and robbery of the Catholic property and the Catholic Church of Ireland. (Great cheering.) (*A voice:* 'Down with Bradigan and the Orangemen.') (Cheering.) Rev. Mr. Gavin: The people of England were not acquainted with our grievance and their eyes were opened by a continuous rebellion. (Hear, hear.) The question of disestablishment and disendowment of that Church which was placed upon your shoulders is now understood in England to be a grievance in this country, and the question for you is—Will you give your voices against it? Up to a very recent period he had not intended to identify himself with the politics of the town; but when he saw a man—by the way a most respectable and an educated man—of the name of Mr. M'Clintock, coming into Drogheda to be returned by the voices of the Liberals and Catholics of Drogheda, his blood rose to his face, and he blushed for shame that such a man would get a chance of becoming representative for the town. (Hear, hear.) All that he wanted to tell his hearers, in conclusion was, that on yesterday, in the City of Dublin, some of the *friends of ascendancy* in this town hired 300 assassins to come and butcher the Catholics of Drogheda. (Tremendous uproar, and loud cries of 'Down with the Orangemen.') He asked them would they meet them? (Several voices: 'We will, we will,' and vehement cheering.) He assured them, on the word of a priest, that what he said was a *fact*, that some party in the favour of the Orange candidate here went to Dublin, and purchased the tag, rag, and bobtail of Orangedom to come down and butcher them to-morrow. (Loud manifestations of emotion.) He did not want the people of Drogheda to treat those hirelings as they deserved; but he merely wanted to show to what extremes the Orange party are capable of going, seeking for victory, in order that M'Clintock may be member who will, by his vote, assist to perpetuate that badge of conquest and blot on the English Constitution—the Protestant Church. (Cheering.) Did any of them know the Irish language? Did they know what a ranthan was? He would explain it to them; it was a calf with a dirty tail—no matter, although Mr. M'Clintock may be a gentleman and a man of education, he called him a ranthan; for from many of those of his supporters, it was clear he had a dirty tail. (Loud cheers and laughter.) No matter how learned a man and great sailor Mr. M'Clintock may be, he may sound well with his plummet remarkably well; but when he comes to us here, seeking for sand and dirt, he will find amongst us adamantine rock to the bottom." I have read that speech for you, and you intended that the people should meet those 300 assassins?—No; but I say that they would meet them as certain they were to come. I say that is what I said there, and I swear it that I said "you will meet them," that is, you will certainly meet them and despise them, and there is a displacement, as far as I recollect. The next part of my speech was, that I did not want that the people of Drogheda should treat those hirelings as they should be treated, only so far as those persons in the interest of Mr. M'Clintock want to perpetuate that badge of conquest.

2992. You pledged your word as a priest to the matter of fact, that the 300 Orangemen were coming to butcher the Catholics?—I did.

2993. Did you intend that the people should assemble at the railway station?—Certainly not.

2994. Will you swear that?—I swear it upon my oath, and it never came into my head.

2995. And

2995. And you never thought it would occur? —Never, never.

2996. Did you say some time ago that some of them said, "we will meet them"?—Yes; but that was before they gave me time; they interrupted me. As soon as I said "you will meet them to-morrow," some parties in the crowd said, "we will." "But you will despise them," said I.

2997. When you used the words "you will meet them," they said "we will meet them"?—They interrupted me in that part of the sentence. Some few of them said, it in the crowd, and then I finished the sentence.

2998. And what brought you there in the early morning?—The first place I went to was to the bench, and when I went up I heard the magistrates had made an arrangement. I went to the magistrates, and spoke to them of the propriety of having the police there to search them, or take precautions against letting people into the town on unsuspecting people.

2999. What brought you there again in the morning?—I was told they had police there to search them, and to take arms or knives or any wicked instrument they had with them. I saw the police there, and I was fully certain when the train came in that that was to be gone through; the magistrate was at the station with me, and he told me it was to be done, and I waited there to see it.

3000. And you now swear that, having told the people to meet them, and you having heard the people say they would, you went to see the process gone through of the magistrates and police depriving these men of their knives and dangerous weapons, and anything else?—That is what I swear.

[The Witness withdrew.

Rev. T. [illegible].

18 January 1869.

The Rev. Thomas Langan, sworn; Examined by Mr. Heron.

Rev. T. Langan.

3001. Are you a Roman Catholic clergyman? —I am.

3002. Are you a parish priest?—I am.

3003. Where?—Of —— lately called ——

3004. Do you know the men named Usher and Devine?—I know Devine well; I don't know the other by name, but I identified them here.

3005. Did you have any conversation with those two men before the election?—I had.

3006. Was a third man named McDonnell there?—I don't know; they were the two men that were examined next after Devine.

3007. What conversation had you with them? —I met them at the Balbriggan station, between 9 and 10 o'clock.

Mr. McDonogh objected to this, on the ground of its being recriminatory evidence, the seat not being claimed.

Mr. Justice Keogh overruled the objection.

3008. Mr. Heron (to the Witness).] Where was the conversation?—Partly in the waiting-room at Balbriggan, partly on the platform outside.

3009. On what day was it?—On Wednesday, the 18th of November.

3010. That is two days before the polling?—I believe so.

3011. Will you tell his Lordship what happened?—Am I to detail the conversation? I cannot do it without repeating what I said myself.

Mr. McDonogh requested his Lordship to take a note of the objection which he had raised.

Mr. Justice Keogh did not think it necessary to do so.

3012. Mr. Heron (to the Witness).] Tell us shortly what you said?—We were talking of politics, and I said as a rule, I preferred the Tory landlords and Tory agents to what is called the Liberals, the Whigs. I specified the names of Colonel Taylor, Mr. Woods, and Mr. Cottington, and their respective agents; and I asked them who or what they were, and they said, that unfortunately they were tenants-at-will, having votes in Drogheda; that they were pressure or something equivalent to that in Balbriggan, to go down to the elections in Drogheda to vote; and to my remark that there was no great difference between one candidate and the other, they said that they would vote for the man that gave the employment, Whitworth, if they were left free. I said, "if you make this statement to Mr. Harry Hamilton he will not ask you to go; I believe him to be an honest and an honourable gentleman." That occurred inside, and one of the men followed me out when I got into the carriage, and put in his hand and shook hands with me, and burst out crying, "For God's sake speak; do something for us, do something for us." It was not until afterwards that I thought he meant to save him from voting. I believed at the time that he meant he would not object to a little coercion, in order that he might not vote. I cannot swear to that, but that is my impression; he wished me to speak to Mr. Harry Hamilton.

3013. That is the only conversation you had with him?—Yes.

[The Witness withdrew.

Mr. John Devitt, sworn; Examined by Mr. Heron.

Mr. J. Devitt.

3014. Are you the court-keeper?—Yes.

3015. Before the day of the nomination, was this placard about the town (pointing to a placard)?—Yes; in several places.

3016. Was it in that form, with a cross on a green ground?—It was.

3017. In many places?—In many places.

3018. Was this one also (handing a paper to the Witness) placed about the town?—It was, in many places.

3019. Where was that board taken from?—A board similar to that was taken from the court-house.

3020. Was it posted on the court-house?—It was posted on the board, and the board was up against the court-house.

3021. Did you direct the police to remove it? —Yes.

Mr. Heron proposed to hand in these placards.

Mr. J. Devin.

13 January 1869.

Mr. *M'Donogh* objected.

Mr. Justice *Keogh* characterised the placards (which had been brought into court) as abominable attempts to prejudice the minds of the people, but ruled that they could not be produced.

[The Witness withdrew.

Mr. Henry Garvin, sworn; Examined by Mr. *Heron*.

Mr. H. Garvin.

3090. Are you the Clerk of Petty Sessions?—Yes.

3091. Is this the Petty Sessions Book (*showing a book to the Witness*)?—Yes.

3092. Do you produce the book of the records of conviction after the 20th of November?—Yes; the Petty Sessions were held on the 23rd of November.

3093. Is there any conviction for assault?—

Mr. *McDonogh* objected to the reception of this evidence.

Mr. *Heron* supported the admission of the evidence on the ground of precedent before the Committee of the House of Commons.

Mr. Justice *Keogh* allowed the objection.

[The Witness withdrew.

Mr. *Fallon* was heard to sum up the case on behalf of the sitting Member.

Mr. *Plunket* was heard in reply.

[Adjourned to To-morrow, at One o'clock.

www.ingramcontent.com/pod-product-compliance
Lightning Source LLC
Chambersburg PA
CBHW031440270326
41930CB00007B/809

* 9 7 8 3 7 4 2 8 1 8 8 1 2 *